Pax Americana?

Transnational Institute Series

The Transnational Institute is an independent fellowship of researchers and activists living in different parts of the world, who develop innovative analyses of world affairs.

It serves no government, political party or interest group.

Other titles in the TNI series:

Short Changed:
Africa and World Trade
Michael Barratt Brown and Pauline Tiffen

Dark Victory:
The United States, Structural Adjustment
and Global Poverty
Walden Bello

People and Power in the Pacific:
The Struggle for the Post-Cold War Order
Walden Bello

The Debt Boomerang:
How Third World Debt Harms Us All
Susan George

Paradigms Lost:
The Post Cold War Era
Edited by Chester Hartman and Pedro Vilanova

Pax Americana?

Hegemony or Decline

Jochen Hippler

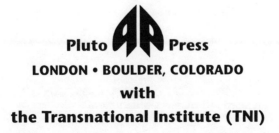

Pluto Press
LONDON • BOULDER, COLORADO
with
the Transnational Institute (TNI)

First published 1994 by
Pluto Press
345 Archway Road
London N6 5AA
and
5500 Central Avenue
Boulder, Colorado 80301, USA

in association with the Transnational Institute
Paulus Potterstraat 20, 1071 DA Amsterdam, The Netherlands

British Library Cataloguing in Publication Data
A catalogue record for this book is available from the British Library

Library of Congress Cataloging in Publication Data
Hippler, Jochen
    [Neue Weltordnung. English]
    Pax Americana? : hegemony or decline / by Jochen Hippler
    203p. 22cm. – (Transnational Institute series)
    Includes bibliographical references and index.
    ISBN 0-7453-0695-0 (hb). – ISBN 0-7453-0696-9 (pb)
    1. World politics–1989- I. Title. II Series.
D860.H5613 1994
909.82'9–dc20   93-47173
                                                                 CIP

ISBN 0 7453 0695 0 hb
ISBN 0 7453 0696 9 pb

Designed and produced for Pluto Press by
Chase Production Services, Chipping Norton, OX7 5QR
Typeset by Stanford DTP Services, Milton Keynes
Printed in the EC by The Cromwell Press, Broughton Gifford

Contents

Preface

When I began this book, everybody – including myself – thought it was a slightly crazy project. With the current pace of world history, writing a book on the changes in the international system should only be done in a format that allows continuous updating, I realised. But that's not what publishers expect from authors, even as remarkable a publisher as Roger van Zwanenberg of Pluto Press.

The whole thing started two or three months before the second Gulf War, when my German publisher called. She wanted me – and fast, she always wants books fast – to write about the Middle East, Western policy towards the area and the war itself. I replied that I might consider writing another book, but that its scope would be broader. It would aim to address the restructuring of the whole international system, the ideology and reality of the 'New World Order'. The Middle East would be covered, but only as part of the whole picture, not the central focus. The idea would be to place these developments in a historical context, going back to the Cold War and what lay behind it in order to foster a better understanding of the era that was to succeed it.

My publisher agreed, and the result was published in Germany in September 1991, under the title *The New World Order*.

After mailing the manuscript to the publisher in late July 1991 I felt quite happy at having produced such a timely work. A week later this warm feeling evaporated: the coup that eventually overthrew President Gorbachev and triggered the breakup of the Soviet Union had occurred. Even though my manuscript speculated about the danger and possible results of a coup in Moscow, I was less than pleased that the book referred in several places to 'President Gorbachev of the Soviet Union', when this country would soon be history, along with Mr Gorbachev's presidency. And this was just the beginning of my dissatisfaction. I had written in general terms about the possibility of war in Yugoslavia – the wars in Slovenia, Croatia and then Bosnia were very much in the headlines soon after. My words on Afghan President Najibullah's chances of survival made less sense after his government disintegrated in April 1992. And, finally, the intervention in Somalia in December 1992 was mentioned nowhere in the book, since it happened long after publication.

Then Pluto Press declared they wanted an English version of my book. This, I thought, would allow me to try and update the material, as well as to add a chapter on Somalia and former Yugoslavia.

But the headlines kept overtaking my writing. Every time I put a full-stop to a chapter and handed it on to the translator, there would be another dramatic event in Russia, the Middle East or somewhere else, forcing me to return to one section or another. This would delay the process, and by the time I had managed to alter the relevant passage, history would move on and the whole absurd process would begin all over again. Only the encouragement of my colleagues at the Transnational Institute kept me going.

Today this process is over; the book is out. Its goal is still to provide the reader with background information and an analysis of the current restructuring by putting it into historical perspective. The emphasis is on the Third World and North–South relations. But since East–West conflict and the Soviet Union played such an important role in world politics, this aspect too is dealt with at length. Developments within the Western camp, that is the changes in the power relations between the US, Western Europe and Japan, are also covered, but to a lesser extent.

Jochen Hippler
January 1994

List of Acronyms

ANC	African National Congress
CDU	Christian Democratic Union of Germany
CENTO	Central Treaty Organization
CIS	Commonwealth of Independent States
Comecon	Council for Mutual Economic Assistance
CPSU	Communist Party of the Soviet Union
CSCE	Conference for Security and Cooperation in Europe
EBRD	European Bank for Reconstruction and Development
EC	European Community
EFTA	European Free Trade Agreement
EU	European Union
FMLN	Farabundo Martí National Liberation Front
FRG	Federal Republic of Germany
FSLN	Frente Sandinista de Liberacion Nacional/Sandinist National Liberation Front
GATT	General Agreement on Tariffs and Trade
GDR	German Democratic Republic
G7	Group of the seven most important industrial nations
IMF	International Monetary Fund
LIC	low-intensity conflict
MPLA	Popular Movement for the Liberation of Angola
NAFTA	North American Free Trade Agreement
NATO	North Atlantic Treaty Organization
NGO	non-governmental organisation
NIC	newly industrialised country
NPA	New People's Army (Philippines)
NVA	National People's Army (GDR)
OPEC	Organization of Petroleum Exporting Countries
PLO	Palestine Liberation Organisation
SEATO	Southeast Asia Treaty Organization
SPD	Social Democratic Party of Germany
UN/UNO	United Nations/ United Nations Organization
UNITA	National Union of Total Independence of Angola
WEU	Western European Union
WTO	Warsaw Treaty Organization

Introduction

The Cold War is over. The Warsaw Pact and the Soviet Union no longer exist. Even the continuing existence of Russia in its present form is anything but certain. This disappearance of one of the two superpowers, taking with it a whole military alliance and alternative social system, means that a new structure for the international system, a 'New World Order', must and will evolve. And it is evolving. Just how 'ordered' or chaotic it will be is not yet clear, nor is it clear which regions will be included in the New World and which may end up excluded or ignored. In any event, the Gulf War of 1990–1, the civil war in former Yugoslavia, the threat of collapse in Russia and the death of hundreds of thousands of people in Somalia are all evidence that we are witnessing a process of evolution in which neither the birth of a New World Order, nor its future, promises to be either peaceful or easy.

This much-discussed New World Order is not simply a descriptive term for changes actually taking place in the world. It is also a tag which can be made to serve the propaganda purposes of governments and politicians.

It was the Gulf War which led American President George Bush to proclaim a New World Order. This in itself is enough to awaken scepticism as to what may lie behind the concept. Something thought up to justify a war is not necessarily a valid formula for peaceful world development.

This book has two main aims. The first is to trace the current of change within the previous international system, because to understand how a New World Order can come into being, we must first of all examine those conditions which had already fundamentally altered relationships within international power politics before the end of the Cold War. The second is to examine the New World Order in action. What does the US government understand by this Order and how will it see its role as sole superpower in dealing with regional conflicts in the Third World or elsewhere? How will the US conduct its relations with Russia and the other countries of the CIS, perhaps against a background of increasing economic, political and military chaos? What are the present effects in Europe and the Third

World of the dissolution of the Soviet Union? What will the Gulf War prove to have meant in this context? What shifts are taking place in the power relationships between Japan, the US and Europe? What will become of NATO and the EU? Will Europe be completely dominated by a united Germany? The answers to such questions will determine the future of the international system.

This book is not an attempt to work out global models or structures, or to try to make concrete proposals for political action. This is not because such considerations are not necessary but because the intention is to fulfil a different function: to help create a meaningful basis for a serious discussion by clearly setting out both the course of historical events up to and including the Gulf War and the end of the Soviet Union, and the choices facing the world today, which will remain constant no matter how fast and surprising the pace of events proves.

It is essential to keep these conditions clearly in mind if useful political conclusions are to be facilitated.

Part One
The Old Order

1

The Birth of the Postwar Order

The First World War, in Europe at least, produced a highly unstable international order which ended in another world war only 20 years later. This Second World War had two principal results. On the one hand a 'Pax Americana' was established in the West and most of the Third World; on the other there emerged a second great power which regarded itself as an alternative to a US hegemony and became the counterpoint to the US in the Third World and in Europe. Even though many states and movements were of great importance in Europe, Asia, Africa and Latin America, the basic structure of the postwar period was bipolar, marked by the split between the opposite systems of West and East, dominated and symbolised by the two superpowers, the United States and the Soviet Union. Almost all areas of global politics, whether East–West, transatlantic or North–South, were structured by this bipolarity for decades.[1]

The establishment of the postwar order in Europe constituted the provisional conclusion of a process of restructuring the international system, which had been going on for well over half a century. In essence it was a matter of transforming the Pax Britannica of the mid-nineteenth century into a new and stable international order. For a long time this lengthy and painful process had little or nothing to do with East–West conflict or opposition between the systems of capitalism and state socialism. The relative decline in British supremacy, which had been at its height for a few decades after the Congress of Vienna (1815), had already begun in the last quarter of the nineteenth century, although this decline was slow to be recognised, particularly in Great Britain itself, where it was wilfully and cheerfully ignored. British supremacy had been based on the combination of a number of factors which by the end of the nineteenth century had almost ceased to apply. These included Britain's economic and technological superiority, resulting from its leading role in the Industrial Revolution; the supremacy of the British fleet on the oceans of the world; the existence of a functioning balance of power on the continent of Europe which facilitated British policy; the absence of any power outside Europe offering any credible threat to British claims; and the international standing of sterling – which was associated with the importance of London as a centre of world finance.

By the time of the First World War a number of the conditions on which the Pax Britannica was based had ceased to exist. The British economy was no longer as competitive within a Europe where the balance of power was itself unsteady, the rising German Reich was constituting a serious economic as well as a political and strategic threat, and the US economy was already way ahead of the British. It was the 1914–18 war which made these altered international power relationships clear.

Great Britain, France and Russia together were not able to defeat the Kaiser's Germany despite the fact that the latter's allies, Austria and Turkey, were in a state of internal decay. Only the entry of the US into the war enabled Germany to be defeated. In other words, Great Britain was only able to overthrow a dangerous European rival with the help of an even more powerful rival from outside Europe.

The restoration of the old British order was impossible after this war. The old powers had been weakened but no really new order emerged, either in the sense of a new supreme power or in that of a working multipolar system. The consequence of this was further instability in Europe and a renewed attempt by the German Reich, in the shape of the Nazi regime, to exert hegemony over Europe.

During this historical phase the US, despite its greatly increased economic and political weight, was not yet thinking of playing any permanent role in the ordering of European affairs, militarily or otherwise. It limited its actions to making loans, generally short-term, and to economic penetration and military intervention in the Third World, predominantly in Central America and the Caribbean.

The Second World War had very different consequences. It did indeed bring about a new international system. Although Great Britain and France were still, as after the First World War, numbered among the victor nations, any thought of British (or French) predominance in Europe or globally was inconceivable. In particular, Great Britain's days as a world power were over. Dependent in Europe on American protection against Germany and the Soviet Union, both France and Britain endeavoured with very little success to rescue what they could from their colonial empires. France suffered humiliating defeats in Indochina and Algeria, which tore the heart out of its empire. Great Britain found itself obliged to grant independence to India (including Pakistan) as early as 1947, and gave up its African colonies one by one. In 1970 it withdrew militarily from areas east of Suez, that is from its zones of influence in the Near and Middle East.

The US played a somewhat contradictory role in this process. On the one hand, in some cases it supported its European allies in their efforts to hold on to colonial control, particularly when liberation movements were suspected of being under 'left' or even 'communist' influence. American funding of the French Indochina war up to 1954 is evidence of this policy. On the other hand, Washington employed an anticolonial rhetoric, appealing to ideological and economic resentment, in the interests of improving its access to markets in former colonies. In some cases it went even further. When in 1956 British, French and Israeli forces seized the Suez Canal after its nationalisation by Egypt, the US, with the agreement of the USSR, forced its allies to withdraw. Limiting NATO's sphere of action to the zone north of the Tropic of Cancer also primarily served to deny France and Great Britain any scope for colonial adventures outside US control.

The strikingly dominant political and military role of the US in global politics had a solid economic basis:

The sheer economic dominance of the United States in the global economy in 1950 added to the sense of invulnerability that most Americans shared. Per capita income in the United States was substantially higher than that of every European country, and six or eight times higher than that of Japan. The U.S. balance of payments recorded large current account surpluses in spite of a heavy outflow of foreign aid; indeed, in 1950 the United States was the only large industrialized country that was free of balance-of-payment problems and related import restriction. The U.S. economy, with nearly 40 percent of the output of the industrialized world and over half of its monetary gold, seemed economically impregnable at the time.[2]

The U.S. position was extremely strong throughout the 1950s. Powered by a thriving domestic economy tripled in size by the war and its aftermath, the United States held a clear competitive advantage in nearly every market for industrial goods in which it cared to compete. Indeed, the primary challenge to American foreign economic policy was to keep the combination of U.S. financial and productive power from stifling the recovery of the other potentially major players in the world economic system.[3]

Thus in the late 1940s and throughout the 1950s only the United States could fulfil the role of leader in the West. In the new bipolar context the country was generally accepted as the provider of a protective shield against the Soviet Union. This economic, political and military domination, not only over the defeated nations of Japan and Germany, but also over the allied victor states of Western Europe, meant that in the Western camp the US alone decided the rules of the game, even though some of its allies occasionally protested against this.

Alternatives

The impression should not be given that the form this reconstruction of the international order took was inevitable. There were alternatives. Looking back on the years 1944–50 in the United States we can discern at least three different ideas about possible postwar systems. All three currents of opinion had the common aim of serving US interests, but they varied in their interpretation of these interests and came to conflicting conclusions.[4]

The first line of opinion was most strongly represented in the Roosevelt administration, and was greatly weakened by Roosevelt's death in spring 1945. It aimed at American hegemony on a global scale, to be achieved through free world trade and strong international ties. With free economic competition the United States, with its exuberant economic strength, would dominate as a matter of course. An important aspect of this concept was the integration of the Soviet Union in this global system, possibly even allowing it the status of a junior partner. Splitting the world into two antagonistic power blocs was incompatible with its vision. The idea was to solve the 'Soviet problem' via integration, not overthrow.

The second element in the debate within America differed from the first in that special emphasis was placed on the aim of containing the Soviet Union. The American diplomat George F. Kennan robustly represented this opinion.[5] According to him the Soviet Union was a repressive and unacceptable politicoeconomic system which had to be kept in its place behind its own frontiers. In doing this, however, reliance could not be placed solely on military forms of containment, but rather and above all on the economic and political recovery of the countries of Central and Western Europe. These were considered to be at risk not so much from direct Soviet conquest as from their internal instability, due to revolutionary and communist movements within their own borders. Kennan compared world communism to an 'evil parasite, which can only feed on diseased tissue'. He conceived of the United States as having a somewhat limited part to play in the postwar order, with Western Europe adopting a more important role. He was especially critical of the increasing militarisation of the

East–West conflict and the corseting of the US in a tightening system of military aid obligations. The communists were to be hemmed in, of course, but by non-military means and with maximum European participation, to avoid the US taking on unnecessary security obligations. Such a view was based on the judgement that the communist threat was more political than military.

Neither of these two views made their mark in history, except for the traces left by the first in the setting up of UNO, the IMF and GATT, and by the second in the drawing up of the Marshall Plan. The Truman administration, which had already used the atom bomb at Hiroshima and Nagasaki more as an anti-Soviet demonstration of power than as a military action against Japan, decided against the indirect securing of US interests advocated in different ways by Roosevelt and Kennan, preferring instead a policy of empire-building. The core of this American empire was to be a military alliance, the North Atlantic Treaty Organization, although NATO was not an isolated phenomenon but was accompanied by a whole network of bilateral and multilateral military agreements which globalised the military role of the United States, including the 1947 Rio Pact, SEATO and CENTO.

The network of military bases which were set up across much of the globe became the material expression of this concept. In Europe NATO (very much against Kennan's advice) was greatly enlarged both geographically and politically. The chain of bases now extended from the north of Norway through the middle of Europe to eastern Turkey. In the Near and Middle East, Asia and the Pacific through to Australia, there was a web of US military installations, many of them having close links with the armed forces of the countries where they were established. The influence of the United States, which was already considerable because of the country's economic weight and the overwhelming competitive strength of its industry, was, after the Second World War, further reinforced by this more or less global military presence. No other country in the West had the capacity or the will to make such an effort.

The United States in Victory

During and as a result of the war the US economy reached previously unknown heights, and the country emerged in 1945 with increased strength and dynamism. France and Great Britain were weakened by the war; they had only been able to survive thanks to American help and above all to the Soviet Union, whose efforts had kept most of the German army tied to the Eastern Front. Germany and Japan were militarily defeated and occupied, controlled by the victor powers. Power relationships within West–West relations during the late 1940s and the 1950s were obvious to all. A common ideology and broadly common interests camouflaged overwhelming US domination over its allies. There was no area where the strength of Great Britain, France, Germany or Japan could even approach that of the United States. In the Western camp American predominance was politically and economically indisputable and therefore virtually forced on its European allies. It was also willingly accepted by them because they felt threatened by the Soviet Union, which, although bled dry by the time the war ended, still had a substantially intact military apparatus and in Eastern Europe and some parts of Central Europe was operating a policy of establishing a zone of maximum influence. Acceptance of US supremacy in the Western camp (symbolised by NATO) would, it was hoped, allow Great Britain and France to continue to pursue their former colonial interests with indirect backing from the US. Only if these two countries could feel secure in Europe would they be able to think about recovering and stabilising even a reduced empire. But the security problems in Europe – in Germany and the Soviet Union – were immense. In both these contexts, involving the US in Europe was useful. On the one hand, it helped to integrate West Germany into the alliance and thus also kept Germany divided; on the other, it kept out the Soviet Union. If the victorious European allies had had to perform both these tasks alone, their success would have been open to doubt at least, and in any event a great strain would have been placed on all the material, political and military resources of Western Europe, making it impossible for the old colonial rulers to play any part whatsoever as world powers.

The stability of the postwar order in Europe was thus based on the following principles:

- the general acceptance of US domination and leadership in the West;
- the implicit acceptance of a Soviet sphere of influence in Eastern Europe and parts of Central Europe, with the simultaneous limitation of this sphere;
- the solution to the German problem by dividing the country, and by making its economic, political and military rebuilding part of the development of the two blocs.

The Cold War was an important factor in this stabilisation of the postwar order, in that it legitimised the American leadership role in Europe (within American domestic politics as well as in Europe itself), while also legitimising the West's 'containment' of the Soviet Union and thus the division of Europe into two camps – with the inevitable consequence of a divided Germany.

The unstable international order of the years between the wars, characterised by rival states which were often highly nationalistic in spirit, was thus transformed into two hostile orders, each dominated by a superpower, forming blocs which despite their hostility to each other guaranteed stability and thus resolved the problem of any German threat to the postwar system.

2

The Shifting Centres of Power

Strength through Integration: the German Federal Republic

The process of rebuilding Germany, both West and East, was already well under way in the 1950s. It was linked to two conditions. The first was the thorough integration of each country into a supranational system (NATO or Warsaw Pact), in order to prevent independent nationalistic action and thus to exclude any new threat. The second was a greater military contribution to the Cold War. Germany, especially West Germany, now had a considerable military potential once more. This was in a sense the price which the Federal Republic had to pay, under US pressure, for membership of the club of Western nations. Naturally in both West and East Germany there were rightwing circles which were only too willing to pay such a price, since for them rearmament was not simply a tactical necessity but an end in itself. The new West German military potential was of course limited on a strategic level (no nuclear or chemical weapons, or missiles) because of public opinion in neighbouring countries, while at the same time it was to be directed solely against the East via integration in NATO. An analogous process took place in East Germany. Thus, whether seen from the East or the West, the respective 'good' Germans could be used to frighten off the 'bad' Germans from threatening their respective neighbours. In terms of security policy this was an attractive solution to the German problem from the French, Polish and Soviet points of view.

Thus at first West and East Germany were essentially passive objects of victor-nation policy. However, this relationship altered more rapidly than many contemporaries realised. The two political and military blocs' wish to use West and East Germany as tools in the context of the Cold War increased the importance and freedom of action of the two Germanies. They were no longer puppets in the hands of the victor nations who were now their respective allies or enemies, because the latter were very anxious to have the support of their respective German state in the Cold War. The Cold War thus smoothed the path of each Germany towards acceptance, at least within its own alliance, as a more or less 'normal' country. This process was considerably facilitated and accelerated by economic recovery, although that of the GDR was less dramatic than the FRG's and took place under different conditions. Both countries were soon numbered among the economically most dynamic and important countries within their respective alliances. At the same time they remained frontline states in the Cold War, which made them from an early stage key elements in the European postwar political order. Without the membership of the Germanies, both NATO and the Warsaw Pact Organisation would have assumed different characters.

The process of integrating of West Germany in the EC and East Germany in Comecon, as well as in NATO and the Warsaw Pact, respectively, was ambivalent in more ways than one. It defused the threat not simply of German revenge for defeat in the war but also of the destabilisation of the postwar order, with whatever consequences that would have brought. It also led to the 'normalisation' of the two Germanies by legitimising them again after the period of fascism and the Holocaust. This legitimisation was in itself a precondition for economic resurgence and for a new, militarily strong Germany, integrated in two bloc systems with a consequent partial loss of independence. Thus West German military strength was under the command of American NATO generals, while its economic strength was closely interwoven with that of the other countries of Western Europe within the framework of the European Coal and Steel Community, and – it was fervently hoped – could no longer be turned against them. However, membership of NATO enabled the Federal Republic to be more influential than it could have been otherwise. Its impact on NATO policy and on the policies of various NATO states, as well as on states outside NATO, is proof of this. The same is true of the country's EC membership. It is true that the West German national economy was closely linked and integrated with those of its Western neighbours, but the enlargement of a quasi-domestic market and the improvement of export opportunities provided one of the essential conditions enabling West Germany to become an important economic power again. In both cases the restraining and the strengthening of the Federal Republic, and of the GDR in different circumstances, were closely linked processes, with the strengthening process becoming increasingly more significant.

Gradually West Germany became the strongest economic power in Europe, while the former world power Great Britain fell behind even Italy in terms of economic strength, and France could barely keep pace.

This economic success story was flanked politically in that West Germany became almost militant in its support of the Atlantic Alliance, while at the same time it sought to establish closer links with France and greater integration into the EC. These two postures were sometimes difficult to combine, for example during the 1960s when Paris was trying to loosen its ties with the US, but essentially the Federal Republic managed this balancing act successfully. The formation of a German-French axis within the EC and close links with Washington constituted the core of German foreign policy in which economic and political interests served each other. From the end of the 1960s onwards the normalisation of relations with Eastern Europe was put on the agenda, further increasing the FRG's influence and scope for action in the West too. West Germany decided on and maintained this change of course against considerable mistrust among some quarters in Washington and in some European capitals. It was precisely this new Ostpolitik of the 1960s and 1970s that enabled West Germany not just to become an economically strong country but also to pursue a really independent foreign policy. 'In October 1979, West German unwillingness to support the dollar and to import American inflation was a vital factor in causing the United States to change its domestic economic policy and to shift to a tight monetary policy'.[1]

In economic and monetary policy the US was now obliged to cooperate with West Germany. It would of course be nonsense to think there was unilateral German domination of the EC or of transatlantic relations. Nonetheless, compared with the initial political and economic position at the end of the 1940s and beginning of the 1950s the changes were striking. The figures in Table 2.1 illustrate the trend, demonstrating the increasing importance of France and above all of West Germany within the EC economy. In 1979 the two countries combined accounted for 55.6 per cent of total GDP in the EC, a rise from 52.1 per cent in 1970, within a nine-member community.

There is, however, little point in comparing the economic potential of some of the neighbouring countries with that of Germany, because the latter's dominance over them was such as to make them practically part of the West German economy itself. The central role of the deutschmark as an instrument of power is also not evident from Table 2.1. However, even this limited representation does clearly indicate the strength of West Germany, with an economy that was becoming more than twice the size of the British and more than four times that of the Spanish, and with a GNP that was more or less equivalent to those of Great Britain, Spain, the Netherlands, Belgium and Denmark taken together.

Table 2.1 Growth of GDP per Working Head of Population, 1970–1979

Country	Per cent change
West Germany	+35.8%
France	+35.1%
Netherlands	+31.1%
Belgium	+29.4%
Italy	+26.3%
Great Britain	+20.6%
EC total	+30.2%

Source: *Eurostat-Revue*, Luxembourg 1980.

Relative Weakening of the US

Shifts in the relative strengths of the industrialised great powers were not restricted to Europe. This process began in the economic sphere primarily as a result of the Japanese economic miracle, and only secondarily through the economic recovery of Western Europe. During the 1960s and 1970s it became increasingly clear that the position of the United States was gradually weakening and that its period of sole domination of the Western world could not last:

> Indeed the relative loss of power of the US from the fifties to the start of the nineties has been one of the decisive factors in international policies, although naturally in real terms the US is no weaker now than twenty or thirty years ago. Economically and militarily it is much stronger than it was then: it can produce more and better goods, and the military power of its armed forces is substantially greater. If we speak of a relative weakening of the US we mean the worsening of its position in relation to other countries, above all in economic vitality, in that '(I)n the early 1950s, the United States, with 6 percent of total world population, accounted for approximately 40 percent of the gross world product; by 1980, the American share had dropped by half to approximately 22 percent' ... Whereas the United States in the early postwar period produced 30 percent of world manufacturing exports, by 1986 its share had dropped to a mere 13 percent. American productivity growth, which had outpaced the rest of the world for decades, declined dramatically from a growth rate of 3 percent annually in

the early postwar years to an incredible low of 0.8 percent in the 1970s (Sawhill and Stone, 1984, p.73). As American productivity lagged behind that of other advanced economies, particularly Japan, West Germany, and the NICs, the result was a less competitive economy and a substantial lowering of the American standard of living. In capital formation, technological leadership, and the quality of the labor force (human capital), the United States was falling behind in a growing field of industrial competitors. Even in the raw materials, which throughout its history had been a source of competitive strength, the United States was decreasingly self-sufficient ... ; only in agriculture and certain high technology industries did it retain its previously unsurpassed economic strengths ... By the mid-1980s, in almost every other category of economic power the position of the United States had declined greatly.[2]

Table 2.2 GDP and Percentage of GDP of the EC as a Whole, 1970 and 1979 (in billion ecu)

	1970		*1979*	
	GDP	*GDP as of % of EC-GDP*	*GDP*	*GDP as of % of EC-GDP*
West Germany	181	29.6	558	31.8
France	138	22.5	417	23.8
EC total *a*	613	100.0	1,754	100.0
US	960	156.5	1,715	97.8
Japan	200	32.6	738	42.1

a Nine member states.
Source: *Eurostat Revue*, Luxembourg 1980.

The figures in Table 2.2, although they are only intended as a rough guide to an overall trend, demonstrate that while the US economy in 1970 was still 56 per cent bigger than that of the EC, by 1979 it was already somewhat smaller. The weakening dollar was naturally an important factor in this. Most striking is the rise of Japan, whose economic strength grew during the period under consideration from less than one-third of the total EC economy to over 40 per cent, and this at a time when the US economy was far from able to keep up with the EC.

Also interesting is the change in GDP per head of working population in those years, providing a guide – however rough – to the growth in productivity of the countries in question (see Table 2.3). Here again it is clear that the US economy in the 1970s, that is during the period of continuing bloc confrontation within the postwar order, was losing ground overall. Such a development did not occur without conflict. In the final analysis, shifts in competitive strength meant changes in real power, accompanied to some extent by serious conflicts over economic and monetary policy or over trade matters.

Table 2.3 Growth in GDP per Head of Working Population 1970–1979

County	Per cent change
West Germany	+35.8%
EC total	+30.2%
US *a*	+ 9.6%
Japan	+40.9%

a 1970–8.
Source: *Eurostat Revue*, Luxembourg 1980.

Trade disputes between the US and Europe began in the 1960s with the so-called Chicken War, over US exports of frozen poultry to the EC. Although this and a number of other subsequent disputes, for example the Spaghetti War, may have appeared somewhat bizarre and irrelevant, the underlying conflict was very serious. In 1987 the North Atlantic Assembly, a NATO body, published a document to the effect that trade conflicts had become regarded as a direct threat to the North Atlantic Alliance. Trade had become so closely interwoven with politics that a worsening of the trade relations between two trading partners necessarily had political repercussions and vice versa.[3]

There has been no lack of fields of conflict, which have included those relating to agriculture, steel, telecommunications, machine tools, semiconductors, the Airbus and technology transfer, as well as differences over economic and monetary policies. These disputes have had widely varying backgrounds. In the agricultural sector they have included fierce arguments over fundamental issues, with the EC subsidies policy the preeminent source of a series of disagreements. EC–US competition in outside markets has been another factor, as

EC preferential treatment for the countries of Southern Europe has had negative effects on US farmers, particularly with the enlargement of the Community following the entrance of Spain and Portugal in 1986 There have been differences of opinion and interest in industrial policy, and disputes with a strategic background or relating to security or the political aspects of technology, as well as conflicts due to differing levels of development in economic productivity and efficiency.

The main competition to the US economy during the 1970s and 1980s, however, did not emanate from Europe. There was a tendency for US foreign trade to shift increasingly towards the Pacific region and therefore for the major rivals of the US to be located in this area. First among these was Japan with its fast-growing economic strength, but the 'four small dragons' of East Asia – South Korea, Taiwan, Singapore and Hong Kong – were also significant competitors. Because of the scope and special nature of US-Japanese relations, in 1989 the US ambassador in Tokyo was able to say that the most important bilateral relationship in the world was that between the United States and Japan.[4] However, it was also in this region, as it become more and more crucial to the US economy, that 'U.S. power to influence and control Pacific economic factors is at its lowest since World War II'.[5]

This was a bilateral relationship which had altered dramatically since the early 1950s, when the US economy was some 25 times larger than the Japanese and it was of overwhelming technological superiority. Today, the US economy is still bigger – the population of the United States is after all twice as big as that of Japan – but the gap has been greatly narrowed.[6] But quantitative comparisons alone give a very inadequate idea of the power shift. Qualitative changes in the relationship have been of greater importance, particularly in the field of high technology. In the computer chip industry, for example, Silicon Valley thought itself invulnerable until the Japanese broke into the unsuspecting US home market in 1979 with the 16K DRAM, immediately snatching a 40 per cent market share. Moreover, Japanese chips proved to be of a higher quality than those made in America. By the end of 1979 the Japanese were producing 64K DRAMs and by the end of 1982 they had won a 70 per cent share of the world market for these. The Americans improved their position in 1983 and 1984, when they began to manufacture 64K DRAMs themselves, but in 1985 demand dropped by 12 per cent and in a pitiless price war the Japanese swept the American manufacturers from the marketplace. On 9 October 1985 Intel, which had invented the integrated memory circuit, declared its withdrawal from the DRAM market.[7] The Japanese extended their lead in the further development and production of memory chips of growing capacity, with European producers falling even further behind than their American counterparts.

The Japanese export offensive also covered a whole range of other key products: cars, entertainment and office electronics, photo-graphic and video equipment. In these sectors too there were devastating effects on the American and European industries, some of which were extremely antiquated.

Even before the end of the Cold War, there was hardly anything left of the 'postwar order' as it existed among the main capitalist powers. America, it is true, was still the strongest state economically, politically and militarily, but this was increasingly due to its size rather than to its qualities. Its principal allies had become its competitors, and there could no longer be any question of US domination of the world economy or of its allies. By 1987 the former US ambassador to Bonn, Richard Burt, was admitting that Japan and a Europe led by West Germany were now equal partners with the US in economic terms; Japan and West Germany alone accounted for nearly a fifth of world trade. What was decided in Tokyo or Bonn had worldwide repercussions. The world economy had become multipolar and it was therefore essential for the leading industrial nations – West Germany, Japan and the US – to work together in controlling world market forces.[8]

The Soviet Union

What essentially stamped its mark on the postwar order was the fact that the Soviet Union was not simply a competitor or opponent, it was above all the enemy in the Cold War. Not only was it competing for concrete positions of influence and power, it was also making a rival ideological claim: that of constituting an alternative to the capitalist world system as a whole, a system of which the United States was a part. This would have been less threatening had it come from any power other than the Soviet Union. The USSR, however, had been the decisive European victor power in the Second World War and was a country to be reckoned with because of its size and potential resources alone.

The Second World War saw the Soviet Union breaking out of its previous isolation. More than that, it led to the establishment of a buffer-zone of states subject to Soviet control between its own frontiers and those of its potential opponents in Europe. From the Soviet point of view the Eastern bloc was a historical achievement in both military terms and in terms of political and economic power. The 'socialism in one country' of the Soviet Union had become a 'socialism in many countries'. Nonetheless, the USSR itself had emerged from the war drained by the loss of 26 million dead, whole regions laid waste, and an industry and infrastructure almost completely destroyed west of the Urals. No less than 1,710 of its towns and 70,000 of its villages had been destroyed.[9]

After the Second World War the Soviet Union was a partly industrialised developing country under harsh dictatorial control, bled dry by the war but with greatly strengthened foreign policy positions. With this went an ideology that was progressive in principle but deformed by a dogmatic Leninism which was the antithesis of Marxian theory. Out of this material the West was able to generate an impressive alien image of a huge, mighty and menacing state, a brutal oriental despotism whose show trials and activities in Eastern Europe were already frightening enough, let alone when viewed in combination with an anticapitalist threat of world revolution.

Given this background, the East–West conflict was always peculiarly dual in character. On the one hand there was a 'battle of the systems', the ideological rivalry. On the other, there was the competition for supremacy and concrete advantages between the two states which dominated their respective systems. It is not always easy to distinguish between what was US–Soviet rivalry and what was rivalry between systems. All too often 'ideological' arguments were used to justify power politics, and just as frequently the opposition between the systems manifested itself in the guise of state and power politics.

If the immediate postwar period is taken as a starting point, then the economic progress made by the Soviet Union by the mid-1950s was highly impressive. In any event the Soviet economy expanded much faster than that of the US, and this at a time when the latter was still very dynamic. A CIA report calculated an annual Soviet economic growth of 4.7 per cent on average, while the US achieved only 3.4 per cent growth over the same period. As a result, in 1950 Soviet GDP was only 32.7 per cent of US GDP, but by 1975 the figure had reached 57 per cent. Per capita consumption in the Soviet Union in the period 1950–81 increased by an average 3.4 per cent yearly, representing an almost threefold increase in the average Soviet citizen's standard of living.

This impressive dynamic impetus, which naturally has to be measured against the comparatively low starting point, slowed down in the 1970s; by the early 1980s virtual stagnation had set in. In spite of all the quantitative advances made by the Soviets, they failed to achieve technological innovation or economic acceptability. Yet despite the continuing shortfalls compared with the West, the economic gap narrowed significantly, so enlarging the Soviet Union's scope for manoeuvre in foreign policy. At the same time the USSR invested massively in building up and maintaining large-scale armed forces, and although their equipment was only relatively modern, any technological deficiencies were made up for by their sheer weight of numbers as compared with those of the West.

Nuclear weapons acted as a deterrent, but also lent prestige. In the decade following the Cuban missile crisis of 1962 and the Soviet capitulation in the face of an American ultimatum, the Soviets, through enormous efforts, even achieved nuclear parity with the US. These successes were attained even though in many sectors and regions the USSR's level of development was barely that of a Third World country. Nonetheless, it could, at least to some extent, claim equal rank in principle with the United States as a world 'superpower'. Without this economic and military rise of the Soviet Union after the Second World War, which compared with the preceding period was a new expression of the relatively weakened US position in the world as a whole, there could have been no talk of a serious East–West conflict, a Cold War or above all a bipolarity in international relationships.[10]

How Bipolar was the Postwar Period?

Almost all disputes on the international stage took place within the grid of the East–West conflict. The North–South conflict was viewed from this angle. Relationships between Western powers were also shaped within this framework, such as the US-Japanese military relationship and the American security guarantee, the setting up of NATO and its role as an instrument of US influence in Europe, and even Western technology policy.

The postwar period, now officially and publicly over with the dissolution of the Soviet Union and the reunification of Germany, was, however, even by the 1980s no longer simply bipolar. It was also not yet multipolar. In other words, the power centres were already differentiated enough no longer to fit into the simple bipolar model. Western Europe, Japan and key countries in the Third World were becoming significant powers with their own power bases; in some sectors of central economic importance they were often ahead of the two superpowers. On the other hand, the continuance of the East–West conflict and the renewed Cold War of the 1980s, especially during President Reagan's first term of office (1980–4), hindered the coming into being of a truly multipolar world order. Despite the process of

3

The Postwar Order in the Third World: Regional Conflicts

The Cold War in the South

Conflicts in the Third World during the postwar period often involved a complexity of problems on different levels. First, naturally, there were internal or localised conflicts of a political, economic, ethnic or social character. Then came the tendency to interpret such local or regional conflicts in terms of East–West conflict, or even to force them into this framework. Purely limited and local disputes could thus become events of global importance, involving the risk of a direct confrontation between the superpowers. Regional conflicts in the Third World also frequently led to contradictions within the Western or Eastern camps, or exacerbated them. The development of conflicts within the Third World was therefore frequently influenced not only by the hostility between East and West but also by rivalries between allies, either making the disputes worse or, less often, damping them down. Finally, it should not be forgotten that regional conflicts in the Third World were and are closely linked with the structure of world market exchanges, such as the falling prices of raw materials, debt crises, a drop in the demand for certain export products resulting from technological changes, or other global economic influences.

For the great powers after the Second World War, the Third World was a crucial field of struggle between the rival systems, but it is noteworthy that different regions were drawn into these struggles to a widely differing extent. During the first decade after the war, Latin America was an area which from the US/Western point of view could be regarded as completely 'safe'. The Soviet Union was a long way away; it had hardly any political or economic presence in the region, and no military presence at all. In Africa the position seemed just as favourable for the West at first, until decolonisation brought contradictory results: pro-Western regimes came to power or were installed, but anti-imperialist forces gained ground. Nonetheless Africa was not an area which caused special strategic worries to Washington or Paris in the immediate postwar period.

The picture was very different in Asia, where the old European-dominated colonial system had been greatly shaken by Japanese conquest and the subsequent Japanese defeat. Attempted recolonisation produced serious conflicts, amounting to wars. The French attempt to reclaim its former colonies in Indochina after the Japanese withdrawal met with armed resistance, particularly from the Vietnamese, who had become experienced in waging a war of liberation in their fight against the Japanese. In 1954 France suffered an annihilating military defeat and withdrew from Indochina. During the final years of this war the United States had been paying three-quarters of the French war costs, because it considered the Vietnamese liberation forces to be 'communist'. However irrational this was at the start of the conflict in 1947 (Ho Chi Minh wrote eight times to the US government asking for support, without even receiving an acknowledgement of his letters), it was nonetheless the mainspring of American policy towards Indochina following the Japanese capitulation. Thus after 1954 French influence in the region was replaced by American influence. By the early 1960s the US was already deeply involved in internal Vietnamese politics. It participated in the coup which deposed dictator Diem, whom Washington had previously supported. Under President Kennedy the US began a rapid military build-up too, with the initially small number of its military advisers being continually increased. Finally the US became the active warring nation and by 1967 had some 537,000 soldiers stationed in Vietnam.

A second breeding ground of conflict was China. In 1949, after a long struggle, the Chinese Communist Party triumphed over the US-backed Kuomintang of General Chiang Kai-shek and the country with the largest population in the world underwent a social and political revolution. In US eyes this was almost the greatest catastrophe imaginable, apart from the possible loss of Europe, since the new Chinese People's Republic was viewed as a close ally of the Soviet enemy, as indeed it was during the first ten years of its existence. The 'yellow peril' was soon categorised as being even more dangerous than the Soviet threat; 'Red China' became the most hated enemy of US foreign policy for almost two decades, elevated to this position by its revolutionary rhetoric and militancy.

Asia proved to be a central theatre of the Cold War in a third instance too, when in 1950 a 'hot war' broke out between the two power blocs, although it was limited to Korea. The United States and the Soviet Union had divided Japan's former colony into two zones of influence, each under their respective control, and each with their respective favoured governments in power, communist in the North and right wing in the South, on either side of the 38th parallel. In 1950 North Korea invaded South Korea in an attempt to reunify the country by force:

> [T]he North Korean attack was not merely an episode in the struggle amongst Koreans. On another level, it represented a clash between the Soviet and American power systems. The war amongst Koreans was soon overshadowed by the war between the blocs. When the fighting ended in 1953, a solution was imposed on both Koreas by the great powers. Unification, their common war aim, remained unrealised.[1]

A British scholar has remarked: 'Ironically for Koreans, liberation brought not self-determination and peace, but a vicious civil war, enmeshed in great power rivalry, which was to bring the country death and destruction on a scale it had never known during World War Two.'[2]

The United States had looked at Korea solely from the viewpoint of the East–West conflict, of its confrontation with the Soviet Union. It had accepted the division of the country along a demarcation line favourable to its interests and had taken over the apparatus of Japanese colonial repression, using it against the opposition to such effect that in 1947 the number of political prisoners was already twice as high as it had been under the Japanese occupation. At about this time an Australian diplomat was reporting that the torture and murder of political opponents by the ruling group were publicly accepted and general practices.[3] Even before the start of the war, the policy of containment was all-important in South Korea, with the aim of limiting Soviet influence via foreign policy measures coupled with the goal of shaping of Korean domestic policy to achieve total repression and control over any opposition. The foreign policy requirement of security was the justification claimed for the establishment of a police state, characterised by a brutality exceeding that of its model in the former Japanese colonial administration. The attack from the North in 1950 was then taken as a further legitimisation of these methods.

The conflicts in Asia during the postwar period were so fierce and dramatic that they often led to the brink of nuclear war. In both Korean and Chinese contexts the possibility of using nuclear weapons against China was discussed or threatened many times. The question of whether such attacks might not also lead to a nuclear war with the Soviet Union did not always produce a clear answer.

For many Third World countries, the postwar period was far from being as stable as it appeared from the European perspective. A series of changes took place slowly and by stages, almost behind the backs of the actors and observers. Social upheavals, closer integration in world markets, nation-building in the decolonised countries, as well as ethnic and tribal conflicts, all led to radical changes in many of these societies.

There were striking contrasts in the development of Third World countries. From the start the term 'Third World' disguised a fiction; what was really meant was simply a collective category within which to lump together those countries of Asia, Africa and Latin America not belonging to either Western or Eastern blocs. Even in 1945 it made no sense to talk about common lines of development in the Third World, as there was such great economic, social and trade variations. The evolution of a number of states to the level of 'threshold countries' and even NICs (newly industrialising countries) – that is, countries with their own industrial base and even a nascent technological and industrial potential for further take off – did not take place overnight, but can often be traced back to starting points in the 1950s or even earlier. In the course of this growing heterogeneity the balance of importance shifted about within the South, and also between North and South, although this was given less attention for a long time.

The attention of the North, and that of the US in particular, was instead concentrated on spectacular changes. The first of these was the Chinese Revolution discussed above, whose victory sent a shockwave through the US political establishment. For many years China had been regarded by the United States as strategically the most important country in Asia, as a potentially huge sales market for US consumer goods, and as a country which because of its internal weaknesses was amenable to US influence. This was the open-door policy that had already been applied to competition with other countries at the turn of the century. The loss of a country of such key importance to the US position in Asia was not simply painful, it was felt to be a national catastrophe. The active role played by China in the Korean War reinforced this feeling.

The second shock came in 1958–9: the Cuban Revolution. The US had always considered Latin America as a 'secure' zone of influence, and with good reason. No 'serious Soviet threat' existed there, it was thought, and since the turn of the century Cuba had been little more than a semi-colony penetrated and controlled by American companies and politically dominated by the American government. An anti-imperialist revolution here of all places alarmed the US government greatly. It was a shattering indication of its own complacency and also therefore a sign that communism (that is, the Soviet Union) was even more dangerous in the Third World than hitherto assumed.

The third shock was America's defeat in the Vietnam War. The gradual escalation of the military involvement did not bring the victory that was repeatedly predicted, but simply reinforced a military stalemate. The poor undeveloped country of North Vietnam inflicted the first military defeat suffered by the Americans in war, although this would hardly have been conceivable without Soviet and Chinese support. This defeat was of course also very much related to political as well as military factors. The US did not lose the war in Vietnam in the technical military sense; rather it was domestic opposition to the war which the US government could no longer resist. The Nixon administration surrendered on the home front because it was unable to achieve victory on the battlefield, or at least not at an acceptable cost.

These three defeats – China, Cuba, Vietnam – influenced US policy far more than the subtle and longer-term changes which were fundamentally altering the nature of the Third World and which made such revolutions possible.

Reaction

The reactions to the three major defeats differed. The initial reflex reaction to the loss of China was a further hardening of ideology, with the consequent establishment and securing of additional anti-communist outposts and regional deputies. The importance of South Korea to the US, or the latter's support for Taiwan with its claim to represent the whole of China, can only be understood against this background. The same world view is also evident in the Vietnam War. The Domino Theory used to justify the war was based on the view that each 'loss' of a country, however insignificant in itself, would lead to further 'losses', until finally the whole region would fall under the hegemony of the People's Republic and/or the Soviet Union. The establishment and extension of a geostrategic network of client states and military bases was therefore desirable, and even necessary, not only politically but also militarily. It was the Cuban Revolution, however, which shook the US out of its conventional thinking. Cuba was proof that an extremely 'safe' small country within the East–West context could break up, because of internal instability, and that US military bases or political influence within such a country were no guarantee of this not happening. The Kennedy administration lost no time in drawing its political conclusions from this experience.

Basic to these conclusions was the not entirely new perception that the 'global security' of the United States in terms of East–West confrontation depended not only on relations with other governments and on weaponry, but also on the internal conditions within other countries. The US-backed coup in Guatemala in 1954, and the CIA-inspired fall of the Iranian Premier Mossadegh the year before, were after all by no means the first cases of United States foreign policy involving interference in the internal affairs of other countries. President Kennedy was following a well-established course, although taking it to very different levels.

On one level Kennedy continued similar types of operation. The invasion of Cuba at the Bay of Pigs in 1961 by CIA-trained Cuban exiles was, however, a fiasco, carried out on the basis of related experience gained in the successful operation against Guatemala, but without the realisation that internal conditions in Cuba were totally different. After a few days of bitter fighting, the invasion force was wiped out. President Kennedy's enthusiasm for such operations was greatly dampened as a result; he even felt himself to have been duped and led into error by the CIA.[4]

But the president did not restrict himself to dubious adventures such as the act of aggression against Cuba. His administration drew from the Cuban Revolution the conclusion that the US would have to pay increased attention to security and stability within Latin and South America. The greatest threats to stability in these regions were, as Cuba had shown, to be expected not from outside but from inside societies characterised by instability and 'subversion'. Certain conceptual parallels with the arguments of George Kennan about post war Europe are unmistakable here.

From this viewpoint, lasting control over Latin America depended on making its societies healthy and economically dynamic. Only on this foundation was political stability possible. Within the context of this logic, the Kennedy administration launched its ambitious programme for an 'Alliance for Progress' in Latin America. The United States and the countries of South and Central America would combine in a big common effort to develop the hemisphere economically and socially, so as to cut the ground from under revolutions before they could happen. This plan was to be financed mainly by the US. The years between 1961, the year in which the Alliance was founded, and 1969, did indeed see some US$10.3 billion flow into Latin America, supplemented by a further $4.6 billion from other bilateral sources and $5.8 billion from multilateral sources. But in net terms, less than half US financial aid actually went into the building-up of Latin American economies – that is, $4.8 billion. The rest had to be spent on debt-servicing and other obligations in the US. Consequently almost no economic and social objectives were achieved, although there were other reasons for this too. Instead of a target annual economic growth rate of 5 per cent (not less than 2.5 per cent per head of population with a population growth of around 3 per cent) the actual growth was barely 1.5 per cent. The programme which began with fine rhetoric and ideological commitment, and which was officially aimed at supporting the 'democratic left' in Latin America, had already run aground by the mid-1960s at the latest.[5]

The economic policy and social reform aims of the Alliance for Progress thus came to nothing, but this was not the case with the political objectives that lay behind the programme. The antirevolutionary policy of the US in Latin America had shown great success by the end of the 1960s. It had prevented the feared spread of the Cuban Revolution to other countries and had isolated Cuba. This was due not so much to any success of the social and economic reform efforts of the Alliance as to the opposite – that is, the repressive policy operated in parallel with these efforts.

This repressive policy was known 'counterinsurgency', and as such it even contained a certain amount of social reform rhetoric. Counterinsurgency and the Alliance for Progress were from the Kennedy administration's viewpoint two sides of the same policy. While military measures in the widest sense of the term were intended to control, contain or defeat existing insurgencies, the Alliance was to serve to bring about economic and social reforms with the aim of forestalling revolution. In effect the results of the reformist Alliance were as unimpressive as the results of counterinsurgency were sometimes spectacular. The failure of the attempt to export the Cuban Revolution to Bolivia in 1967 was of symbolic importance, when Che Guevara was tracked down and killed by an army counterinsurgency team accompanied by US advisers.

During the 1960s the practice became established of ensuring continuing control over the Third World through the application and combination of different methods. These included the creation of an overall global economic framework of conditions guaranteeing US domination at minimum cost, for instance via free trade or bilateral agreements; integrative 'soft' forms of influence on and within other countries, perhaps by appropriately designed forms of 'aid' through programmes like the Alliance for Progress; repressive 'hard' forms of influence, such as counterinsurgency itself or a coup d'état (Philippines and Guatemala); and direct intervention by US troops, although this of course only occurred in emergencies and within appropriate contexts (Korea, the Dominican Republic, Vietnam).

Revolutionary Waves

Revolutionary changes in countries and societies of the Third World did not occur continuously and uniformly, but in waves. The British scholar Fred Halliday has described three such phases for the period after the Second World War:

> In the post–1945 period, there was one such wave in the years 1944–1954 (Albania, Yugoslavia, China, Korea, Vietnam, Bolivia, and many unsuccessful ones in, among other countries, the Philippines, Iran, Malaya and Guatemala). A second postwar wave come in the years 1958–1962 (Iraq, North Yemen, Congo, Cuba, Algeria). After 1962, and despite many upsurges in the third world, no state fell to revolutionary forces, with the single, remote case of the British colony of South Yemen in 1967. But from 1974 to 1980 there was a third revolutionary wave, covering no less than fourteen countries, across the whole geographical span of the tropical south: Vietnam, Cambodia, Laos in Indo-China; Afghanistan and Iran in Central Asia; Ethiopia in the Horn and Zimbabwe in the south of Africa; the five Portuguese colonies – Angola, Mozambique, Guinea-Bissau, Sao Tome and Cape Verde; and, in the western hemisphere, Grenada and Nicaragua.[6]

During the 1980s there were no successful revolutions in the Third World, although in some countries revolutionary or prerevolutionary 'situations' did exist, as in El Salvador, the Philippines, Haiti and Burma. Instead, the 1980s saw a whole series of non-revolutionary transformations, including the overthrowing of various dictatorships which had established themselves in the 1970s – for example in Peru, Argentina, Uruguay, Brazil and the Philippines – while dictatorial powers were significantly reduced in South Korea and Pakistan.

This poses two related questions. Why should Third World revolutions have occurred in 'waves', although internal conditions in these countries have often been so extremely different? And how did conditions during the 1974–80 period differ so substantially from those in the 1980s, when the third revolutionary wave was so completely stopped? Revolutions are such drastic social processes that they obviously cannot succeed easily or frequently. In retrospect there is much to indicate that their success depends on the simultaneous presence of two complex conditions. First, a combination of revolutionary economic, social and political conditions must exist within a society, so that within a specific country the revolution can move from being the wishful thinking of the dissatisfied to becoming a real possibility. But this alone is generally not enough. It is also important that the international situation should not make a revolutionary development a priori impossible. Revolution can be made impossible by regional factors, such as the military intervention by the Shah of Iran against the uprising in the Dhofar province of Oman, or by reason of the policies of extra-regional big powers. The actual success of a revolutionary movement in the Third World thus becomes essentially dependent on whether the powers which exercise hegemony can and will oppose the revolution. The third revolutionary wave in the post war period (1974-80) makes this clear. The power exerting the greatest external influence over the Third World, the United States, had just suffered its crippling defeat in the Vietnam War and for a number of years was not in a position to act energetically to impose its hegemony for reasons which had to do with domestic politics. This was a combination of factors which became known as the 'Vietnam syndrome': the paralysis of a superpower. The classic example of this was perhaps the victory of the MPLA in Angola.[7] Without the military assistance of Cuba this victory would have been almost unimaginable, and if the US had opposed Cuban military aid neither Cuba nor the Soviet Union would have been able to do much about it, but as a consequence of the Vietnam War the US Congress forbade its government to authorise any American intervention in Angola.

The administrative expression of the Vietnam syndrome crippling the US in its role as dominant power was seen during the first two years of the Carter administration. During the final phase of the Nixon administration the president had been hindered by his part in the Watergate scandal and by the proceedings to remove him from office. His successor, Gerald Ford, was shackled by Congress in his foreign policy.[8] When Jimmy Carter was elected, however, he set about drafting a foreign policy based on 'morality', marking a fresh start after Watergate and My-Lai. In May 1977 he formulated his aims clearly enough:

Being confident in our own future, we are now free of that inordinate fear of communism which once led us to embrace any dictator who joined us in that fear. I am glad that it is being changed ... For too many years we have been willing to adopt the flawed and erroneous principles and tactics of our adversaries, sometimes abandoning our own values for theirs. We have fought fire with fire, never thinking that fire is better quenched with water.[9]

At least in principle Carter, from this perspective, initiated a policy at the start of his period of office which was officially based on four objectives. These were:

- to respect the countries of the Third World as sovereign states with fundamentally equal rights;
- to renounce military intervention;
- to promote economic development;
- to advance human and social rights.

These principles were naturally at no time meant to be taken at face value, but they were one reason why freedom movements in the Third World found themselves with greater scope for action. They took away legitimacy from future US interventions and gave progressive movements in the Third World arguments which could be used against foreign intervention. By February 1979 at the latest, however, the Carter administration was once again applying Cold War logic to the Third World. 'Protection of the oil flow from the Middle East is clearly part of our vital interest', the then defense secretary, Harold Brown, declared in 1979. And 'in protection of those vital interests we'll take any action that's appropriate, including the use of military force'.[10]

This effectively shelved the principle of non-intervention. Summer 1979 saw the beginning of a large-scale military build-up which was directed against the Soviet Union, and which also involved a massive expansion of US potential for intervention in the Third World.

The wave of revolutionary movements in the Third World after 1973–4 took place within a variety of contexts. First, in many countries social conflicts had reached a prerevolutionary intensity. Second, the defeat of the United States in Vietnam acted as a political and psychological encouragement to freedom movements in the Third World, and as a spur onwards since the myth of American invincibility was suddenly destroyed. Third, the US will to make further massive interventions in the Third World was weakened for a few years, undermined by the domestic political climate resulting from Vietnam and Watergate. Carter's initial policy was primarily the expression of these circumstances, not their cause, and the clumsiness of his administration in its contradictory and naive foreign policy tended to increase the Third World countries' freedom of manoeuvres. Fourth, during the 1970s the Soviet Union was playing a more active role in the Third World, supporting freedom movements to an ever-increasing extent. Vietnam had also given it greater scope for action in this sense. Yet these contexts in themselves suggest why the 1980s were not to be a particularly favourable period for revolutionary movements in the Third World.

Under Ronald Reagan the unambiguous aim was to overcome the Vietnam syndrome. Great ideological and material efforts were made to revitalise American capacity for intervention, both physical and psychological. The latter aim was achieved by transporting Cold War ideology wholesale into the Third World, for instance to Central America. The former was achieved by evolving the concept of 'low-intensity conflict', or LIC, to streamline American capacity for more efficient intervention. This became a global policy of containment, based on the use of military power, with the purpose of reversing the Soviet advances in influence in the Third World during the 1970s. It was to be a 'geopolitical offensive'.

The Ideology and Instruments of the Cold War in the Third World

The postwar period and the Cold War were a time of increasingly fierce conflicts of interest, but they were also characterised by the increasing importance attached to ideology. The justification for a foreign policy was not simply that it was regarded as the best expression of a country's own interests. The policy was also given a moral justification. In saying that the Soviet Union was 'the Evil Empire', that the Cold War was being waged 'between the powers of light and darkness', Ronald Reagan was speaking in earnest. In his first press conference as president, Reagan declared that the Soviet leadership was constantly seeking 'world revolution and a single socialist or communist world state', and that to this end it 'reserved the right to commit any crime'.[11] Religious or pseudo-religious phraseology was used. The Cold War was to be waged as a 'Crusade'.

Paranoia set in. The Soviet threat was everywhere. The Soviet Union was using the peace movement to infiltrate Europe. It was establishing military colonies in Africa and Asia. Soviet forces in the guise of advisers were already on the American continent. Only the Rio Grande stood between the United States and Soviet tanks.[12] Popular magazines such as the *Reader's Digest* were referring to Cuba as a puppet, or as a 'knife in Soviet hands held to America's throat'.[13] The Committee of Santa Fe[14] had already provided the Reagan administration with an ideological basis for this view of the US as being under constant attack from within and without:

> The Americas are under attack. Latin America, the traditional alliance partner of the United States, is being penetrated by Soviet power. The Caribbean rim and basin are spotted with Soviet surrogates and ringed with socialist states ... The Americas are under external and internal attack. Latin America, an integral part of the Western community, is being overrun by Soviet supported and supplied satellites and surrogates.[15]

Three ideological elements constantly recurred in the picture of the Soviet Union as the enemy in the Third World. The first was the 'proxy thesis': the assumption that the Soviet Union was the driving force behind revolutionary changes in general and anti-American activities in Third World countries in particular. Secretary of State General Alexander Haig declared that 'Soviet promotion of violence as the instrument of change constitutes the greatest danger to world peace'.[16] (It may be noted in passing that this was the same military man who shortly afterwards did not want to exclude the use of 'nuclear warning shots against the Soviet Union'.) According to his thesis all the threads of 'social change' led to the Kremlin, even though the theoretical existence of an internal and regional potential for conflict in Third World countries was not denied. Such potential conflicts were in any event being stirred up, used and turned against America and Freedom by the Soviet Union and its 'proxies' (for instance, Cuba).

The second tenet of belief was that the Soviet Union had a comprehensive plan for world conquest. In the Caribbean and Latin America, for example, it was assumed that the USSR and Cuba were aiming at not just Nicaragua but also El Salvador, Guatemala and Honduras, in order to bring these countries under Soviet control and from there to undertake a 'drive' towards the north and south. Moreover, this gradual conquest of Central America represented only a stage in the worldwide plan of aggression. This perception of Soviet policy was based on the assumption that there existed a real plan for world domination, to be put into action by creating and above all exploiting 'opportunities', a plan whose core was the isolation of the West from its sources of energy and raw materials, a plan based on growing Soviet nuclear superiority to make the Caribbean a 'Marxist-Leninist sea'.[17]

Brigadier Joseph E. Hopkins explained the Soviet plans in more detail:

The Soviet goal of a world communist community directed from Moscow remains doctrine ... A major conflict in the near term with either China or the United States could result in formation of an American-Chinese pact, with disastrous consequences for the Soviet Union. Accordingly, the Soviets have sought an interim expansion objective which might be attained without directly confronting either China or the United States. The interim objective is the conquest of Eurafrica. To avoid confrontation with China or the United States while seizing Eurafrica, the Soviet Union has chosen the technique of employing proxies or surrogates.[18]

He named Cuba, Vietnam, North Korea and Libya as the most important proxies.

The third ideological element was that the alleged Soviet strategy was a twin strategy made up of external aggression and internal subversion, policies that were essentially identical and simply two sides of the same coin. In the words of the Committee of Santa Fe: 'Given the Communist commitment to utilize every available means to overthrow the capitalist order and to transform the world, internal and external security become inseparable'.[19] This was to set up an ideological mechanism enabling virtually any internal radical change, any social transformation in a Third World country, to be depicted as an 'external' threat.

This ideological intensification of the Cold War in the Third World brought further consequences. Secretary of State Haig had not restricted himself to making threatening nuclear gestures towards the Soviet Union; like other senior US government figures in the White House and the Pentagon, he had also argued strongly for an American maritime blockade against Cuba – which would have been an act of war under international law.

Haig's successor, George Shultz, was soon using arguments reminiscent of those which President Carter not many years previously had declared to be no longer acceptable.[20] The protection of human rights and freedom was made a pretext for American action, with prevention cited as a justification for intervention, and definitions of dictatorship were twisted to suit the requirements of Reaganite ideology. Thus the US government was able to legitimise its support for the Contras in Nicaragua, the Mujahedin in Afghanistan, UNITA in Angola – indeed for almost every military or paramilitary intervention by the US in the Third World. After all, the policy of the US in the Cold War was not simply based on naked self-interest but also on 'morality', a 'morality' which was always intended to be a political counterplan to the alleged Soviet plan, an active ideology constituting part of an anti-Soviet strategy. These rhetorical exercises always implied that the Soviet Union was an overwhelming force, in many regards more powerful than the West. The structural weakness of the USSR, which would make it disintegrate just a few years later, was wilfully ignored.

The Instrument: Low-intensity Warfare

The intensified anticommunist ideology of the 1980s, giving a new impetus to the Cold War, drew the South even further into the East–West conflict than it had been in the preceding decade. This was not a question of rhetoric alone. Washington was working to develop a range of political and military instruments to suit its ideological purposes and the new realities of a 'disturbed' Third World. The new concept for the 1980s went under the heading of 'low-intensity warfare'. It was based on the argument that the strategic situation between the United States and the Soviet Union, particularly in Europe, was now stable. The Soviet Union had nothing to gain by direct aggression against the US or its NATO allies and was therefore trying to ensnare and damage the leading capitalist countries via the Third World, a 'flanking manoeuvre' according to Secretary of State Shultz.[21]

This argument contained two interesting components. On the one hand there was an implicit and sometimes also explicit assumption that the USSR was not more powerful in terms of nuclear and conventional armaments but at best equal, and for this reason it was bypassing confrontation in Central Europe by moving into the Third World. On the other hand stress was laid on the importance of the Third World to the United States per se, or rather the importance of specific regions for specific economic, political or strategic reasons.

In the US view, the real significance of unstable areas in the Third World was the security problem they presented. The 'nuclear impasse' between the superpowers had shifted confrontation between them to the Third World. A US army document advised:

The nuclear stalemate at the strategic level and the threat of escalation to nuclear confrontation serve to confine the confrontation to low to mid intensity conflicts within Third World countries, such as Afghanistan and Vietnam, or support for third parties against clients of the other.[22]

Responsibility for these trends was frequently shifted on to the Soviet Union, which was allegedly using LIC strategies quite deliberately as forms of low-profile warfare against the United States, in order to avoid massive US reaction. LIC was also a Russian strategy to enable global warfare to be waged against the US without the latter knowing that war was going on, according to Secretary of Defense Casper Weinberger:

> The world today is at war. It is not global war, though it goes on around the globe. It is not war between fully mobilized armies, though it is no less destructive for all that ... Tonight, one out of every four countries around the globe is at war. In virtually every case, there is a mask on the face of war. In virtually every case, behind the mask is the Soviet Union and those who do its bidding.[23]

Two other factors entered into the ideological and politico strategic classification of LIC. First, LIC was a frequent phenomenon, while actual wars in the sense of medium/high-intensity conflicts were rare, and were always very unlikely to occur in certain instances. (Since the Second World War US soldiers have been deployed in some 300 cases of conflict in the Third World classified below the threshold level of acute warfare, while conflicts deemed to be full-scale wars – as in Korea, Vietnam and the Gulf – have been few and far between. Second, US military planners were forced to the unwelcome conclusion that their armed forces were in fact extremely poorly prepared for such frequent outbreaks of low-intensity conflict.

This was explained in a study commissioned by the US armed forces:

> The Army's dilemma is that the conflict least likely to occur – extended conventional superpower hostilities in Europe – nevertheless dominates Army thinking, training, and resource allocation. The hostilities most likely to engage the Army's attention will be those small but critical low-intensity conflicts proliferating at the periphery of the great powers; whether indigneous or externally driven, many of these conflicts – or protoconflicts – engage important U.S. interests – in the Gulf, in the Caribbean, in Africa, in the southern Pacific, and potentially, even within the U.S. itself. This low-intensity conflict environment is not one for which the Army is currently prepared.[24]

The function of the discussion around low-intensity warfare was to adapt the foreign policy apparatus of the US government and, vitally, of the US armed forces to altered conflict conditions. The aim of the discussion within the military was to define the conditions and circumstances for low-intensity warfare, to evolve a military doctrine related to this, to adjust military thinking within the forces to these requirements, and to translate the new doctrine into practical terms in the selection and training of military personnel and in the arming of these troops with appropriate weaponry and equipment.

The conclusion that the US armed forces were poorly equipped for low-intensity warfare naturally implied that conflicts of 'low' and 'high' intensity differed not only in their scope but in a qualitative sense as well. In other words, these were not simply differences between 'big' or 'small' wars: completely different types of conflict were involved.

Conflicts of low intensity differ from those of medium/high intensity in that the latter are of a conventional military or nuclear type, where firepower, large numbers of troops, high technology and related variables are decisive. In the case of low-intensity conflicts these factors are in the main frequently irrelevant or secondary, and thus the classic rules of warfare can only be applied to a limited extent. This is something of a simplification, but conflicts of medium and high intensity are chiefly aimed at the military destruction of the opponent's concentrations of power and/or at winning or defending territory. The Gulf War is the most recent example of a war of medium intensity. In LIC situations such troop concentrations are the exception rather than the rule, either because the opponent does not possess them and only carries out operations involving small numbers of fighters, or because they cannot be found or cannot be attacked. Guerrilla warfare provides classic examples of this. Firepower is of secondary significance in such circumstances. LIC situations are generally unconventional and personnel-intensive, characterised by their long duration and small-scale skirmishes. 'The aim is no longer to gain and hold territory, but to maintain political and economic access to the Third World by preempting the Soviets from achieving their expansion aims.'[25]

LIC situations are generally of a highly political nature. This is demonstrated by the proverbial struggle for the hearts and minds of a civil population, within the context of counterinsurgency campaigns. It is clear from this that troops whose fighting strength was optimised for tank battles in the borders between the two Germanies, or for nuclear warfare, are not necessarily useful in LIC situations.

Counterinsurgency
LIC politically is clearly a form of conflict in which counterinsurgency is aimed primarily at preventing or hindering open civil war, uprisings or similar types of conflict. The existence of such a campaign is an indication of the political and socioeconomic nature of the

conflict, an admission that a 'military solution' is either impossible or achievable only at unacceptable cost. Counterinsurgency is aimed predominantly at first winning over and obtaining control of the population, with all other aspects, even including direct military confrontation with a guerrilla force, simply a means to this end.

Counterinsurgency has two fundamental related objectives. The first is the transformation and 'modernisation' of a Third World society and its apparatus of state government on the basis of criteria which leave that government capable of functioning, and which at the same time guarantee US control. Second, it is aimed at driving a wedge between the guerrilla forces or other forms of radical opposition and the population, either by introducing politico-economic stimuli and/or through military coercion and geographical division. That these are not the functions of military forces used in a 'classic' way is obvious. Counterinsurgency therefore requires stronger elements of economic assistance, development aid, psychological back-up and diplomatic initiatives. In all these attempts to 'reform' and 'modernise' the Third World countries concerned, and thus to establish a status quo which can both function and remain stable, the military aspects of the campaign must naturally not be overlooked. After all, such attempts have not infrequently to be made within the context of an escalating civil war. The military forces of the client country are frequently the driving force behind this escalation, with the US military assuming important advisory and training functions and taking part to some degree in military operations as well as in 'civic action' projects to develop the infrastructure or support the population by drilling wells, providing medical aid and so on. Of course these diverse political and economic programmes can only be successful if a minimum level of military 'security' can be achieved. A strategic problem in counterinsurgency is often that its military and repressive side and its development-orientated elements contradict each other in the course of a campaign.

LIC situations can, however, involve more than just counterinsurgency operations. They can require the organisation or supporting of rebellions, for example those of the Nicaraguan Contras or the Afghan Mujahedin. The counteracting of real or alleged terrorism, the freeing of hostages, the 'drugs war' and the deployment of actual or would-be peacekeeping forces all come within this category. LIC is a generic term for militarily appropriate measures below the threshold level of an actual war.

It is important to remember here that the essentially political nature of LIC means that neither it nor its precise implementation were or have been accepted within the US government or the armed forces without disagreements. On the contrary, LIC is still anything but a uniformly defined concept, and the question of how strong the military element within it should be has been disputed. Thus at an Airpower Symposium in 1985, discussing counterterrorism, a certain lieutenant-colonel argued that there was no military solution to terrorism,[26] while another colonel urged the use of B52 bombers to combat terrorism militarily, demonstrating that he obviously thought along completely conventional military lines and took no account of the basic concepts of LIC.[27]

Furthermore, the priority assigned in theory to the political aspects of LIC is frequently not maintained in practice, and the concept is clearly subject to increasing militarisation. This means that political, sociopolitical and economic means are sacrificed to military purposes.This tendency became apparent under the Reagan administration in the 1980s, and there is no evidence at all that it changed under the Bush or Clinton administrations. LIC does not mean the substitution of political for military solutions, but rather the removal of the distinction between 'military' and 'civil'. Thus within LIC situations non-military events such as strikes and demonstrations can be regarded as 'acts of war', while the military may be occupied in giving medical aid to rural populations or in setting up infrastructures for civic improvements. In this sense, under LIC conditions civilian aspects can become completely militarised and military activities completely politicised. Both the military and non-military measures that are implemented by the armed forces of the US and/or a local government are of course of decisive importance for any LIC programme, while the establishment of military and police 'security' is also a prerequisite without which any pacification programme must fail.

The Lesson of Vietnam
Low-intensity warfare is fundamentally a concept based on the lesson of Vietnam, which is that large-scale interventions by the US using its own troops are often inappropriate to guarantee US domination. Even the Gulf War has not changed that feeling. During the 1980s low-intensity warfare was intended to enable the US to pursue an active and even military Third World policy, without becoming involved in a second Vietnam. Correspondingly, LIC campaigns are designed to keep any US engagement small-scale while optimising its efficiency. For the US, LIC is, compared with direct military intervention, substantially cheaper in terms of both cash and casualties, because mostly local troops are used. It minimises the risk to the US itself. At the same time, and this is the essential aspect, all other things

being equal LIC is more efficient than conventional intervention in many cases. It can be aimed directly at the causes of conflict, allowing the use of 'appropriate technology' available for military tasks in the Third World and completely avoiding the counterproductive effects of direct US intervention – such as the generation of an increasingly costly military stalemate, or a nationalistic reaction uniting the population against the invaders. It thus in general avoids the risk to the United States of military overreaction and conflict developing into full-scale conventional warfare. The purpose of LIC is to use specific methods with increased efficiency to make direct intervention by the US unnecessary.

There are also factors related to US domestic politics, in that one of the main problems for the country's foreign policy is that since Vietnam American public opinion is no longer prepared to wage a war in the Third World which will result in heavy US casualties.

This constitutes a considerable constraint on the capacity of the US to exercise an active and dominating foreign policy, since it not only hinders specific military options but also in many cases makes the threat of the use of full-scale military force lack credibility. The difference between a virtually risk-free airwar against Iraq and the unattractiveness of an involvement in a ground war in Bosnia illustrates the point. LIC is the attempt to find a way out of this difficulty. Low-intensity warfare in the final analysis is the kind of warfare that the United States can carry on in a particular Third World country for years, without even attracting especial attention from public opinion. This minimises criticism. Relatively small US commitments in terms of troops and material do not give rise to the growth of political opposition, let alone to a polarisation of US society such as occurred as a result of the US involvement in Vietnam.

> Popular support is not absolutely essential, but there must be at least benign indifference, especially on the part of the mass media. Otherwise, congress will feel compelled to end U.S. involvement, regardless of the stakes. If LIC can be kept controlled at the lower levels of violence, with very little carnage for the TV cameras, then possibly public support, and as a minimum, benign indifference will accrue. Something so pedestrian as Internal Defense and Development [another word for counterinsurgency] especially when it is relatively successful, will never make the 6 o'clock news.[28]

This argument has been proved correct. If the US carries on LIC campaigns in two or three dozen Third World countries at the same time, generally centred around programmes of economic and military aid and training, and generally avoiding the commitment of US troops, American public attention remains unfocused and can be more easily contained than it could if the US were to commit a substantial force of its own soldiers and related losses were felt directly and powerfully. The time factor also plays a role, in that in the case of direct military intervention on a large scale domestic political opposition generally grows as time goes on, but with low-profile LIC operations public opinion quickly becomes accustomed to them. The counterinsurgency campaign in El Salvador, for example, evolved from a highly controversial undertaking in the years 1981–3 to become generally accepted even by Congress in the years following 1985. The reasons for this were a degree of political and military success in the campaign, and the fact that the direct US military intervention which critics feared was avoided.

The discussion outlined above concerning low-intensity warfare in the 1980s had little connection with traditional, mainstream military thinking, which was focused on Europe, NATO and war against the Soviet Union. It was not simply the expression of a structural change in US interests as reflected in its foreign policy, nor merely evidence of a slowly widening distance between the US and its partners. It was also an indication of the increasing significance attached to the Third World in the maintenance of the United States' role as a world power now and in the future. LIC doctrines are a military reflection of this new world view.

The fundamental assumptions of the US government in the 1980s were, first, that the strategic situation in Europe could be considered stable; second, that differences between the US and Western Europe were liable to grow; third, that Europe was not prepared to increase its share of the defence burden to a necessary and reasonable extent, and was using the United States as guarantor of its security; fourth, that the strategic significance of the Third World, particularly that of specific regions such as Asia and the Middle East, was constantly increasing; and fifth, that the Soviet Union had made significant gains due to Western negligence and was following a strategy of 'encircling' the West and trying if possible to cut it off from its supplies of raw materials and energy.

A scaling-down of US commitments in Europe and increasing emphasis on commitments in the Third World appeared to be an almost inevitable conclusion to these assumptions. Low-intensity warfare was a logical extension of this conclusion. For some this meant a shift to 'interests instead of allies', but that this was to be a gradual shift of emphasis and not an abrupt change of direction in foreign and military policy orientation was self-evident.[29] Even the most belligerent supporters of LIC strategies in the 1980s regarded it not as a substitute for but as complementary to a commitment to Europe and NATO.

A very interesting aspect of the whole discussion on low-intensity warfare has only become apparent some 15 years after its inception. It was born as an instrument of the Cold War, as an anti-Soviet tool. Low-intensity warfare was developed to create an appropriate means of fighting the East–West conflict in the Third World. In this sense it became obsolete a decade after it had begun. But at the same time it provided the instruments that the US would use in the New World Order, after the Soviet breakdown, to control and dominate the Third World. Justifications changed, but the instruments and strategies remained in place with the disappearance of anticommunist sentiment and superpower rivalry, which had both created and legitimised low-intensity warfare, the 'drug war', ethnic conflict, 'peacekeeping', 'humanitarian intervention' and other catchwords were easily substituted for them. The new era ushered in by the end of the Cold War, together with the new interventionism, was able to utilise all the devices that had been developed in the final phase of the East–West conflict.

Part Two

The New World Order

4
The Conditions

The End of the Postwar Order

At the end of the 1980s the postwar order, which was already crumbling as a bipolar system, finally collapsed. It would have done so earlier had it not been held together by the disciplining effect that the East–West conflict had on new powers rising in the East, West and South, because no sooner had the system been established than the process of its erosion had begun. The 'New World Order' being formed in the 1990s within the international system will therefore be shaped not only by the end of bipolarity, but also by the rise of other countries to become centres of power – a phenomenon which has been evident for some time. It would be wrong to think of this New Order simply in terms of how a different structure of relations between the 'old East' and the 'old West' can be established, of how the US and Western Europe can relate to Russia and the other nations of the former Soviet Union, because North–South and East–West relationships too can never be the same again after the end of the Cold War. Nonetheless it is logical to take the disintegration of the Soviet Union as a starting point for an analysis of the current situation.

Gorbachev's speech to the United Nations in December 1988 bore testimony to the ideological surrender of the second superpower. In that speech he announced further comprehensive and unilateral disarmament measures, which in practice abandoned the Soviet claim to military parity with the US and explained the Soviet withdrawal from the Third World. Between April 1988 and February 1989 the Soviet Union took its troops out of Afghanistan. In November 1989 the political system in the German Democratic Republic collapsed and the country vanished from the map, becoming economically and politically part of West Germany in 1990. In April 1991 the Warsaw Pact dissolved itself, a logical consequence of the anti-communist revolutions in the states of the former Eastern bloc.

Within the Soviet Union there was the most serious crisis since the Second World War, with the economic position becoming increasingly desperate. In August 1991 the old guard attempted a coup against perestroika. Although this failed, it very soon meant the end of Gorbachev's presidency – and the end of the Soviet Union as well by the time the year was over. The old state disintegrated, with Russia and most the other former Soviet republics forming a fragile 'Commonwealth of Independent States' (CIS). This process of disintegration may not yet be over; the CIS and even the Russian Federation itself may well go the same way. But in any case one of the two military and power blocs of the postwar period has vanished, while the other remains intact.

Again it must be emphasised that to say the postwar order lost one of its two main pillars in this way should not be taken to mean that its structure had been determined only by the rivalry between the two superpowers. As already indicated, for some time previously other trends had begun to erode this bipolarity. Nonetheless it had remained a sine qua non. The disappearance of one of the poles of the bipolar system fundamentally altered all the parameters of the international order. The Western powers were faced with the task of redefining their relationships with the Third World, as well as with the countries of the former Soviet Union and other Eastern bloc countries, and with each other. Without a widely felt 'Soviet threat', irrespective of how real this threat in fact was, neither the close partnership of the West, nor strategies in the South, were self-evident any longer. Furthermore, if the threat to the West as a whole no longer exists, does it still need a protecting leader? Ideological points of reference are necessarily altered by changes in the political and military framework. Now that 'world communism' has been abandoned and no longer exists as a menace, what happens to militant anticommunism? And without anticommunism how can the Western policy of maintaining a hold on the developing countries and of repeated military interventions continue to be justified?

These and many related questions have suddenly been put on the agenda in the 1990s. They constitute the core of the propaganda surrounding the concept of a New World Order, particularly as expounded in Washington. The concept as formulated by President Bush and his administration contained the basic answer to some of these questions. The Washington version of the New World Order means carrying over as much as possible from the old order into the new age. This is to be a world order which, not surprisingly, is based on the self-interest of the remaining big powers.

It would nonetheless be premature to regard the New World Order as nothing but propaganda. Even though it was introduced into the debate for tactical reasons to legitimise certain actions, behind it, there lies a very real problem for international politics, which is that a fundamentally new structure has to be found in the 1990s to fill the vacuum left by the end of the previous international system. In some ways the situation is comparable to that in the second half of the 1940s, with the actors on the international stage enjoying considerably greater freedom of action and initiative in foreign policy for a time, until a new system has been solidly established. This does not simply mean that any new international order that is desirable or conceivable in theory can be established in practice. Rather, the new order must grow out of existing fundamental structural conditions, including the interests of the main participants.

The most important of these conditions are: first, the multipolarity among the Western capitalist and industrialised countries that already exists; second, the West's gradual loss of control over internal developments in Third World countries; and third, the disappearance of the alternative system at one time offered by the Soviet Union as a superpower, however inadequately realised and flawed in practice that system was.

The End of a Superpower: the Soviet Union and its Foreign Policy

At the end of 1985 a Western academic established the following:

> The Soviet Union's current form of organisation inhibits the creative powers of its scientists and engineers, managers and employees. From the beginning of the first Five-Year Plan at the end of the 1920s right up to the 1960s, the Soviet Union was able to reduce the USA's industrial lead as a result of high economic growth rates. Since the end of the 1960s, however, the process of catching up with the USA economically has made no progress. The rapid technological change that has been experienced in the Western industrial nations and in other fast-developing nations carries with it the danger of undermining the Soviet Union's economic position the world over.[1]

At the end of the 1970s the Soviet Union saw the rate of increase in its GNP, (which had been falling for some time) halved to under 2 per cent, and in 1982/3 the situation worsened as the growth rate fell almost to zero.

All economic sectors were affected by this recession in a way unprecedented in history. To the chronically inefficient agricultural system were added previously unknown bottle necks in industry, transport and construction. Consumption stagnated, and the rate of capital accumulation fell sharply. Even growth in arms expenditure went down.[2]

The Soviet leadership was aware that the first half of the 1980s constituted a period of stagnation and that there was growing danger of an acute crisis – possibly one that threatened the whole system. This awareness of a looming crisis was the background to Gorbachev's appointment as general secretary of the CPSU and later as president. The crisis however, was anything but ended by the beginning of perestroika.

'It is not only in the West, but here too that you hear ever louder voices [warning] that the USSR is turning into a second-class Power, into a "developing country with the atomic bomb"... No help is to be expected from the allies', wrote two important Soviet academics in 1988.[3] The aim of Gorbachev's policies was to introduce economic reforms to prevent the USSR from sinking to the level of a developing country. With this in mind he consciously accepted that the Soviet Union had to give up its position as a world power. Retreat from many regions in the Third World, massive unilateral disarmament and the relinquishment of Eastern Europe as a politically and militarily controlled buffer-zone reduced the Soviet Union to the status of a regional power.

The Starting Point
During the postwar period, many Western experts repeatedly depicted the Soviet Union as, militarily at least, the most powerful country in the world; one that was aiming at global expansion and world conquest under the heading of 'world revolution'. Such statements were often politically loaded, and they were used to justify the arms race. The continual conjuring up of 'missile or bomber gaps' between the resources of the two superpowers, and the constantly reiterated fictional lead of the Soviets in this sector or that – for example in space weaponry – were good propaganda but no more than that.

The Soviet Union was always a world power with feet of clay and a superpower whose claims to that position were never backed by real strength. Apart from nuclear parity, there was hardly any sector in which the Soviet Union could come anywhere near matching American power.

On a very general level the Soviet Union completely lacked the power base for this. That is not to say that it lacked the physical resources. The power of the US, and of the capitalist powers of Western Europe and Japan, was not primarily based on military might but on control of the world market, the world monetary system, international trade relationships, and on the penetration of the economies of other countries. Rarely, then, did the US have to use, or threaten to use, military power to maintain its domination, because the power relationships had already been established in other ways. The most effective way of controlling another country was to take over its economy and local means of production. Such instruments of domination were never available to the Soviet Union to a significant extent, not even within Comecon. Just as limited was the ability of the Soviet Union to support more than a few countries with large amounts of economic and development aid, so binding these countries to itself materially. The experience of subsidising the Cuban Revolution after 1960, at an estimated cost of US\$25 billion including price subsidies in trade, provided the Soviet leadership with dramatic evidence of the limit to its capabilities that was set by its own economic difficulties. The role of the Soviet Union as a world power was based almost entirely on its military might, particularly on its ability to maintain nuclear parity with the US. Even in the military sector, however, there was no real substance to the claim of Soviet superiority. It is true that in the conventional arena the USSR did have the advantage of greater numbers in some areas, but the combat strength of its units, which is what counts in the case of conflict, was considerably inferior to that of Western armed forces. Neither its military hardware and technology nor the level of training and motivation of its troops or those of its allies came near NATO standards. In the late 1980s *Jane's Soviet Intelligence Review* considered 'that the basic fighting formations of the Soviet army are poorly led, poorly trained, poorly motivated, poorly treated and even poorly equipped'.[4]

A large number of Soviet tanks, obsolete and of limited reliability, would have been fairly ineffective against the high-tech antitank weaponry of NATO (rockets, helicopters and the like) if war had broken out. The equilibrium which existed in terms of nuclear strategy even before Gorbachev came to power was thus far from giving the Soviet Union parity in an overall military context, compared with the combat strength of the NATO armed forces. Although this was irrelevant in a practical sense, considering mutual nuclear overkill capacities, the Soviet armed forces during the late 1980s were in such a poor state that it was extremely doubtful whether they would have been capable of withstanding a serious military conflict. They finally proved unable even to organise a coup d'état. Now that the Soviet Union has disintegrated their situation has worsened still further. Increasing misery, social and political discontent, and growing ethnic conflict within the armed forces, together with the setting up (or splitting off) of independent forces in the Ukraine and other states have left the Russian or CIS armies today more a potential force for civil war or for war against each other's forces than a factor in a foreign policy.

The structural weakness of the Soviet Union as a world power meant that it could only achieve and maintain this status through great economic and political efforts. The concentration of excessive resources in the arms and military sector when between 10 per cent and 13 per cent of GNP was allocated to defence (some claims put the figure much higher),[5] with a corresponding deformation and weakening of the national economy and inevitable political consequences, were the price which the Soviet people had to pay for the superpower status of their nation. Just two examples make the specific economic weakness at the time when Gorbachev took office very clear. First, between 20 and 25 per cent of agricultural production was lost annually because transport and storage facilities were inadequate; second, by the mid-1980s about 60 per cent of Soviet exports to countries outside Comecon consisted of oil and gas supplies: a foreign trade structure which is more reminiscent of a Third World country than a superpower. The economic consequences of the fall in oil prices were correspondingly overwhelming[6] when between 1985 and 1988 the price plummeted from 160 to 60 roubles per tonne, a drop in earnings of 25 billion roubles from exports to the West alone.[7]

The lavishing of resources on the maintenance of foreign policy positions tended to undermine the material foundations for these same foreign policy stances. Edward Shevardnadze, after his resignation as Soviet foreign minister, said:

> In the final analysis we had become a superpower solely thanks to our military strength. The limitless build-up of this strength however brought us to the situation of a third-rate country, and even more than this our defense policy resulted in processes which brought our nation to the brink of a catastrophe...We occupy a leading position on the world market for arms, with 28 per cent of total sales, and we have made the Kalashnikov the symbol of our high technology, but so far as the living standard of the population is concerned we are in 50th place worldwide, in 32nd place for average life expectancy, and 50th place for child mortality. How can this be called national security?[8]

The Situation up to 1988

In spite of the huge economic and military efforts that were made, the overall result of Soviet foreign policy was on balance negative.

Successes in maintaining a secure position of power vis-à-vis the West were contrasted with blatant failures elsewhere. At the time when Gorbachev came to power, the foreign policy of the Soviet Union looked successful, so far as the maintenance of its hold on Eastern Europe and securing the stability of the postwar order were concerned. But this success depended on the ruthless use of all political and military means, including armed intervention, a means, which the United States never had to use in Western Europe.

A second apparent success of Soviet foreign policy was of course the achievement of nuclear parity with the US only ten years after the Soviet humiliation in the Cuban crisis of 1962. After that time the USSR became capable of inflicting direct nuclear destruction on important centres in the US and the extent to which it was vulnerable to nuclear blackmail by the US was correspondingly reduced, the US having hitherto been capable of threatening the destruction of the USSR without being seriously threatened itself. During Nixon's presidency the Soviet Union was almost officially given the status of a second superpower with fundamentally equal rights in terms of East–West relations.

In general, however, the Soviet Union as a world power was a fiction which it invented for itself as an objective, and which simultaneously provided a bogeyman for Western propagandists. A threat to Western Europe through subversion or conquest was repeatedly conjured up by Cold War ideologies, but it may be doubted whether the Soviet leadership itself ever considered this to be a real possibility.

Another Soviet aim was to promote revolutions in the Third World, with governments following the 'Soviet model'. However, the organisation of leftwing governments to constitute an anti-imperialist system and build up a 'socialist world market' in the Third World, although proclaimed very loudly and emphatically by the Soviet Union in the 1950s and 1960s, came to little in practice.

Khrushchev's aim of 'burying the West in the Third World' proved to be empty boasting. When Allende's government in Chile was bloodily overthrown in 1973, the Soviet Union had neither the will nor the ability to offer any serious help. The Cuban Revolution was not exported to the rest of Latin America, but simply became subsidised by the Soviets, whose ability to maintain discipline over Cuba remained limited despite all the financial expenditure. In the Middle East, the alliance with Egypt came to a spectacular end when Sadat threw out the Soviets in 1972, while the latters' 'friends' Syria and Iraq were not only extremely hostile to each other but also only really interested in receiving Soviet arms supplies; otherwise they remained somewhat cool towards Moscow. The Soviet Union was in fact unable to establish solid strongholds anywhere in the Middle East, except perhaps in Aden (South Yemen), and with the reuniting of the two Yemens in 1990 even this stronghold vanished. Furthermore, by the time Gorbachev took office, the Soviet Union had lost most of its credit in the Islamic world because of its war in Afghanistan, a war which it could not even win.[9] Things looked no better in Africa, where the friendly countries Angola and Mozambique were refused entry into Comecon in 1981 and 1985, respectively, neither the USSR nor Comecon was ready to accept the economic burden of supporting them. These countries received only US$250 and $400 million respectively in economic aid from the Soviet Union.

The list could be continued almost ad infinitum. Almost always when alarm bells rang in the West over a 'Soviet penetration' of the Third World, this proved to be either premature, shortlived, untenable over a longer period, a tactical manoeuvre, or once again propaganda on the part of one side or the other. It is true that the Soviet Union managed to obtain positions of influence in some areas of the Third World, but it was unable to establish positions of power, or even to achieve the establishment of socialist societies in the Soviet sense. The influence of the Soviet Union over Third World countries remained generally external, and could be shaken off relatively easily – which was not the case for countries under American influence and domination.[10] This was accepted by the Soviet leadership in the course of the 1980s, and it adapted its foreign policy accordingly.

For the countries of the Third World, and for the freedom movements, the attractiveness of the Soviet model decreased to the extent to which it became clear, first, that the USSR was neither able nor willing to supply significant economic assistance; and, second, that the classic Soviet economic concepts (for example state farms) had failed. The Soviet Union remained attractive only in two cases: where a progressive developing country, particularly one geographically close to the United States like Cuba or Nicaragua, was politically or militarily threatened by the Western superpower; or where Third World countries were anxious to secure supplies of arms which the West would not supply. No global power role in the Third World could be built up or maintained over the long term on such narrow bases of support.

Real Soviet domination over other countries was maintained into the 1980s only in Eastern Europe, Mongolia and Afghanistan. In these areas, which were adjacent to the USSR, Soviets at least in principle had the resources and the will to impose their rule and hold on to it, provided that appropriate conditions existed within these countries. In Finland, Turkey, Iran, Iraq, Pakistan, China and Japan, such domination could not be achieved, despite their geographical proximity to the USSR. The structures and capabilities of the Soviet armed forces were a key factor in this too. Up to about 500 kilometres from their own frontiers these forces enjoyed substantial strength. But neither their ability to deploy over greater distances and in greater numbers, nor their ability to hold their own against a significant opponent far from home, could be considered great. They were handicapped by their structural and logistical limitations, in spite of a substantial build-up of the Soviet fleet. The Soviet Union was never capable of anything like the rapid and massive military intervention over a great distance that was achieved by the US in the Gulf War. During the 1980s, the Soviet Union was a superpower in a regional rather than a global sense, and its efforts to maintain even this regional role overextended it as time went on, leading to what was once described with reference to the US as 'imperial overstretch'.[11]

To quote Edward Shevardnadze again:

The war in Afghanistan alone cost 60 billion roubles. At a conservative estimate, the confrontation with China swallowed up some 200 billion roubles, the cost of building up a colossal military infrastructure over three decades over the 7500 kilometres of frontier with China. Who can say how costly the many years occupation of Czechoslovakia, Hungary and Poland by our troops was? Or the increasing production of chemical weapons, which the Americans had already stopped making in 1969? What did the Cold War cost us politically? The last two decades of ideological confrontation with the West alone saw an increase in the cost of this military confrontation amounting to 700 billion roubles, according to some estimates, and this was in addition to the resources which were necessary to maintain military parity with the United States and the West as a whole.[12]

Adjusting to Realities

The main problems facing the Soviet Union when Gorbachev came to power were its rotten national economy and its ossified political and administrative system. Both problems were aggravated by the burdens of a foreign and military policy aimed at maintaining superpower status.

The decisive changes in Soviet policy under Gorbachev were made necessary because of economic stagnation and the risk of economic catastrophe internally, coupled with the geographical and strategic overstretching of resources externally. Internally it was necessary to initiate a process of revitalising the economy, and at the same time to adjust the foreign and military policy burdens to the limited material resources available. These changes were regarded as interrelated. In this context, a revitalisation of the national economy depended on a reduction in outside pressure and on fewer resources being wasted on arms. This in itself required an understanding with the West. According to Soviet thinking at the time, the hoped-for revitalisation would be facilitated, or indeed only made possible, by loans, technology and management methods imported from the West. Such assistance could naturally only be obtained by dismantling the confrontational system between the blocs. Within the USSR, market mechanisms needed to be installed and the sociopolitical superstructure adapted to the concurrent changes within the organisation of production – democratisation and openness – since the antiquated political structures and control mechanisms were hindering any further development of the national economy. The links between domestic and foreign policy were clearly emphasised at the 19th Party Congress in July 1988: 'Foreign policy must make an increasingly substantial contribution to the freeing of resources, in the cause of peaceful development as well as of perestroika'.[13] Foreign policy was thus to be subordinated to domestic policy.

Related new initiatives were already taking place before the advent of Gorbachev. They were aimed above all at preventing any further expansion of the Soviet Union's global responsibilities, particularly if they involved either economic burdens or foreign policy risks. The refusal to accept Cuba into the Warsaw Pact at the beginning of the 1970s, the refusal to integrate Angola and Mozambique into Comecon, the limited and diminishing material support given to Nicaragua, as well as the gradual and defensive rethinking of policy towards the Third World as a whole, were an indication of a cautious opportunist policy of making careful use of events in the Soviet Union's own interest rather than proof of an offensive strategy of expansion, world revolutionary endeavour or planned world conquest.

The Soviet leadership under Gorbachev went even further in this adaptation to circumstances, showing an almost amazing determination to cut its coat according to its cloth. From the mid-1980s onwards virtually all significant and burdensome aspects of an overextended world power role, and its ideological justification, were gradually eliminated in obedience to the imperatives of domestic and economic policy. In addition to its readiness to enter into disarmament and arms control negotiations, the USSR embarked on a programme of unilateral disarmament, reducing its armed forces by 500,000 soldiers, 10,000 tanks, 8,500 artillery and 800 fighter aircraft.

The unilateral nature of these reductions must be emphasised. These measures related to a sector which hitherto had been the sole foundation of the Soviet claim to be a superpower; that is, its military strength. Only the full realization of the suicidal costs of the military build-up, in addition to the equally powerful peace policy considerations, could have led to this step.

It was made very clear to the Soviet Union's allies in sub-Saharan Africa that no significant economic assistance was to be expected, that they would do better to turn to the West and to reorientate themselves towards the world market structures dominated by the West. Since then Mozambique has joined the Lomé Convention and the IMF. There were also cautious but unambiguous changes to the policy adopted towards South Africa. After 1986, signals were repeatedly given which even a short time before would have been unthinkable, and which also led to lively discussion within the Soviet Union. The ANC was informally criticised for talking too often and too loudly about socialism, although in fact it kept a very low profile in this respect. Soviet advisers counselled against any large-scale nationalisations after the removal of the apartheid system, and demanded related 'guarantees for the bourgeoisie'. The head of the Inkatha Movement, Chief Buthelezi, was referred to as a possibly inevitable partner for talks and negotiations, although without much enthusiasm.

As early as September 1986 the Soviet Union, together with the United States, was opposing a request from Nigeria and other countries that South Africa be excluded from the International Atomic Energy Agency in Vienna. The previous strategy aimed at weakening the apartheid regime through concerted international isolation was thus modified. Even though the Soviet Union continued to support the ANC politically, shifts of emphasis and a closer alignment with Western positions became clearly evident. The building of socialism in South Africa, according to the new official doctrine, could hardly be expected to take place within 25 years, and perhaps would not happen for 100 years.

In Central America and the Caribbean no offensive policy could now be discerned. The Soviet Union was projecting itself much more discreetly as a force for 'moderation' and caution, and it brought corresponding influence to bear on Cuba, Nicaragua and the FMLN in El Salvador. This moderating role was of course successful only to a very limited extent, and both the Reagan and Bush administrations repeatedly expressed their reservations about Moscow's new line. During the first Gulf War (1980–8) between Iraq and Iran the Soviet Union adopted a very cautious position, aiming to maintain its political and economic links with both combatants. In spite of massive fleet movements into the Persian Gulf by the US and the Western European countries in 1987–8, the USSR kept to a policy of disciplined restraint and de-escalation, almost completely renouncing any policy of demonstrating military power. During the second Gulf War between the US and its allies and Iraq in 1991 the Soviet Union to all intents and purposes followed no active independent policy, supporting Washington although sometimes verbally disapproving of the war. Moreover in Afghanistan, following the Geneva agreement of 1988, the Soviet Union withdrew its occupying troops within the agreed time, although the United States and Pakistan consistently violated the letter and spirit of the agreement.

In the Third World, by the mid-1980s at the latest, the Soviet Union was concentrating on improving its political and diplomatic relations with other governments, for example the Arab countries and Iran, using arms supplies as an instrument. The aim of this policy was the establishment of 'normal' relations with other countries, based as far as possible on cooperation, with no imperial penetration or domination intended. Geopolitical positions were also abandoned because they were regarded as politically and economically disadvantageous when costs were weighed against profit, for instance in the countries of sub-Saharan Africa, or because they were regarded as quite simply untenable, as in Afghanistan. In material terms this withdrawal was rational, and politically it made possible a better climate in East–West relations. If relations with freedom movements and some of the progressive movements of the Third World were made difficult, this was irrelevant to the process of political and economic transformation within the Soviet Union.

Eastern Europe
The situation in Eastern Europe was more complicated, at least by the end of the 1980s. At the beginning of Gorbachev's period in office, the member countries of the Warsaw Pact constituted a political, military and geostrategic buffer-zone around the Soviet Union, an indispensable guarantee of the protection of its own frontiers and of the political and economic system whose control was regarded as the core of Soviet foreign policy. From 1985/6, the Soviet Union had an interest in reforms in the countries of its allies, not just for political reasons but also because the revitalisation of Eastern European economies promised to offer advantages and stimuli for Soviet reforms. Initially this encouragement of reform in Eastern Europe was made conditional on these countries' remaining true to the Warsaw Pact, and on the maintenance of Eastern bloc discipline, as a guarantee

that the reform process would not get out of control. Nonetheless, and particularly in Hungary and Poland, the pace of reform became so rapid that the preset limits were soon exceeded. In 1988/9 the unequal pace of change, with democratisation and a move towards a capitalist economy in Hungary and Poland while various forms of Stalinist regime continued to survive in Czechoslovakia, East Germany and Romania, was making it impossible to talk about a 'socialist camp' or an 'Eastern bloc' any longer. In Hungary there was soon open discussion about leaving the Warsaw Pact, and by the end of the 1980s the reform-oriented countries' economic dependence on the West, and on the world market, was almost irreversible. Their foreign debt was becoming very similar in structure to that of Mexico.

During the last months of 1989, the regimes in East Germany, Czechoslovakia, Bulgaria and Romania finally collapsed. This eliminated their resistance to the policy of perestroika in terms of foreign policy, and at the same time brought into being a bloc of non-socialist countries within the Warsaw Pact who began energetically to establish capitalist democracies on the Western model, even if by the mid-1990s it is still unclear how democratic some of these countries will be.

Despite the effects of these developments in the Soviet Union itself, Moscow was becoming less and less capable of putting a stop to the dissolution of its hegemony in Eastern Europe. Without military force it was no longer possible to bring Eastern Europe into line; by 1988/9 such a military solution was already becoming unrealistic. Quite apart from the difficulties involved, and the economic consequences, both domestic and foreign policy considerations made it impossible for the Soviet Union to take this course of action. Soviet control over Eastern Europe was thus irrevocably lost and with it went the foundations of its previous role as a superpower. It ratified this evolution politically by giving its blessing to the most far-reaching reform processes in Eastern Europe, and by declaring that the Brezhnev doctrine (of the limited sovereignty of socialist countries) was no longer valid. In East Germany the government's self-liquidation, together with integration into the Federal Republic, completed and symbolised the loss of Eastern Europe as a preeminent geostrategic area. The essential territorial gains of the Soviet Union after the Second World War were thus lost and the loss accepted. The term 'end of the postwar period' takes on its full meaning in this context in Europe. By mid-1991 not only had the German Democratic Republic vanished from the political map, but the Warsaw Pact and Comecon had also been dissolved and Soviet troops had withdrawn from Hungary and Czechoslovakia. The voluntary dissolution of the

USSR and the coming into being of new states in Eastern Europe within the CIS, of which Russia and the Ukraine are the most powerful, mark the radical end of this process of dissolving the former Eastern bloc. Well before this, by 1990 at the latest, there was clear evidence that the Soviet leadership's abandonment of empire and its costly military apparatus had failed to revitalise the economy. This was not surprising, considering that the country's economic crisis was not primarily due to a shortage of resources, but to structural failures. No matter how successful and logical certain aspects of the political reforms were, the picture remained just as hopeless for economic reform within the framework of glasnost and democratisation. After more than five years of perestroika, the Soviet people were even less able to obtain basic goods than they had been during the period of 'stagnation', and there was no sign of economic recovery.

The supply position was extremely poor. Even by Soviet standards, the shops were empty. There were shortages of foodstuffs which had once formed part of normal stocks; where they did appear for a short time, long queues formed immediately. Although in Moscow the supply position could be regarded as still just tolerable, in the provinces it was desperate. Official Soviet statistics for 1990 showed a real drop in production for the first time since the Second World War. The CIA estimated:

Although it has become harder than ever to make estimates of the Soviet economy, we believe the GNP fell by around 4–5 percent last year. Official Soviet statistics indicate that the decline accelerated sharply during the first three months of 1991 compared to the same period a year ago.[14]

This was primarily due not to the notorious resistance offered by the bureaucratic apparatus but to a conceptual failure. The Soviet leadership had recognised that a late-Stalinist model was structurally incapable of solving the economic problems of the country, but, for understandable reasons, simply to take over capitalist economic models was rejected as a solution. Nonetheless a positive, independent and working concept of reform for the economic system was never developed, so that the changes and reforms which were undertaken always fluctuated between necessary repair and limited reform within the Stalinist model on the one hand, and some degree of copying the capitalist model on the other, for example the plan to transform the economy into a market economy within 500 days. The end result was that the old regulatory system was destroyed without a new economic system to replace it. In such a situation the resources that were gained from the changes in foreign and military policy could not be put to fruitful use. This development was particularly dramatic because as the Soviet Union continued to decline economically, the chance for independent, non-Western-style economic development disappeared. The greater the disintegration of the economic system, the more sharply the alternatives for action became limited to a choice between re-Stalinisation and the complete transformation of the Soviet economy into a capitalist system. Political developments within the USSR, however, meant that the only possible development was the capitalist one, provided there was no coup or civil war. The failure of the 1991 coup left Russia with capitalist development as its only option. But what form will it take?

Such a process is very unlikely to be reversed now that the Soviet Union has collapsed. In the new states which have succeeded it, development will naturally be much slower and more difficult than in the smaller countries of Eastern Europe, because political, historical and economic conditions across the former Soviet Union are full of contradictions.

Thus Mikhail Gorbachev would appear to have been right in a sense when he said in his speech before the United Nations in December 1988, that the 'world economy is becoming a single organism, and outside this organism no individual state can develop normally, no matter what social system it belongs to, and on what level of economic development it may find itself'. The complete integration of the CIS states within the world economy is no longer avoidable today, following the crippling of the system under decades of Stalinism, and the failed perestroika of Gorbachev. There is a price to be paid for this, however, in that the CIS states will indeed 'develop normally' – that is, driven by the determining forces of world market structures, but also by their own inner problems and conflicts.

In autumn 1992 the conservative *US News and World Report* summed up the social consequences of restructuring in Russia:

The economy is in free fall. Inflation is running close to 2000 percent a year – with no monetary discipline to prevent it from going even higher. The ruble has been destroyed, wiping out the life savings of teachers, accountants, the military, retirees, and the elderly. The decline in production has been twice as severe as in the great Depression. Foreign trade has collapsed. Average real wages have dropped by about 50 percent. More than half the people live below their poverty line – ours would be luxury in Russia – without a solid safety net. Only a small group of ex-Communist party types and a new mafia are doing well. The rest suffer an unforgiving primitive capitalism not seen even in the 19th century.[15]

The rapidly worsening economic crisis in the Soviet Union was accompanied by a process of political disintegration that was initially slow but then overwhelmingly fast. Two aspects of this are of particular importance. First, the Soviet Union became increasingly federal in character, with the central government losing many decision-making powers to the republics, and this not only in matters of economic policy. Even before the attempted coup, this process had gone so far that some republics were thinking about the independence of their own armed forces, or had in fact already initiated this. In the Baltic states, Georgia and Armenia, according to Soviet Defence Minister Jasow, the Soviet authorities in 1990/1 were not able to conscript more than 6 per cent of those liable for national service in the Red Army. Second, all the indications were that the relationship between the Soviet central government and the Russian Republic would be very complicated. Because of the preponderant importance of Russia, any conflict between the two would inevitably handicap Soviet policy. In 1990/1 the Russian Republic was already setting up a strong executive government and becoming capable of action as an independent nation. The different ideas held by the Soviet and Russian governments made it difficult to see how any related conflicts could be resolved. For example, Boris Yeltsin's Russia seemed to be more prepared than the Soviet Union to return the Kuril Islands to Japan, after a Soviet occupation which had lasted since the end of the Second World War. Furthermore, in 1990 Yeltsin proposed direct negotiations between Russia, Kazakhstan and the United States over a nuclear test ban, bypassing the Soviet government without consulting it.[16] These developments were already taking place under the last Soviet president, Gorbachev. With the dissolution of the USSR at the end of 1991 these contradictions vanished and were replaced by deeper disagreements between Russia and the other CIS states, especially the Ukraine.

The former Soviet republics have other problems apart from their relations with each other. In the Russian Federation, for instance, some 100 peoples and nationalities live together, 22 of these numbering more than a million each. The risk of conflicts within individual republics, amounting in some cases to civil wars along ethnic lines, has become considerably greater since the early1980s. Conditions inherited from the colonial and Stalinist past, a freer political climate in which opposition and resistance can speak out and organise more easily, as well as the increasing seriousness of economic difficulties, constitute an explosive mixture. Nationalistic or ethnic conflicts in or between some of the successor states of the Soviet Union, particularly in the south, are already raging. The struggles in Tadzhikistan, Moldova, Georgia, and between Armenians and Azerbaijanis, are perhaps only precursors of catastrophic development within the Russian Federation. The possibility that the CIS and then Russia will also disintegrate in their turn cannot be discounted. Indeed, worsening nationalistic and ethnic conflicts in combination with a disastrous economic situation make such a scenario quite feasible.

In leaving the world stage, therefore, the Soviet Union has left the world with a number of major problems, not least of which is the nuclear arsenal it once held. Out of one nuclear power several new nuclear powers have emerged, the most important of which are of course Russia, the Ukraine and Kazakhstan. Suddenly the world has been faced with the dissemination of warheads and technology in highly unstable regions, not only within the former Soviet Union but outside it as well. Since early 1992 there have been reports that Iran has bought three nuclear warheads from a central Asian CIS republic, paying US$150 million for them.[17] The West's euphoria over its victory in the Cold War has soon given way to new worries. But, as we shall see, the West's reflex action unfortunately seems to be to rely on old solutions.

The Western Response

In the Soviet reform process, and now in the further evolution of Russia and the other CIS states, it is East–West relations which have been of vital importance, with the Third World becoming completely irrelevant once the Soviet Union found itself able even to abandon Eastern Europe itself.

While the Soviet Union was still in existence as such, the accepted necessity to abandon confrontation and to cooperate with the West led not only to material concessions but also to ideological modifications which found expression in the 'new thinking' of Gorbachev and others. Gorbachev himself, in a speech to the United Nations in December 1988, spoke of the 'de-ideologising of inter-state relations', of their 'harmonisation'. In his opinion 'global politics would have to be ruled by world-wide human values', instead of the former class interests. The entry of the USSR into a 'united world characterised by mutual interrelationships' naturally had consequences for internal Soviet reforms. According to Gorbachev, the maintenance of any kind of 'closed society' was now scarcely possible, and in order not to lose its place among the developed countries the Soviet Union would have to adapt itself to the new economic, scientific, techno-logical and other realities of the world.[18]

In such a world in which common human interests were to be given priority over class interests, there would naturally be little room for confrontation – cooperation would be the order of the day.

Early in 1987, in a speech to the World Economic Forum in Davos, Switzerland, West German Foreign Minister Genscher was already bluntly reducing these ideological metamorphoses to their concrete meaning, and sketching out a Western strategy of response:

> The East is still a trading bloc essentially turned in on itself. This will not enable it however to join in the economic and techno-logical development of the world. Gorbachev appears to see this. He knows that in order to modernise his country he needs economic and technical cooperation with the West, that he needs entrepreneurial cooperation on a broad basis, and that he – initially in any event – also needs loans. Conversely, this will open up to the West a huge economic space, a huge commercial market, the exploitation of which will and can become a motor of growth for the world economy as a whole.[19]

From this point of view, Western help to the Soviet Union and the Eastern European states was indeed in the West's own interest. Genscher's statement expressed the tendency of Western politicians to support Gorbachev's reforms and make these a lever for a reinte-gration of the Soviet Union in the world market. The opposite view, held mainly in Washington, disagreed with what was disparagingly called 'Genscherism', (being soft on Gorbachev), maintaining that pressure should be kept up on the Soviet Union so that the latter could be forced into more and more concessions.[20] The US positions changed late and slowly.

The Bush administration's starting position was clear, and had been formulated time and again by almost all relevant high-ranking government officials. According to a senior State Department official speaking before a Senate committee in May 1989: 'It would however be premature to consider the Soviet threat to be considerably reduced,[21] (that is, despite the change in the politics and position of the Soviets). He was not alone in thinking this. The comments of the President's adviser on national security, General A.D. Brent Scowcroft, did not reveal any desire for further clarity. Shortly after he took up his post in the government, he explained in an interview:

I believe that he [President Gorbachev] wants to make trouble within the Western Alliance. And he assumes that he can best achieve this by launching a peace offensive rather than through the noisy ranting of some of his predecessors ... The Cold War – I do not believe the Cold War is over. There might be 'light at the end of the tunnel' as the saying goes, but our behaviour will determine whether this light is the sun or whether it is an oncoming train.[22]

In this way Scowcroft – as one of the two or three most important politicians involved in foreign affairs in Washington – took the Soviet policy of disarmament for a particularly perfidious way of undermining NATO and compared Gorbachev to a train that could soon run the West over. This could hardly be called the dismantling of the concept of the enemy; it was rather more an attempt to keep the carefully cultivated concept of the enemy alive at any price.

Scowcroft was asked in the interview: 'The West Europeans, the Germans and others clearly appear to be more open to Gorbachev's peace offensive than we do. Do you know why that is?' He replied: 'I believe they are more susceptible to wishful thinking than we are. They are more threatened by bad Soviet-American relations, by threat and conflict and so on.'[23]

The head of the US Defense Department, Paul D. Wolfowitz, made rather more sober comments a month after the Berlin Wall came down:

We want the reform process in the Soviet Union to succeed: but we must also be prepared for a world in which it does not. Even if reform continues in the Soviet Union as we hope, we are still likely to face a long-term competition with the Soviet Union, albeit in different forms and at a different level of intensity than in the past.[24]

This position, which indeed clearly differed from that of most of the European allies (especially France and West Germany), visibly began to soften in the course of 1990. The political implications of the collapse of the Wall and the rest of the Eastern bloc, as well as the readiness on the part of the Soviets to tolerate these developments and the Soviet support for the US in the Gulf War, contributed to this.

Internal and external politics made it increasingly difficult to maintain the image of the Soviet Union as the enemy in its old form, and the ideological position was therefore complicated. In official announcements the Soviet Union at times appeared to be threatening, as a result of its military power, and at others to be a new if somewhat uncertain partner. In the autumn of 1990 American Secretary of State James Baker gave his view of the Soviet Union:

> The image of a single totalitarian monolith which predominated in the Cold War has now disappeared and been replaced by a confusing, disordered mosaic that holds both hope and danger ... Soviet-American relations will always have a unique character, but our relations could however, more closely resemble those we entertain with many other governments. Cooperation could be the norm, with differences of opinion limited to specific areas of conflict. A 'normal' relationship or perhaps even a real partnership could be within reach.[25]

Secretary of State Baker mentioned three areas where he saw the first signs of need for a partnership. The first was concerned with the removal of the 'relics òf the Cold War' in Europe. This included the task of adapting NATO and the EC to the new needs, but also the task of taking a few steps forward with regard to arms control.

> Secondly, the United States and the Soviet Union need ways and means of overcoming new threats to the emerging World Order ... The condemnation of Iraq by the international community demonstrates ..., that others will probably follow when the United States and the Soviet Union take the lead. Soviet-American and multilateral cooperation must anticipate regional conflicts and try to resolve them before they lead to war. The prevention of regional conflicts must be the aim of Soviet-American cooperation.[26]

We should once again be careful not to take such statements at face value. This speech was given by Baker during a phase of the Gulf conflict (the end of October 1990) when the US administration was trying hard to get the Soviet Union's support for its policies. Without the support of the Soviet Union in the UN Security Council Resolution 678, which was interpreted by the US as the UN's authorisation to wage war against Iraq under certain conditions, would never have been adopted – as it was at the end of November. It was with this in mind that Baker's friendly words about mutual settlements of conflict in the Third World by the US and USSR were formulated, with a political and tactical aim. After the Gulf War, such visionary statements were hard to find. Nevertheless the US was interested in avoiding or resolving certain conflicts and crises in the Third World with and through the Soviet Union. The Gulf War, which had been used as a starting point for focusing on other regions, was one example of this, although what was envisaged was naturally not a US-Soviet alliance, nor an equal partnership, nor the altruistic settlements of conflict for the greater good of all, but the exploitation of the Soviet Union for Washington's own interests. The aim of US cooperation with the Soviet Union in the Third World, was to use the old connections of Soviet clients for US interests, and to gain Moscow's cooperation in the liquidation of its own positions. This had already been demonstrated in the joint efforts to resolve conflicts in Afghanistan, Angola, Central America and Cambodia.

It was only in the summer and autumn of 1990 that the US government was prepared to speak of the 'end of the Cold War', although it remained considerably more cautious than its European allies. It has already been pointed out that the Bush administration wished President Gorbachev's perestroika complete success, but was not prepared to offer serious help itself. The following reasons were instrumental in this decision:

1. Considerations of military security. It was argued that even a Soviet Union that had taken steps towards unilateral disarmament still had considerable forces and strategic nuclear potential at its disposal which continued to threaten the US and its allies.
2. Uncertainty about the success of perestroika. Members of the American government never tired of pointing out that Gorbachev's restructuring could fail and that the Soviet regime which followed could prove to be more hostile than ever before. Thus American assistance might serve a future anti-American Soviet Union.
3. Ideological and economic reasons. Materially significant help for the Soviet Union from the US did not make sense yet, for practical reasons, since the Soviet Union could not make productive use of it. The USSR was still dogged by bureaucracy, was ineffective and a planned economy. Aid would therefore fall into a 'bottomless pit'. US aid could only flow to a Soviet Union with a real market economy. This hypothesis was sometimes based on technocracy ('efficiency') and sometimes on ideology ('Soviet Union: still communist').
4. Budgetary and fiscal considerations. In the early 1990s the US could not set up a really significant aid programme, as it did not have any financial leeway. This was a result of the monumental budget deficit (a consequence of the Reagan administration's military Keynsianism). This is evident primarily in the purely symbolic scale of help provided to those countries from the former Eastern bloc, such as Poland and Hungary, which had been completely reorganised into market economies. Although

the previous three reasons did not apply to these countries, the extent of aid they received was nonetheless very limited.

In 1991 in particular, the arguments which had already been outlined in the previous year, but which were quietly set aside during the Gulf War, began to gather strength. As US Defense Secretary Cheney explained in Brussels at the end of May:

Great uncertainties continue to exist regarding future developments in the Soviet Union. With its considerable economic problems, the Soviet Union desperately needs fundamental reforms. However, it is not yet clear if the government will be in a position to carry these out. This situation would lead to great instability in the Soviet Union and such instability would necessarily affect Europe.[27]

It is of no small significance that Cheney made this statement as NATO's planning committee and nuclear planning group were meeting. He saw Soviet instability as a new threat with relevance for NATO. This coupled with risks/threats in the Third World (sometimes he used the more old-fashioned word 'threat' and sometimes the word 'risk') led him to conclude that NATO would in future 'lay greater emphasis on mobility and flexibility than on static defence in the structure of her forces'.[28]

Six months earlier US Secretary of State Baker had also, with great tact, broached this delicate subject to the North Atlantic Council in Brussels. He had formulated a variety of tasks for NATO's future security policy, of which the first two dealt with the Soviet Union:

While, in the last forty years, the attention of our security policy has mainly concentrated on the immediate Soviet threat from the East, today and in the future, we must turn our attention to a wider [field] ...

Firstly, we must continue to offer our members [those of NATO] continued security against the Soviet threat and its other considerable conventional and nuclear capabilities. The nature of this danger has undoubtedly changed, and our first task is to deal with present and future Soviet powers in such a way as to include the Soviet Union in a European order that promotes democracy and stability.

Secondly, we have a strong mutual interest in the promotion of a stable security structure in the whole of Europe – particularly in Central and Eastern Europe – based on the growth of democratic institutions and commitment to peaceful resolutions of conflict.

This European security [that is, in the sense of West European/NATO security] has indeed in the past often been threatened by the effects of political uncertainty and conflicts in countries on our borders. These challenges – of a political and economic nature and concerning security policy – that are faced by the struggling nations of Central and Eastern Europe are also our challenges [that is, NATO's]. It is in our interest that these countries do not have to repeat the dark chapters of their history'.[29]

If we look at both these statements from the Defense and State Departments – and they are entirely typical – then it appears that the US saw three threats from the old Soviet Union: first, its continued military might; second, its internal instability, which the US feared could spill over its borders; and third, the direct and indirect threat from the Central and East European countries through the Soviet Union (through its strength and instability), which Washington believed would directly affect the US and NATO. These three risks/threats were flexibly manipulated in diplomatic statements, with one aspect or another stressed according to the foreign affairs situation and tactical aims. What is most fascinating about this new pattern of argument is how the image of Moscow as the enemy, and the threat from the Soviet Union, did not disappear but was modified. Where before it had been the *strength* of the USSR, its monolithic and dominating character and its military might, that formed the core of the Soviet threat, it was now the USSR's *weakness* and instability that constituted the danger. Thus the Soviet threat continued to exist. Equally fascinating is the argument that although the USSR posed a threat to European stability and security as a result of its internal weakness, at the same time the West had to protect itself from the Soviets' continuing military *strength*. This was at a time when the Soviet Military was still perhaps capable of a coup, but certainly not of launching large-scale military operations.

In the course of 1989 and 1990, the differences in the opinions held by Washington and Western Europe were increasingly ironed out, with the hardline position becoming less and less justifiable as a consequence of the overwhelming nature of the changes in Eastern Europe and the series of unilateral disarmament decisions taken by the Soviet Union. Even before the Berlin Wall was breached in November 1989 'Genscherism' had become the accepted NATO position. Any pressure on the USSR was therefore scarcely to be expected now, except as a matter of tactics. Instead, Western governments were concerned to offer economic inducements to the

Soviet Union to go down the path chosen in Poland and Hungary, with partial economic penetration to follow the abandonment of empire.

Of course, the disagreements between the United States and Western Europe over how to deal first with the Soviet Union and then with Russia did not vanish altogether in 1989. Washington was still not ready to make major offers of assistance to the USSR, and continued to concentrate on the formulation of additional conditions relating to the Baltic states, the adoption of Western economic models, Soviet disarmament and so on. Whether the US actually had the economic strength to put a new Marshall Plan into action is another matter. The countries of Western Europe, in particular the enlarged Federal Republic, placed the emphasis elsewhere, maintaining that economic support would help to prevent a failure of perestroika, and that to apply pressure over the question of the Baltic states or other issues must take second place compared with this vital necessity.[30]

The tug-of-war between Washington and Bonn/Paris over the question of Gorbachev's participation in the 1991 world economic summit in London was evidence of the continuing differences within the Western camp. Only in spring 1992 – in other words after the disintegration of the USSR – were these differences of opinion overcome. Washington was now ready within the framework of the group of the seven most important industrial nations (the G7) to contribute US$4.5 billion to an aid package worth $24 billion. By this time, the Bonn government alone had already handed out $40 billion worth of aid to the Soviet Union/CIS.

The Clinton administration finally proclaimed Russia to be a central focus of its foreign policy. Secretary of State Warren Christopher was quite clear on that: 'No relationship is more important to the long term security of the United States than our strategic relationship with Russia'.[31] And Christopher's ambassador-at-large and special adviser for the new independent states (NIS), Strobe Talbott, told a Senate committee 'that support for reform in the NIS would be the No. 1 foreign policy priority' of the Clinton administration.[32]

But all these speeches and the figures of assistance tend to overemphasise the Western financial commitment. Often the official figures included monies that would never be spent in Russia or be of any direct help, and much of the G7 package simply consisted of funds that would come from the International Monetary Fund, not from bilateral aid. Some other assistance was intended more to subsidise Western exporters than to help Russian economic reconstruction.

Steven Rosefielde has observed:

> The G-7 has embraced the mission of saving Russia without committing itself to providing the aid and knowhow to get the job done. Its plan amounts to little more than a decision to allow Russia to join the IMF, World Bank and EBRD...[This is a] minimalist approach insofar as it is anything more than an expedient attempt to seize the moral high ground, while allowing matters to sort themselves out.[33]

5

Initial Trends in the Third World

The Balance of the 1980s

For the Third World, the 1980s were a decade of disappointment. Disorientation and resignation followed the withering of the hopes and ideological dreams that had blossomed in the 1970s. The social, economic and political effects of the overwhelming debt crisis were brutal. Moreover, the Reagan administration's policy of reviving the Cold War in the Third World and using this to restimulate an old imperialist policy met with significant success, while the Soviet Union abandoned its role as a world power and counterweight to the US.

At first glance it is not clear why such despondency should have set in. The Reagan doctrine, and the policy of counterinsurgency and low-intensity warfare of the 1980s, had failed to achieve many of its declared objectives. The Contras did not militarily overthrow the Nicaraguan Revolution; the guerrillas in El Salvador were neither militarily defeated nor estranged from the population. Similarly, after the fall of the Marcos dictatorship in the Philippines an effective, stable regime could not be established there, nor the NPA defeated. Despite efforts throughout the decade to remove Gaddafi from power in Libya, he remained in control, while the planned overthrow of the Afghan government by the Mujahedin alliance was no more successful. This list could be considerably extended. Nonetheless it would only describe part of the reality, because despite these demonstrable failures in many individual areas, overall the US could look back on a positive result. The Contras might not have been able to dislodge the Sandinista government, but they did fundamentally disrupt the Nicaraguan economy and infrastructure, establishing the basis for the defeat of the FSLN in the election of 1990. Nicaragua did not become a 'model' for revolutionary change in Latin America. In El Salvador too, the guerrillas may not have been annihilated, but their victory was prevented, a victory which had seemed imminent at the end of 1983 and in early 1984. In the Philippines the US might not have completely achieved its objectives, but any revolution in the foreseeable future was prevented. In Afghanistan, US policy might not have brought about the downfall of the Najibullah government in the 1980s, but the Soviet Union was left with a 'bleeding wound', according to Gorbachev, and with a strategically significant defeat. And in early 1992 President Najibullah lost power because of the disintegration of his party and government. This list too could be continued.

In a period during which Soviet Third World policy had already slowly come to the limits of its resources, and was virtually withdrawn, the United States succeeded in halting the revolutionary wave of the 1970s and at least in part going over to the strategic offensive. In this sense the 1980s saw a shift of power in the Third World towards a stabilisation favourable to the US. Freedom movements and revolutionary governments were put on the defensive.

Freedom movements had generally believed that the problems of developing countries could be solved by revolution followed by the increasing independence of world markets, and by nationalisation of the means of production accompanied by assistance from the Soviet Union or China. By the end of the 1970s these ideas had been shaken. During the 1980s any such confidence was severely weakened and often vanished altogether, particularly in the light of the economic, political and military experiences of the countries concerned.

One revolutionary government after another was forced to recognise that to proclaim substantial independence from world market structures was easier said than done. The chopping and changing in Cuban sugar production policy during the 1960s was an early indication of the problem. Initially cane fields were burnt in order to make room for vegetables and other products, with the aim of increasing self-sufficiency instead of producing for the world market. This strategy had failed, by 1963 since the loss of revenue from the sugar sector meant that resources for financing industrialisation and other sectors were insufficient. The Cuban government was compelled to go back to full dependency on sugar production, a policy which subsequently had to be modified yet again.

In almost every case, breaking away from the world market depended on long-term substantial financial support from the Soviet Union; even then success was not guaranteed, as the Cuban example demonstrated. In the later 1970s and throughout the 1980s, however, the lesson was that the Soviet Union was neither willing nor able to supply such comprehensive aid over the long term, a dilemma which was further reinforced by the very success of the revolutionary wave of the years 1974–80. The number of applicants for Soviet aid grew significantly at the very time when there was a greatly increased awareness in Moscow of the paucity of Soviet resources. This restricted the freedom movements' scope for action. It also led them, however discreetly at first, to rethink their own political ideas, to seek greater ideological flexibility and to reassess the role of the Soviet Union.

The Sandinistas in Nicaragua are a good example of this. In spite of massive US aggression, they ceased to place all their eggs in the Soviet basket and instead began to broaden their foreign policy and diversify their trade relations. Cuba played an important role here in convincing the FSLN of the necessity for this.

Particularly in the second half of the 1980s, and into the early 1990s, this gradual reorientation became increasingly urgent, as Soviet support for Third World governments and freedom movements was rapidly reduced, and a number of regimes saw their very existence threatened. Vietnam was a country in point.

During the period of harmony between Vietnam and the USSR, Moscow supplied the former with goods whose value was four times greater than those it received. Development aid was doubled every five years. But then the Soviets began to insist on an equal balance of trade, and in addition demanded the repayment of loans amounting to 9 billion roubles. Whereas previously 3 million tonnes of crude oil, 2.5 million tonnes of fertilisers and 400,000 tonnes of iron and steel were made available annually at 'friendly prices', Hanoi now had to pay for these with its own exports at world market prices or in hard currency. Inevitably, imports were reduced and the rice harvest consequently endangered. The IMF estimated the value of previous Soviet aid to Vietnam at an annual US$250–300 million, corresponding to 4–5 per cent of Vietnamese GDP. The removal of this support exacerbated the economic crisis dramatically. The year 1991 was the most difficult year since independence, requiring the complete reorientation of foreign, security and economic policies – according to views widely held in the country itself.[1]

The 1980s were thus a period when the weakening of the Soviet Union in the Third World coincided with an ideological and politico-military offensive by the US in the area, and with conceptual, political and in some cases material crises affecting many freedom movements or progressive governments.

The crisis in the Soviet Union and its withdrawal from the Third World did not just mean a shifting of political parameters and a loss of political support against the West. It often also signified a very decisive weakening in material terms. Soviet arms supplies and economic aid, at best comparatively small scale in the international context, dwindled and then vanished altogether. The fact that in the past a considerable percentage of such support went to repressive and undemocratic regimes does not alter the fact that, viewed as a whole, the freedom of action of the Third World was correspondingly reduced.

Regional crises and conflicts in the Third World will not stop now that the East–West conflict is over, just as the causes of these local problems often had very little to do with the rivalry between the blocs. Crises in the area occurred before the American-Soviet conflict even commenced, and for that matter even before the founding of the Soviet Union. The expectation that such crises and conflicts would end with the end of the 'postwar period' was never realistic. Nonetheless, the political framework determining the conditions for regional Third World conflicts have fundamentally altered since the end of the 1980s, and this will certainly have its effects on the course of many future disputes. The first evidence of such changes is already apparent.

It has frequently been overlooked that long before the end of the Cold War was officially proclaimed, the basic model of superpower conflicts in the Third World did not apply in all cases. A glaring example of this was the 1956 Suez crisis, in which the United States and the Soviet Union acted together to force France, Great Britain and Israel to abandon their military seizure of the Suez Canal and get out of Egypt. Although of course lines of conflict were rarely so clearcut, there are sufficient other examples of how the principal East–West rivals were very careful not to encroach on each other's preserves in the Third World, or at least to reduce the potential for escalation to a minimum. The Soviet Union's endeavours to exert a 'moderating' influence on Cuba and Nicaragua, and the readiness of the US until 1978/9 to regard Afghanistan as part of the Soviet sphere of influence, were part of this scheme of things.[2]

During the 1980s it became clear that the superpowers were handling regional crises in the Third World in a different way. It was noteworthy how the Reagan administration, at a time when it was notoriously vigorous in prosecuting its version of the Cold War, was careful to avoid any suggestion of involving its confrontation with Libya in the East–West context. Although Libya was obtaining most of its arms from the Soviet Union and other Eastern bloc sources, and was at the same time indulging in fiery anti-imperialist rhetoric, the US government rejected the normal propaganda temptation to paint Libya as a tool of the Kremlin. The bombardment of Tripoli and Benghazi in April 1986 was justified not on anticommunist grounds, but as part of the fight against terrorism. Furthermore, there are substantial indications that Washington not only avoided such ideological attacks on the USSR, but informed the Soviets of its intentions before informing most of its own allies. Soviet warships based in the port of Tripoli were all out at sea, a safe distance from the US attack, when the bombardment took place.

The US intervention in Panama followed very similar lines of ideology and legitimisation. Again the opponent, in this case General Manuel Noriega, was not branded a secret communist and accomplice of Moscow – grounds which had previously been suggested as a rational justification for action against Arbenz in Guatemala in 1954, for example, as well as elsewhere. The conventional Cold War legitimisation for action against Noriega would have been to denounce him as an 'accomplice of Cuba and Nicaragua', and thus of Moscow, who with the help of Columbian cocaine was aiming to undermine American capitalist society. Such propaganda arguments had been taken to a point beyond absurdity as a matter of course at times, for instance in the case of Grenada in October 1983, when the tiny island and its airport were inflated into a 'vital threat to American security' and it was claimed that there were 'American hostages' to be freed, ignoring the fact that the US citizens in question had been neither seized nor threatened.

Panama was therefore invaded and occupied on the official grounds that this was a police action, admittedly a massive one, to capture a criminal and fight the drugs traffic. Such arguments may have been just as absurd as an anticommunist claim, but the important point is precisely that of the two lines of argument that might have been used, the one chosen did not fit into an East–West framework.

Thus the bombardment of Libya and the invasion of Panama were early instances of conflicts that went beyond the scope of the Cold War and East–West confrontation. On the other hand, the support given to the Contras and the entire Central American policy of the US under Reagan, the invasion of Grenada, policies vis-à-vis Angola and Cambodia, and to some extent even the massive fleet presence in the Persian Gulf in 1987/8, may all be regarded as having been just as typical of East–West confrontation in the Third World as was Soviet intervention in Afghanistan. In all these cases the real or assumed threat from the enemy superpower played an important role in the other superpower's determination of its foreign policy and its legitimisation.

Afghanistan, Central America, Cambodia

From the mid-1970s to the mid-1980s, regional conflicts in the Third World themselves had an especially great influence on East–West relations. They were responsible for the drastic worsening of relations between the US and the Soviet Union from 1978/9 onwards. Increased Soviet influence in Africa (Angola, Mozambique, Ethiopia), the alleged 'discovery' of a Soviet 'brigade' in Cuba, the Soviet intervention in Afghanistan and the civil wars in Central America had undermined the readiness of the US to pursue a policy of global détente and served as justification for a new policy of confrontation with the Soviet Union. Unlike the first, the second Cold War between the superpowers, which began in 1979/80, was staged almost exclusively in the Third World, whatever the nuclear strategy in the background. The American battlecry in this new Cold War was the Reagan doctrine, a modernisation of the 'roll-back' policy of the 1950s, revamped and transferred to the Third World. In the first half of the 1980s, the time of the first Reagan administration, US–Soviet rivalry had the effect of greatly sharpening regional crises. It was US policy to use these as weapons in the Cold War. This was cynically expressed in relation to Afghanistan, where it was not necessarily in the American interest to see the Soviet Union withdraw, but rather to have it pinned down and bled dry. This would weaken it most. However loudly the US might continue to demand Soviet withdrawal, it was in fact quite happy 'to fight to the last Afghan'.[3]

This militant confrontational policy was slowly modified from the mid-1980s onwards and was complemented by more pragmatic political objectives. In October 1985 President Reagan challenged the USSR, in a speech before the United Nations, to join in common endeavours to try to solve regional crises in the Third World, such as those in Angola/Namibia, Afghanistan, Cambodia, Nicaragua and Ethiopia. Although this may have been a long way from indicating a readiness to come to an understanding with the Soviet Union, or even to move towards it, the discussion was nonetheless raised to a new level.

Reagan's proposals were threefold:

- first, that discussions should be started between the warring parties in the countries concerned;
- second, that following progress in such discussions, the United States and the Soviet Union should talk about possibilities of promoting dialogue between the combatants, that in individual cases the superpowers should consider giving guarantees in order to reach an agreement, and in every case in the American view the aim should be to end foreign military presence and halt the flow of arms from abroad.
- third, following success in these measures and in the context of national reconciliation, generous American aid for the

economic reconstruction of the countries concerned should be planned.

What lay behind these proposals, which sounded so relevant and rational on the surface, was of course the real point that the countries concerned were all Soviet spheres of influence. Implementation of the proposals would have legitimised the Contras in Nicaragua, or UNITA in Angola, while to all intents and purposes eliminating Soviet support for their respective governments. The US was basically asking the Soviet Union to abandon some of its clients in the Third World, a demand sweetened by the offer of giving Moscow a say in the regulation of conflict. This did indeed involve recognising the Soviet Union as a global power with interests in the Third World and constituted formal recognition of a kind of 'political parity', but in reality this amounted to nothing other than the USSR's inevitable cooperation in managing its own withdrawal from the Third World. In other words, it was a friendly request by the US to its opponent to capitulate in the latter's own interests. Under normal conditions this request would presumably have marked the end of the debate. However, the political and economic bankruptcy of the overextended Soviet system, and the resultant 'new thinking' in Soviet policy, resulted in an understanding being reached on several matters.

Afghanistan

The war in Afghanistan was the first and a particularly instructive case of a regional conflict over which the superpowers came to an understanding. In April 1988 in Geneva the governments of Afghanistan, Pakistan, the Soviet Union and the United States signed a series of documents agreeing to terms intended to bring a solution to the conflict nearer. These four agreements were in no way peace treaties, but simply regulated some international aspects of the war. In particular they provided for the complete withdrawal of Soviet troops. The content of what was agreed can be summarised as follows:

1. Afghanistan and Pakistan's non-interference in each other's internal affairs, including agreements not to support armed groups or insurgents (that is, the Mujahedin), and not to undertake or allow any other actions which could be regarded as interference and intervention.
2. Reciprocal undertakings to make every effort to assist the repatriation of Afghan refugees on a voluntary basis 'as far as possible'.
3. An undertaking by the Soviet Union to withdraw its troops from Afghanistan within nine months beginning on 15 May 1988.

The Geneva agreements in essence constituted a deal under which the USSR was bound to withdraw its troops from Afghanistan, while the United States and Pakistan undertook no longer to support or even countenance the operations of the Mujahedin. This settlement also meant that the Afghan war would lose its major international aspects, in that although it would indeed continue for the time being, the conflict would now only be waged between the Kabul government and its internal opponents.

The basic principles of this agreement only existed on paper, of course. Even just before the agreements were signed, Pakistan's military dictator General Zia, declared publicly that he would continue to support the Mujahedin. And US Foreign Minister George Shultz asserted that it was the right of the US in conformity with its obligations as a guarantor of the agreement 'to allow military aid to reach the resistance'.[4] Naturally, the actual agreement guaranteed by the US provided for exactly the opposite.

The background to these positions was an informal agreement between the US and the Soviet Union. The Soviet Union, contrary to the Geneva agreement, would accept American and Pakistani supplies to the Mujahedin provided that it could for its part continue with military supplies to the Kabul government, which was permitted under the agreement. Thus the USSR had informally approved a violation of the Geneva agreement by the other contracting party. This meant that one of the two main principles of the agreement became a dead letter – that is, the single American concession to the Soviet Union in the agreement would not be put into effect.

The Geneva agreements thus did not constitute any settlement involving mutual give-and-take or agreement between equal partners, but were simply a sweetened form of capitulation enabling the Soviet Union to save face. What mattered to Moscow, for reasons of foreign and domestic policy, economic and military policy, was to get out of Afghanistan as fast as possible and at almost any price. The structure offered by the Geneva agreements simply constituted the multilateral political framework for this essentially unilateral objective. The advantage to the Soviet Union was solely political, and its sole function was the avoidance of an overhasty withdrawal that would look too much like a capitulation. In material terms the Soviet Union gained nothing.

Thus for the Reagan administration the Geneva agreements represented a 'victory', the culmination of the 'most successful CIA operation in history'. This assessment was based on the assumption that the Kabul government, once Soviet troops had withdrawn, would collapse within a few weeks or at the most three months. The forces that would then take power would be those which had been militarily supported by Washington for years, at high cost.

This is precisely what did not happen, however. The big general offensive of the Mujahedin against the provincial capital Jalalabad in spring 1989, intended to be a prelude to the capture of Kabul, ended in a strategically important defeat. After this turning point, with the Afghan government defending itself successfully without the support of Soviet troops against the Mujahedin who had been so sure of victory, the prospects of the armed opposition achieving such a military victory became increasingly remote. The US administration took more than a year to recognise this fact. Only when the Gulf crisis loomed in the summer of 1990 did the Bush administration face up to reality and come closer to various Soviet positions. The altered foreign policy requirements resulting from the Gulf crisis, and from the war with Iraq which began in January 1991, together with a series of serious practical problems, meant that no final arrangement was made despite the fact that, in practice, the views of the two powers were almost identical.

Four factors contributed to the US now being prepared to accept a political solution in principle, after having hoped as late as the first half of 1990 for a military victory on the part of its guerrilla allies:

- the political success of the Geneva agreements;
- the changed international climate (these two factors formed the overall political background but were not sufficient in themselves to bring about the new policy);
- the Mujahedin's military defeat and political weakness, in particular the weakness of the seven Mujahedin parties operating from Pakistan;
- the necessity of maintaining good relations with the Soviet Union because of the Gulf crisis, and thus of moving towards the Soviet position on Afghanistan.

The whole chapter was of course to be closed by the disappearance of the Soviet Union as a player on the world stage, and by the entry of the Mujahedin into Kabul in April/May 1992.

The reasons for the Mujahedin's final success lay not in the military or political strengths of the rebels, but in the collapse of the government power coalition. Although until the end of 1991 President Najibullah was extremely skilful in keeping together an alliance of tribes, the different factions of his party and the military – often playing these off against each other – at the end of August 1991 this effective but delicate balance began to break down and by December the alliance had fallen apart. Economic factors played a role in this. For example, the government was no longer able to pay the Uzbeki militia of General Dostum. Ethnic conflicts also surfaced, with fierce disputes in the north between Pashuni officers on the one hand and ethnic Uzbeki and Tadzhiki officers on the other. There was disaffection even within the ruling party itself. Top officials such as Vice-President Mohtad, Politburo member Farid Mazdak and (Tadzhiki) Foreign Minister Abdul Wakil (the last two key figures in the Kabul power apparatus) wanted gradually to distance themselves from Najibullah and began secret discussions with Mujahedin commanders, notably with Ahmad Shah Masood.

Moreover, the power structure of the government was disintegrating from within. When General Dostum's militia finally deserted, and entered into a tactical alliance with the Tadzhiki Mujahedin of Ahmad Shah Masood, the Kabul government collapsed like a house of cards. Najibullah was overthrown by his own people, and shortly afterwards power was handed over to the quarrelling Mujahedin alliance.

It is more than a little ironic that the Afghan government was strongest when the governments of Presidents Reagan and Bush, after the Soviet withdrawal, were making their greatest efforts to overthrow it, whereas once the US government had abandoned this hope and its efforts in this direction the Kabul regime collapsed almost of its own accord. It is scarcely less ironic that the Islamic forces which for over a decade were armed by the West and lauded as 'freedom fighters' lost no time in waging the civil war even more fiercely, this time against each other. Kabul had never suffered such brutal and bloody battles and heavy rocket bombardments as occurred after the fall of Najibullah and after the end of the Cold War. The question now is whether the state of Afghanistan will completely fall apart, and whether Kabul will become another Beirut.

Nicaragua

For some years Central America was an ideologically overloaded focal point for US foreign policy, a location in the Third World where the East–West conflict was being fought with a vengeance. One of the main political elements in the US administration's policy was the establishment, equipping and continuing support of the Contras against the Nicaraguan government. Another was its support for the El Salvador government, in the form of military and economic aid. However, by the time President Bush came to power (if not before) many within the US foreign policy establishment regarded this policy as having failed. A new beginning was thought to be overdue. In any event, the new president tended to want to dampen the ideological enthusiasm of his predecessor where Central America was concerned. As early as spring 1989, the US government took initiatives aiming at a careful change of political course. The Contras were not officially dropped, it is true, but they moved from the centre to the periphery of American policy towards Nicaragua, while at the same time Washington sought a political understanding with the Soviet Union vis-à-vis Central America. It goes without saying that this did not constitute an abandonment of old American objectives, at least not those of primary importance. It was rather a matter of the US extracting itself, through limited cooperation with the Soviet Union, from the political dead end which it had created for itself in Central America.

In March 1989 there was already a perceptible change of direction from the new administration. While the Reagan administration had worked for a confrontational policy on Nicaragua against an important current of opinion in Congress, the Bush administration and the opposition came to an agreement on a common line.

Independently of each other, Secretary of State James Baker and the White House press spokesman, Marlin Fitzwater, declared that the old policy had proved a failure and that now, in agreement with Congress, a new policy was being launched; one that was no longer based on the use of military force to achieve US objectives. The new policy was to 'have a stronger diplomatic than military accent, since we believe that military pressure has simply not worked'.[5] The Contras were to receive no more military aid from the US government, only a monthly US$4.5 million for 'humanitarian' assistance, a term which was to be interpreted very widely, until the Nicaraguan elections planned for February 1990. The agreed line of Congress and the administration provided for the 'reintegration' of the Contras in an increasingly democratic Nicaragua, while the Contras' military offensives were to cease. At the time it was not yet clear whether this common line actually constituted a genuine change in US policy, or was simply a move on the political chessboard to prevent Congress from vetoing any support whatsoever to the Contras. This doubt was fed by the continuing sharply anti-Sandinista language used by top American politicians, including the president, when talking about Nicaragua.

Three days later the Bush administration was already turning to the Soviet Union to propose cooperation on Central America (especially Nicaragua). President Bush wrote to his Soviet opposite number warning that if Soviet support for Nicaragua were not reduced this would have a negative influence on American-Soviet relations.

After this barely veiled threat, came the carrot. Good behaviour on the part of the USSR and Cuba would be generously rewarded by the United States, although what form this generosity would take was left unclear. The Soviet Union's reaction to this vague signal from Washington was cautious. The United States was after all continuing to give substantial support to the Contras. After some informal activity on both sides, Gorbachev sent a signal in early May 1989. He praised 'positive trends' in relation to Central America, 'including the intention of your government and of the American Congress to "give diplomacy a chance"'. Then came the core of the offer: 'to facilitate a peaceful settlement of the conflict and considering the fact that the Contras' offensive has ceased, the Soviet Union has not supplied weapons [to Nicaragua] since 1988'.[6]

A few days later US Foreign Secretary James Baker took this up in discussions in Moscow. He now offered more concrete counterproposals, stating that practical steps taken by a Nicaraguan government to put into effect the Esquipulas decisions (taken at an earlier conference of Central American heads of government seeking a regional solution for conflicts) would lead to an improvement in relations between Nicaragua and the United States. If the forthcoming elections in Nicaragua proved to be fair and free according to US standards, the US government would also accept a victory by the Sandinistas. Furthermore, an overall regional solution including a peace settlement in El Salvador would release comprehensive American aid for the region and relieve the Soviet Union of its Nicaraguan burden.

The US was thus distancing itself from its long-pursued policy of overthrowing the Sandinistas by force, moving towards a policy of influencing internal affairs in Nicaragua by diplomatic and political means. Reliance on military means would be replaced by support given to the anti-Sandinistas as a political opposition. In return, Washington wanted Moscow to stop sending its principally military aid to Nicaragua.

The Soviet Union accepted this deal and used its influence on Managua correspondingly. The processes of reaching agreements between the US and the Soviet Union, and between the Soviet Union, Cuba and Nicaragua, were not without problems, but they did have the result that the American-Soviet consensus was substantially translated into action. In August the Sandinistas and the internal opposition in Nicaragua agreed that the Contras would be disbanded and that elections would take place in February 1990. Two weeks before these elections the US and Soviet foreign ministers, Baker and Shevardnadze, announced that both their countries would 'respect the result of free and fair elections'.

The elections of 25 February 1990 unexpectedly resulted in the narrow defeat of the Sandinistas. The opposition candidate, Violeta Chamorro, took over the presidency from Daniel Ortega. This transfer of power was achieved without friction, a smooth transition facilitated by the new president working as hard for cooperation as the FSLN. On the right wing of the new government coalition, up to and including the vice-president, this policy was watched with severe criticism, as it was in Washington, and even met with open resistance, particularly since the social conflicts within the country were becoming sharper.

Cambodia

The war in Cambodia at the start was shaped first by the defeat of the US-backed government as a result of the Vietnam War; second, by the subsequent bloody reign of terror of the Khmer Rouge; and third, by the Vietnamese military intervention in 1978 which expelled the Khmer Rouge from power. This was followed by the occupation of the country by Vietnamese troops, civil war between the Khmer Rouge and other groups against the government backed by Vietnam, and the increasing internationalisation of the conflict. The Soviet Union supported Vietnam and the Cambodian government which was under Vietnamese control. China supplied weapons and other aid to the Khmer Rouge, while the United States and other countries supported the guerrilla forces of Prince Sihanouk and Son Sann, who cooperated with the Khmer Rouge.

The Vietnamese troops withdrew from Cambodia between April and September 1990. This opened up the possibility of a political solution to the conflict. Preparations for this were made in August 1988 in discussions between the Soviet Union and China. The help given by the United States to the non-communist guerrilla units was intended to put pressure on the occupying Vietnamese forces and thus on the Soviet Union, and at the same time form a counterweight to the militarily stronger Khmer Rouge. While the first of these objectives was fully achieved, the second failed completely. Indeed the opposite effect was obtained in that a significant part of American aid was passed on to the Khmer Rouge. This state of affairs, in combination with the memory of the genocide perpetrated by the former Pol Pot regime of the Khmer Rouge against their own people, resulted in American aid becoming increasingly unpopular in Congress even before the withdrawal of the Vietnamese. In November 1989 a ban was put on American arms supplies to Cambodia, although other forms of aid were for the moment permitted to continue.

In July 1990 there was a change of policy in Washington on three points. Despite continuing differences, the US government declared its readiness to discuss Cambodia with the Vietnamese government, and to extend its humanitarian aid to Cambodia to those areas which were under that government's control. In addition, despite continuing its support for the non-communist guerrilla movements, it would no longer support the claim of the armed opposition groups, including the Khmer Rouge, to the Cambodian seat at the United Nations. Although the US would not openly declare that the Cambodian government under Hun Sen could now occupy its country's seat at the United Nations, the backing given by Washington to the alliance of the Khmer Rouge, Prince Sihanouk and Son Sann was thus terminated.

In August 1990 the five permanent members of the UN Security Council (the United States, the Soviet Union, China, France and Great Britain) agreed on the basic principles of a political solution for Cambodia. This plan had four main points: first, agreement was to be sought on the holding of elections; second, a National Council was to be set up consisting of representatives from all the parties in the Cambodian civil war, these representatives to be 'personalities with acknowledged authority among the Cambodian people' who would be mutually acceptable to each other; third, the transition period and the elections were to be supervised under strict United Nations control, this control to extend over the government and the work of the National Council; and fourth, all the warring factions were to be disarmed by the United Nations. There were also provisions for guaranteeing human rights and the international neutrality of Cambodia.

On paper, this peace plan looked very promising. The disarming of all military and paramilitary units, a strong non-partisan role played by the United Nations and free elections might indeed open up the path to peace. It was, however, more than uncertain whether the plan had any chance of even being implemented. In the first place, it was questionable whether the United Nations was really in a position to be able to disarm the Khmer Rouge if the latter refused to give up its arms. The Khmer still had an estimated 25,000–30,000 troops, and in Cambodia's difficult terrain these would be extremely difficult to disarm. If it came to a conflict it might be necessary to use several hundred thousand soldiers to achieve the desired end. Would the UN member states concerned be willing and able to undertake such a massive commitment? Moreover the United Nations was of course also responsible for the civil adminstration of the country. But unless the Khmer Rouge was disarmed, the whole plan could easily fail or in fact deliver the country into the hands of the Khmer, if the government forces were themselves disarmed. Success thus depended on the disarming of the Khmer Rouge, or rather, since this would scarcely be possible if the group resisted, on the extent of the external pressure which could be applied to the Khmer. In practice this meant that the ability and willingness of China to coerce its Cambodian clients would determine the fate of the peace plan; in other words, a key to Cambodia's future lay in Chinese hands. Against this background it appeared doubtful, to say the least, whether any guaranteeing of human rights could be more than empty words. The role of the United Nations thus became even more of an urgent necessity.

The plan of the permanent members of the UN Security Council, clearly exposed a strategic dilemma. In June 1991 political negotiations in Thailand between the Cambodian government and the three resistance organisations resulted in a provisional agreement being reached, but it still remained unclear whether this would hold.

It was only in June 1992 that the UN plan began to be put into action. Officially the UN was the supreme political and administrative authority in the country, but in practice in many respects the government remained in control. Disarming the parties to the conflict proved mostly impossible, with less than 10 per cent of all soldiers surrendering their weapons. In May 1993 the UN organised general elections, which were technically successful, but the Khmer Rouge boycotted them, remaining a powerful armed oppositon. The formerly Vietnamese-backed government party and the royalists formed a coalition government, albeit a fragile one. And when in the summer of 1993 the new government announced a military offensive against the Khmer Rouge, it became clear that the conflict had not been solved politically.

Solutions to Regional Conflicts: an Intermediate Balance

Obviously the end of the Cold War has and will have direct effects on the evolution and extent of regional conflicts in the Third World. This is already clear from the examples of Afghanistan, Nicaragua and Cambodia. The same is also true of the agreements in Angola; Namibian independence; the collapse of the Ethiopian government; the negotiations between government, army and guerrillas in Guatemala and El Salvador; the 'pacification' of the Lebanon by Syria; and new conflicts in Georgia, Armenia/Azerbaijan and Tadzhikistan. The effects on the Third World have also been evident in the mostly aborted democratisation processes within a number of African countries, and in developments such as the rapprochement between Cuba and China. Other conflicts appear to have been affected little or not at all by the cessation of the East–West conflict. This has been the case with the civil wars and overthrowing of governments in Somalia and Liberia, and in the dispute over Kashmir between India and Pakistan. The Gulf War requires a chapter to itself (see Chapter 7).

The effects of the altered international situation on regional conflicts in the Third World are generally not equivalent to the ending of such conflicts. It has become clear that the control exerted by the big powers over their clients in the Third World was not always as rigid as had been assumed. Thus the Soviet Union could not prevent Iraq from going ahead with its occupation of Kuwait, nor persuade it to withdraw, while the US was not able to control the Afghan Mujahedin. Cuba did not allow the Soviet Union to dictate its domestic or foreign policies. Israel continued to put obstacles in the way of US-inspired Middle East negotiations and then struck a separate deal with the PLO outside the US framework, in secret talks in Norway. Even after the end of the Cold War, control over the Third World by the remaining superpower and other big powers remains anything but certain. For the moment only a very provisional assessment of the situation can be made. There is much to suggest that the US, and the other major powers, are in a much better position today to bring about political and diplomatic settlements of Third World conflicts. This may be an advantage in a number of cases. On the other hand, diplomatic solutions alone are often not solutions at all. They do not equal political solutions, but might be only one of the preconditions for such a settlement. Third World conflicts generally have local causes of a political, economic and social nature, quite apart from religious and ethnic factors. It is precisely such causes of conflict that are often not even referred to in diplomatic agreements. An economic crisis, hunger, riots, the misery of refugees, a culture of violence brought about by years or decades of warfare with no alternative way of life, a destroyed infrastructure, continuing oppression or dictatorship – all such sources of conflict generally go beyond the capacity of diplomatic agreements to deal with them. Outside powers are either not able to solve problems in such cases, having little to contribute to a solution of ethnic and religious conflicts in India, for example, or are not willing to do so because of cost or lack of interest. Big powers are generally in the final analysis not so much interested in solving other countries' problems as in protecting themselves from any harmful consequences of such problems. Afghanistan has provided the classic example of this. Both the big powers involved extricated themselves from the war, which was a decisive political success on their part, but the war itself simply continued.

In this sense, the increasing diplomatic means available cannot constitute anything more than a framework for finding solutions to conflicts. They are not the solutions themselves. Just as during the Cold War the internal conditions within particular regions were of much greater significance for the conflicts than was often realised by the strategists in Washington and Moscow, so these internal conditions are just as significant after the end of the Cold War.

Each individual focus of conflict requires an individual solution which will vary with local interests, structures and conditions – which will themselves vary from region to region. What we may expect with some degree of confidence, however, since this is already becoming clear, is an increasing lack of interest in many Third World disputes on the part of North America and Western and Eastern Europe. Somalia is a case in point: by late 1991/early 1992 mass starvation there was a reality, but any meaningful humanitarian assistance did not begin to arrive before the autumn of 1992. Even then it was woefully inadequate.

6

The Ideology of the New World Order

What's New? Which World? Whose Orders?

With the start of the 1990s a new political phrase entered the discussion to proclaim the era that was to succeed the Cold War: the New World Order. However, it was not launched immediately after the Soviet Union's abandonment of its superpower role. It was the Gulf War that was declared to be the event giving birth to this New World Order, an ideological framework which had its political origin in the White House. In his State of the Union speech at the end of January 1991, President George Bush made the connection clear.[1] Later his deputy foreign minister, Lawrence Eagleburger, claimed that 'we have truly turned a page in the history of relations among nations', and hoped that 'the world community, acting collectively, will no longer tolerate the kinds of terror and intimidation which have blighted the international system since time immemorial'.[2]

It is obvious that such phrases were intended to legitimise the Gulf War in the eyes of the American public and foreign opinion. They could to some extent be classified under the heading of psychological warfare. Times of war are periods when there is a special need for legitimisation; times that require ideological expression heavy with emotional resonance. Clearly one should be seen to be fighting for one's own 'interests', and the US government has blatantly formulated this often enough[3] but it is nonetheless politically advisable to find 'selfless' idealistic grounds for war as well. So to wage a war in which the whole world is united against a single outsider, in order to bring about a New World Order of democracy and peace, ideologically speaking has an almost irresistible attraction.

The ideological grounds for proclaiming a New World Order implied more than simply reordering the Near and Middle East, however. For that, a 'regional peace plan' would have been sufficient, and of course there was talk of that as well. The Gulf War did not simply break out at random; it occurred within the context of the Gulf crisis which started with the Iraqi invasion and occupation of Kuwait. The US representative at NATO, William Taft, stated:

We had a brief peace – four weeks to be exact – from the date of
the London Declaration, July 6, when the Alliance recognized
that the Soviet Union was no longer an enemy, until August 2,
when Saddam Hussein occupied Kuwait. It is the stated policy of
the U.S. to restore and maintain this peace.[4]

Taft was implicitly formulating the material and political core of
the concept of a New World Order. In its own eyes the US had won
the Cold War by 1990 and had achieved undisputed political and
ideological power. After a period of increasing doubt as to the strength
of the American position in the world, the victory over the Soviet
Union and 'communism' restored hope in US world leadership. This
was what was suddenly threatened in August 1990, and this was
precisely the 'peace' that was to be restored.

In April 1991 President Bush expounded the doctrine of this New
Order in another policy speech:

For more than four decades we've lived in an world divided, east
from west – a world locked in a conflict of arms and ideas called
the Cold War – two systems, two superpowers, separated by mistrust
and unremitting hostility. For more than four decades, America's
energies were focused on containing the threat to the free world
from the forces of communism. That war is over. East Germany
has vanished from the map as a separate entity ... The Warsaw Pact
passed into the pages of history last week, not with a bang but with
a whimper, its demise reported in a story on page A-16 of the
Washington Post.[5]

This New World Order under US leadership would be characterised by cooperation between nations, by shared values, by peaceful
settlement of conflicts, by democracy and protection against acts of
aggression, by peace and prosperity and by the reduction and control
of arms.

It would be too simplistic to dismiss this collection of fine-sounding
words as the usual rhetoric of politicians, as so often the most effusive
rhetoric contains a substantial core of truth. Nonetheless all these
fine expressions did not mean that the US was going to renounce
power politics in its own interests and instead work in strict cooperation with other states to solve the world's problems as an equal
among equals. Why should the US renounce the use of its own
power at the very moment when it had overcome its greatest rival?
President Bush had pointed out clearly enough that national

sovereignty and the defence of the nation's own interests would remain paramount:

> For two centuries, America has served the world as an inspiring example of freedom and democracy. For generations, America has led the struggle to preserve and extend the blessings of liberty. And today, in a rapidly changing world, American leadership is indis-pensable. Americans know that leadership brings burdens and requires sacrifice. But we also know why the hopes of humanity turn to us.[6]

Thus we come to the political core of the official statements about the New Order; that is, a reappraising of the US claim to global leadership. The New World Order must not simply happen; it must be organised by the US in that it is conceived of as an American World Order. This is the real meaning of the ideological formulae. 'Shared values' are the American values of the free market economy which can be made to prevail even more strongly after the collapse of the ideological opponent. Similarly the phrase 'international coopera-tion' denotes that the international community must willingly accept American leadership, as it did in the Gulf War. 'Peace' thus defined can very easily include war if the aim is to maintain a regional Pax Americana, as the Gulf War showed.

The American Leadership Role

It is significant that with its concept of a New World Order, and its success in the Gulf War, a shift of emphasis occurred in the official rhetoric of the American government. While throughout 1989 and for most of 1990 the term 'partnership' can be found in countless speeches and declarations made by the administration and its members, with President Bush in May 1989 himself welcoming Europe as a partner for the US 'in the leadership of the world',[7] the Gulf crisis and war led to a shift to 'leadership' reaffirmed as meaning unilateral American leadership. This motif was an integral part of the conceptual structure of the New World Order.

In considering these shifts of emphasis, however, two qualifica-tions must be borne in mind. First, the proclamation of a renewed claim to world leadership by the Bush administration, which only a few months previously had been talking loudly of a partnership and common leadership with chosen allies within the partnership, was not based on a reasoned reassessment of the shifting international scene. It was relatively spontaneous, in that in the unique historical situation of the Gulf War the US was giving free rein to its own wishful thinking. The transition in the rhetoric from talk of partnership to talk of leadership reflected a shift not so much in political analysis as in political feeling. The Vietnam syndrome had at last been overcome; or that was the hope, at least. Walter Russell Mead has called this a 'brief but intense period of triumphalism' after the end of the Cold War.[8]

Second, the political character of the Bush administration must be taken into account. It differed from its two predecessors not least in that it felt no need for 'visions'. Presidents Carter and Reagan had felt it necessary to illuminate their respective periods of office with the ideological trappings of moral enterprises. Carter did this with his 'crusade for human rights' and Reagan with his anticommunist 'crusade for freedom'. George Bush was sceptical about such ideological ornamentation and regarded politics as rather a question of handling and solving problems. He made this difference clear when he somewhat disrespectfully referred to the need for large moral ideals as a basis for practical government activity as 'the vision thing'. If there was one thing that George Bush did not have and did not miss, it was the 'vision thing'. His aim was a hardworking, serious, professional administration, dealing with political and diplomatic problems in a practical and skilful way.

This in itself brought with it the practical problem that by the summer of 1990 the Bush administration had assumed an increasingly pale public image. Bush found himself more and more exposed to the criticism from both left and right that he was a colourless, passive president who had no 'vision for the future'.

The Gulf crisis and war gave Bush a now-recognisable profile and leadership role both in America and abroad. The New World Order which he suddenly discovered and proclaimed fulfilled the function within domestic politics of satisfying those who were demanding 'visions'. Someone who was waging a war to bring about a New World Order – and the future American role as leader of this Order – could hardly be reproached any longer with lacking a vision of the future. The New World Order was George Bush's substitute for the big 'morality' card played by his predecessors. It was his 'vision thing', born not out of a predilection for ideology but out of practical domestic necessities on the political stage.

This explains why Washington left the substance of the New World Order somewhat vague and all-embracing. The term was not worked out in ideological detail, and the concept was never expressed in more than a collection of banal and pleasant-sounding phrases.

After all, a 'vision thing' is not at all the same as a thoroughly thought-out foreign policy. As a public relations exercise it was precisely the generalised nature and woolliness of the idea, a disadvantage in practical terms, that was a great advantage.

As soon as the Gulf War was over the US claim to leadership was played down again, and from April 1991 onwards the term was being increasingly used once more with its normal resonances of 'partnership' with the European countries. But the rhetoric was not exactly what it had been before. Moreover, it remained full of noteworthy contradictions. On the one hand the theme of unilateral American leadership was maintained, with President Bush declaring in his State of the Union address in early 1992 that the goal was to 'move our country forward as the undisputed leader of the world.'[9]

Such declarations were to be made time and time again in 1991 and 1992 and they can hardly be regarded as evidence of moderation. But at the same time more modest statements were being made in other speeches by George Bush, in which he assured his heroes that the US had 'no intention of seeking to impose a Pax Americana',[10] or asserted that 'Where in the past, many times the heaviest burdens of leadership fell on our nation, we will now see more efforts made to seek consensus and concerted action'.[11]

The US government was fully aware of the contradictions. Asked whether cooperation or unilateral leadership constituted the core of American policy George Bush replied: 'it isn't a clear-cut choice of either-or',[12] and his national security adviser ex-General Brent Scowcroft suggested the answer: 'to mix equal parts of leadership and cooperation.'[13] Neither of these statements cleared up the confusion.

The incoming Clinton administration did not change this position. Mixed signals remained. What may have surprised observers is the fact that despite Clinton's emphasis on domestic and economic policies the rhetoric claims to world leadership not only remained in place but were often even expressed in more explicit terms than before. Secretary of State Warren Christopher stressed the point time and again:

> America must lead. And the need for American leadership is undiminished. We are a blessed and powerful nation. We shoulder the responsibility of world leadership. We stand prepared to act decisively to protect our interests wherever and whenever necessary. When it is necessary, we will act unilaterally to protect our interests. Where collective responses are more appropriate, we will lead in mobilizing such responses. But make no mistake: we will lead.[14]

Shortly after these remarks Christopher went so as far to name 'leadership' as a central element of a new 'Clinton doctrine', exclaiming that 'the need for US leadership is one of the fundamental tenets of the Clinton administration'.[15]

Even this tough talk could not hide the fact that confusion remained. In regard to Bosnia, Washington never managed to implement anything resembling a leadership role, while in Somalia the expression 'US leadership' implied the passing of responsibility as fast as possible to someone else – to the United Nations. Not getting oneself into trouble was always a more convincing argument than the 'own leadership' rhetoric. And occasionally it was quite amusing to listen to all the ambitious phrases. The US secretary of state actually managed to describe the US and European helplessness in regard to former Yugoslavia as a US policy 'to lead in a multilateral way'.[16] 'Leadership' obviously can be many things, with the Clinton administration as with its predecessors.

What these contradictions do show, however, is just how unclear Washington's ideas about a New World Order were. Even the extent of its own leadership role was not clearly defined. A 'pragmatic' policy was therefore followed with the aim of maintaining and expanding US power and influence wherever reasonably possible. In situations where cooperation with other parties appeared more advantageous than unilateral action, the emphasis would be placed on cooperation – although, naturally, once again with a view to furthering US interests. Such a political approach can hardly be termed a 'concept', however, since it amounts to little more than the formulation of the banal objective of promoting the interests of US power with whatever means appear to be the most appropriate. There are thus three strands to the leadership role of the United States in international politics: First, to become as powerful as possible, which is hardly an original objective; second, to fill the power vacuum left by the collapse of the other superpower, which is an accidental role allotted to the United States at a given moment in history; third, it is the expression of a simple feeling, concealing the lack of any concrete thinking.

The Future of the Third World

The acid test for all the smooth phrases and fine words about a New World Order, justice and peace is provided by the hard realities of the Third World. In this region considerable differentiation has taken place over the last two decades, with the result that there is no longer a single Third World. Living standards, economic conditions and levels of development in the individual countries vary too much for this to be otherwise. It has become increasingly difficult to consider countries such as Bangladesh, Brazil, Vanuatu, Iraq, Niger, Brunei, South Korea and India as belonging to a single category. It is of course indisputable that countries who may be regarded, on a more abstract level, as belonging to the Third World all have – or may have – interests that are common to all and different to those of the 'First World'. But this does not imply that Saudi Arabia and Bangladesh, for instance, can ever have really comparable interests. The only commonality of the Third World is negative: it consists of not belonging to the North.

Any loss of the blanket validity that the term 'Third World' still had in the 1970s, at least politically and rhetorically in the context of a New World Economic Order proposed at that time, does not alter the fact that poverty, misery and hunger are very far from being eliminated today. Quite the opposite. It was in the 1980s in particular that the world economy was marked by a widening gap between the rich countries and the poor countries, with the losing side experiencing a considerable increase in poverty. Table 6.1 indicates the growth in per capita GNP for selected groups of countries during the period 1965–89. The table makes it clear that the industrialised countries and the upwardly mobile threshold countries and NICs of East Asia achieved a good and in some cases outstanding growth in GNP per head of population, not only in the 1960s and 1970s but also right through the 1980s. On the other hand Latin America, which had satisfactory results during the 1960s and 1970s, dropped back in terms of per capita GNP in the 1980s. In Africa south of the Sahara, after initially positive figures, 1973 saw stagnation set in and the 1980s were a period of drastic setback, as these annual figures show. While the population of sub-Saharan Africa increased by 117 million in the years 1980–9, (that is, by 32.3 per cent), its GDP (at 1980 prices) fell by almost 27 per cent during the same period.

Table 6.1 Growth in GNP per annum and per capita as a Percentage

Group of Countries	1965–73	1973–80	1980–6	1987	1988	1989
OECD countries	3.5	2.2	1.9	2.8	3.7	3.1
East Asia	5.4	4.4	6.6	8.0	8.7	3.1
Africa	3.0	0.1	–2.8	–4.4	0.8	0.5
Latin America and Caribbean	4.1	2.4	–1.6	1.5	0.8	–0.8

Source: World Bank, *World Development Report 1990*, Washington, DC, p. 192.

The conclusion that 'development' on a global scale for the Third World has failed is not contradicted by the fact that individual countries or sections of populations have shown successes and to some extent can already seriously compete with the industrialised countries of the world. As the number of people suffering extreme poverty and hunger rose during the 1980s, and large areas or parts of continents found themselves in a state of permanent crisis, it is hardly possible to talk about development having been a success as a worldwide concept, even though today in certain Third World countries computers are being produced, or at least assembled. Today more than a billion people in the Third World live in absolute poverty, an estimate that is based on the World Bank definition of poverty as an income below US$370 per annum. Even the World Bank itself admits that these people have to 'struggle for their lives'. Poverty affecting the Third World in this way is one of the material conditions in the South which have to be taken into account when considering the New World Order, despite the success stories of astonishing growth in some East Asian countries that are now integrated in the world market. These growth and development success stories, however, are no proof of the success or realisability of worldwide development on the basis of current concepts or practice. Rather, they are evidence of the critical differentiation taking place within the Third World, a differentiation between individual countries, but also between different regions of the same country and between different social groups and classes.

A second condition affecting the situation of the Third World following the end of the Cold War is its inheritance of some 40 military conflicts, which in the mid-1990s continue to exhaust and destabilise the countries concerned. Here again, the proclamations of a New World Order will have to be measured against the real contributions which it makes to improving Third World situations. These countries are moving into the New World Order under catastrophic conditions. Ecological disasters turn into 'natural disasters' increasingly frequently, with famines in Africa or floods in Asia. Debt crises themselves result in more famines, wars and civil wars, partly due to internal social problems and partly due to external influences that either cause these catastrophes or keep them going. There are more and more ethnic and/or religious conflicts which are linked to socioeconomic problems and are virtually insoluble.

Given that the old order was not only incapable of solving this complexity of problems, but in vital sectors even contributed to causing them, then the minimum requirement for a New Order must be 'neutrality in conflict' – that is, it should not make existing problems worse. To go a rational step further, the New Order in the Third World must be measured against its ability to contribute to an alleviation of its difficulties. These are by no means radical require- ments. They offer a very pragmatic yardstick related to the solution of concrete and practical problems, and indeed to those which most obviously and urgently need solving.

So what ideas and proposals do the propagandists for the New World Order have to offer?

What is striking above all is that in important speeches made by politicians in Washington concerning the New World Order, Third World problems are either mentioned only very peripherally, or do not appear to merit any attention at all. In these speeches, all the talk is about Eastern Europe and Germany, the Soviet Union and now Russia and the CIS, the Gulf, and of course the United States itself. Occasionally 'Eastern Europe, Latin America, and other developing countries' are mentioned. Africa and Asia are passed by almost without mention, while Latin America is referred to only within certain limited contexts, such as debt management, foreign trade policy or illegal immigrants into the US.

> The 'New World' that Mr. Bush seeks to order is quite small. It includes Europe, the Middle East, parts of Asia, Canada and Mexico. Mexico apart (and for domestic reasons no American government can ignore Mexico), the administration is not much bothered with what goes on in Latin America. It will vaguely push to expand trade with South American countries, but that is about it. The same lack of interest marks America's policy towards Africa. There is a sense that things are heading in the right direction in South Africa, and that is all. India? Pakistan? Indonesia? Never heard of them.[17]

Exceptions are made only in a reactive way and regarding particular circumstances. Somalia is a case in point. But these are mostly responses to disasters or instances of imperial behaviour, not indi- cations of a policy or strategy for the development of the Third World or for the struggle against poverty or environmental degra- dation.

Not only are no solutions proposed, but the question of how the main problems of the Third World might be solved is completely missing from these draft scenarios for the future. Anyone who does take the trouble to ask what can be done in both North and South to resolve the difficulties of the developing countries is almost always served up with the failed ideas of the 1980s. Integration in the world market, free and open markets, private enterprise, Western investments, deregulation and the dismantling of direct state interventions in the economy, together with crisis management by the IMF/World Bank, private business and governments, are still supposed to lift the Third World out of its poverty. The CIA director-designate Robert Gates, for example, proposed that the US aid programmes 'should be aimed at fostering [the] growth of a private sector in recipient countries and enabling them to stand on their own feet.' Hardly less innovative is the following proposal: 'Our longstanding support of free trade also can play an important role in their economic growth. By helping them gain access to world markets, we can promote the trade and investment on which their economic success depends'.[18]

Such proposals are aimed at both Eastern Europe and the Third World. Yet they are precisely the recipe which in the 1980s was not only unable to remedy the crisis in the Third World, but made it very much worse. To increase dependency on the world market when the real trend is towards declining terms of trade may have been a good idea for Western empire-builders, but has been a catastrophe for most Third World countries. The concept of freeing markets and free trade in the Third World as a cure-all has both political and ideological dimensions. In terms of power politics, it facilitates access to the Third World by the industrialised countries and is structurally reminiscent of British free trade imperialism in the early nineteenth century, and of the US 'open-door' policy at the turn of the century, when a liberal foreign trade policy also represented the most effective foreign policy tool for exerting influence. With free markets and free trade relations, the strongest buyers and sellers necessarily become predominant; a few special East Asian cases apart, these are the Western industrialised countries, and Japan. At the same time, however, it can scarcely be overlooked that the free market policy has acquired the status of an independent ideology. In the course of the 1980s it became a kind of creed, whose application no longer needed examination or proof because it was a priori true. 'Potato chips and semiconductor chips, what's the difference? They're all chips!', said Michael Boskin, chairman of the Bush administration's Committee of Economic Experts, in 1990, arguing that both should remain equally outside state industrial policy.[19]

Today, the ideological enthusiasm of the Reagan years has faded into a more businesslike empiricism. The ideological bombast has died down, but in essence this represents only a modification of style, not an abandonment of the theory. It is striking that although the doctrinaire political aim of freeing world markets has not been made an ideological keystone of the New World Order, in reality it continues to be so.

A further difference compared with the 1980s, and especially with the 1970s, is that the elites and governments in the Third World can no longer make any serious attempt at resisting free market economy offensives from North America and Western Europe. An example of this is the plan for a 'Common North American Market', which in the early 1980s was rejected out of hand by the Mexican government as an attempt by the US to effect an economic takeover of Mexico , but is now about to become a reality under the name of NAFTA.

In terms of positive aid for construction and development the Third World therefore simply does not figure in official presentations of the New World Order.

The same is true with regard to other important and pressing problems of global politics. The end of the Cold War has meant that there is greater freedom of action for solving many of the world's problems. These opportunities, however, are being thoughtlessly thrown away. Here we can consider only a few examples of this, since the scope of this book will not allow further discussion of this theme.

The first involves the greenhouse effect and the destruction of important ecosystems. Climatic changes and the warming of the earth could become a serious threat to living conditions, and indeed in some cases they already constitute a menace. In pious speeches about the New World Order, however, this theme is almost never mentioned. Serious attempts to solve such problems are simply not made. The man who coined the term 'New World Order' flew to the Earth Summit in Rio in 1992, proclaimed to the United Nations that his country was the leader in this field as in others, and then immediately sabotaged the decisions taken at the conference.

Then there is the question of overcoming hunger, poverty and other causes of large-scale mortality in the Third World. This theme is also absent from the ideological exercises of top politicians, let alone from practical government policies. Once again policy is limited to symbolic acts with a figleaf function. Where are the bold plans to solve the problem of poverty in the South, or for that matter in the North too, as a part of this New Order? Where is the bold concept for solving the debt crisis of the Third World after more than ten years? Once the banks of the North were no longer at risk, governments lost interest in this, limiting their action to debt management instead of debt relief or the cancellation of debt.

These are all old questions for which serious answers are long overdue, questions to which answers could have been found and for which new – and this time serious – solutions must finally be proposed.

Global arms reduction is another problem. Instead of decisive initiatives by NATO following the collapse of the Eastern bloc, we have seen the then United States president in the election campaign of 1992 announce one arms deal after another for the Third World, in an attempt to secure his reelection. NATO, it is true, is reducing the size of its armed forces to some extent, but at the same time it is beefing them up with increasingly modern and 'more intelligent' weapons systems. Politicians, generals and publicists are all seeking new enemies now that the traditional opponent has vanished. A New World Order? All these attempts to retain and improve the intricacies of modern armaments cannot conceal the helplessness of those involved. No matter how imposing the military might, there can be no military protection against the possibly hundreds of nuclear warheads from the former Soviet Union now wandering about the world, with no one knowing exactly where they are. What defence can there be against warheads whose whereabouts are uncertain, with no one knowing into whose hands they have fallen or might fall, against whom they may be directed, or even if they exist at all?

These and many other matters have never been on the agenda of the New World Order, although they are problems of absolutely vital importance affecting the lives of hundreds of millions of people.

And with President Clinton assuming office in 1993, even the term New World Order was dropped. The Clinton administration has not changed course or tried to tackle the principal problems that its predecessor left untouched. Instead, it has substituted the more conventional phrase 'Post-Cold War era' for Bush's New World Order and continues to ignore key tasks of global importance.

Looking for New Threats: the South

The Third World looms large in the New World Order only where it poses a threat, as in the strategically vital Near and Middle East, particularly the Gulf. In this context it is the Third World which is seen as harbouring a new menace as real as the old 'Soviet threat'.[20]

After the end of the Cold War, and during the period between the proclamation of the New World Order and the final disintegration of the Soviet Union, there was an attempt to keep the idea of a 'Soviet threat' alive, to provide continuing legitimacy for an offensive and often militarised foreign policy. If a threatening image of an enemy cannot be conjured up, it is difficult to justify continuing high defence expenditure to public opinion. Why an arms race if there is no enemy to race against? In fact, without a credible adversary even a medium-level defence posture, as expressed in NATO terms, may seem like a waste of taxpayers' money. The end of the Cold War and the disappearance of the enemy has thus had potentially disastrous consequences for the legitimacy of the military forces, with corresponding political and economic consequences. Images of new threats, risks and enemies have therefore become necessary to provide continuing justification for the military apparatus and for an interventionist policy.

We have already seen, of course, that the use of scare-images to depict enemies distinct from, however much some of them may have been associated with, the 'Soviet threat', preceded the end of the Cold War by many years. In the 1960s, and again in the 1980s, the internal conditions in Third World countries were regarded as potentially hostile in themselves and as constituting a threat to US national security and to Western freedom as a whole, irrespective of any Soviet role.

Despite the official rhetoric of the early Reagan years it was recognised that the Soviet Union or world communism was not responsible for all threats and instabilities in the Third World, but that within the South there was adequate potential for conflict which in itself was sufficient to put US interests, however concretely or otherwise defined, in jeopardy. Opposition movements, insurrections and freedom movements, political and social unrest and instability in whatever form in the Third World were a threat, quite apart from whether or not the Soviet Union could make use of them.

Once again, a cynical view of US policy would be that it only concerned itself with problems such as poverty, the population explosion, illiteracy and so on if they seemed likely to cause instability and insurrection in areas where there were deposits of natural raw materials of value to the West, which deposits might be threatened.

It was also regarded as a threat if certain dictatorial Third World regimes closely linked to the US or other Western countries were liable to be overthrown, as in the case of the Shah of Iran, President Mobuto of Zaire, King Hassan of Morocco or the Duarte regime in El Salvador.

Above all, and it could be argued even before US diplomats in Tehran were taken hostage in 1979, the threat from Islamic 'fundamentalism' also loomed large on the horizon. This 'threat' became fashionable again with the Gulf War and the end of the Cold War, when the traditional enemies had disappeared.[21]

During the second half of the 1980, political planners and decision-makers in Washington and some European capitals were becoming aware of a whole range of new 'soft threats' to Western security. Their common features were that they were not threats of a conventional military type against which conventional military means could be used, and moreover they were essentially threats from the South – from the Third World.

Since the end of the 1980s a further threat has become the increasing military strength, in terms of both quality and quantity, of key countries in the Third World reaching a level of potential direct military concern to American or Western interests. These in fact are not 'soft' but 'hard' threats to Western interests, arising not from internal disorders within Third World states but from their regimes and military apparatus.

In May 1989, Secretary of State Robert Kimmitt told a Senate sub-committee:

> Certain regional military powers, whose forces are armed with increasingly sophisticated weapons, pose a threat to their immediate neighbours, and, to a lesser degree, the security interests of the United States. Examples of such regional threats are, unfortunately, plentiful. In the Middle East, Iraq has emerged from the Gulf war [the Iran–Iraq War of 1980–8] with larger, more modern forces and increased political aspirations. Iran remains unpredictable, and continues to support international terrorism. Chemical and ballistic missile proliferation – in Libya, Syria, Iran, Iraq, and elsewhere – and the danger of nuclear proliferation, are growing threats.

After listing a series of regional conflicts in the Third World, Kimmitt went on:

> Given these regional tensions, the United States will for the fore-seeable future need the ability to project military power to protect our interests in unstable regions. Our military presence, even on a limited basis is the final guarantee of regional stability in many areas vital to the United States.[22]

Thus even in the final phase of the Cold War countries such as Iran, Iraq, Syria and North Korea were regarded as being the new potential regional opponents of the US ('non-Soviet threats', in Kimmitt's words), quite irrespective of any treaties of friendship some of them might still have had with the Soviet Union.

Kimmitt's defence counterpart, Paul D. Wolfowitz, speaking in February 1990 on 'a national security strategy for the nineties' proclaimed:

A second key fact is that we are facing a world in which military power has come into the hands of a widening circle of states, all of whom reserve the right to use it as they see fit. You are all familiar with our concern over the proliferation of ballistic missiles, chemical weapons, and the technology to produce nuclear weapons. It is not less important that many states in the so-called Third World have highly advanced conventional weapons such as cruise missiles, and have them in quantity. The Iraqi army's tank fleet, for instance, is comparable in size to that of the Bundeswehr. Potential adversaries in the Third World are no longer trivial military problems, if indeed they ever were: Grenada is not the kind of conflict we are likely to see often, nor is it the challenge against which we should measure our requirements.[23]

This was both to define the essential nature of the new threat from the Third World, and to state an important element in the ideology of the New World Order. It was a threefold argument. First, the military strength of Third World countries was growing significantly; second, this was reducing the military superiority of the US; and third, these ambitious countries would claim the right to use their military power 'as they deemed fit'. In other words, the core of the problem was that some Third World countries were determined to step out of their postcolonial situation and demand rights for themselves which the US and other countries of the North had long thought of as being exclusively their own, namely the right to use their power as they thought fit.

Naturally the further proliferation of nuclear, biological and chemical weapons, of missile technology and other modern high-tech military systems, is fundamentally undesirable. This is particularly so in relation to the Third World, where wastage of resources through expenditure on arms is fatal. The political problem in preventing further proliferation is that it is those who produce and own military high technology and weapons of mass destruction who want to disarm the Third World. In the ideology of the New World Order it is potential enemies in the Third World who are to be disarmed, while the US increases its military capability despite reductions in the size of its armed forces. Wolfowitz said:

We should make the investments needed to explore promising new military technologies, including, but not confined to those associated with the Strategic Defense Initiative ... Moreover, as Third World military challenges become more difficult, we will want to ensure that we have decisive advantages over potential opponents.

In particular, we will press ahead in those areas that will enable us to use force without exposing more American servicemen and women to risk than is absolutely necessary.[24]

He was speaking little more than a year before the war against Iraq.

The policy of non-proliferation of weapons of mass destruction as practised by the nuclear powers, and above all by the US within the framework of the New World Order,[25] is primarily aimed not at an overall reduction in numbers of these weapon systems, but at preserving the West's own lead in weapons technology. In this sense a strict distinction is made between 'good' and 'bad' weapons and missiles. President George Bush in 1990 emphatically warned against allowing nuclear, biological and chemical weapons and rocket technology to 'fall into the hands of those whose hatred of America, and contempt for civilized norms, is well-known. We will continue to work hard to prevent this dangerous proliferation'.[26]

According to this view, only in the hands of the West are weapons of mass destruction necessary for the preservation of peace. Such weapons in the hands of the Soviet Union were bad enough, although acceptable in the context of mutual deterrence, but nuclear or other weapons in the hands of Arab or other Third World governments constitute a risk to world peace,[27] the only exceptions hitherto made to this rule having been South Africa and Israel. It is difficult to disentangle ethnocentrism and racism from the simple truth that non-proliferation is of course not only desirable but fundamentally essential, and that the simple criterion should be applied that North and South, East and West must be measured against the same standard. 'Bad' weapons of mass destruction can only be disposed of in the long term, practically speaking, if the 'good' ones are done away with as well.

That the policy of arms limitation in the Near and Middle East is predominantly tactical in nature is immediately evident from the fact that there can hardly be said to have been any let-up in US arms exports to the region. Israel, Saudi Arabia, the United Arab Emirates, Egypt and other friendly countries continue to receive varying quantities of arms from the US and Western Europe, and these are not obsolete systems but the most technologically advanced. It was symptomatic of the situation that while President George Bush on 30 May 1991 was heralding a 'comprehensive and ambitious plan for arms control in the Near East', his defense secretary, Dick Cheney, only five days later was announcing the planned delivery of major weaponry to the United Arab Emirates and Bahrain to the value of some US$2.1 billion, which seems almost modest compared with the planned arms supplies to Saudi Arabia worth almost $20 billion. Cheney in fact stated quite clearly that American plans for arms control in the Near East 'did not mean that Washington was not going to supply more arms'.

This should not be interpreted as a contradiction between Bush and Cheney – there wasn't one. Bush might have proclaimed an initiative to stop a new arms race in the Middle East, but at the same time he had made clear: 'My desire to curb proliferation doesn't mean we're going to refuse to sell anything to everybody'.[28]

The New World Order is a legitimising model, a 'vision thing', and in no way a practical guideline for action or a political concept. The Bush administration was not going to let its proclaimed New Order hold it back from a practical, flexible and energetic foreign policy. The New World Order was going to serve US interests, and not vice versa.

Just exactly what these interests are is now unclear, however. It is true that the US finds itself in a world situation where it is no longer faced by a single major enemy, the Soviet Union, and the ideological challenge of communism. Rather, it is confronted by a confused picture of heterogeneous dangers and risks.

After the Gulf War the US chief-of-staff, General Colin Powell, said: 'We no longer have the luxury of having a threat to plan for. What we plan for is that we're a superpower. We are the major player on the world stage with responsibilities around the world, with interests around the world'. Asked whether US forces would be more or less likely to be ordered into battle in view of the decline of a comprehensive Soviet threat, Powell replied: 'Haven't the foggiest. I don't know. That's the whole point. We don't know like we used to know'.[29] This feeling did not change with the arrival of the Clinton administration.

Occasionally, the emphasis on 'new threats' and future insecurity was even stronger. President Clinton's choice for the new CIA director, James Woolsey, stressed this at his Senate confirmation hearing:

The number and complexity of very serious threats to major aspects of our nation's security and interests have grown, not shrunk. In many ways today's threats are harder to observe and understand than the one that was once presented by the USSR ... Yes, we have slain a large dragon. But we live now in a jungle filled with a bewildering variety of poisonous snakes. And in many ways, the dragon was easier to keep track of.[30]

Secretary for Defense Les Aspin followed up on this, describing the dangers US defence policy would have to deal with in the future. The first is the 'new nuclear danger'. It stems from

> a handful of warheads in the hands of others. The leaders of the Soviet Union may have presided over an evil empire, but they weren't crazy when it came to nuclear weapons. If nuclear weapons continue to spread, we won't always be sure about their new owners. Even though the numbers would be small, the threat isn't. One weapon can destroy a city, a handful can represent a national catastrophe.

This argument basically continued the policies of the previous administration.

Aspin continued:

> The second danger we face is from regional/ethnic/religious conflicts. Here I'm talking about Iraq and Panama and Bosnia. These dangers do not put the existence of the United States at risk ... Rather, the threats posed here potentially threaten America's vital interests, American friends, American allies, and the American sense of decency.[31]

Whatever 'the American sense of decency' was supposed to mean, this was simply a restatement of Bush's policies by President Clinton's secretary for defense.

Aspin's next two points about danger and threats were somewhat more original. He mentioned the danger of a failure of democratic reform, principally in Russia, and declared that 'economic wellbeing is vital to our security'. These were two obvious points, but to raise them under a military heading instead of a political one was a new departure, which set them apart from the previous administration's policy. This represented a shift in style rather than in substance.

When the US Defense Department completed its 'bottom-up review' in 1993, the result was a reduction in the size of the US military apparatus. But its main goal for future military planning was to be able 'to fight and win two nearly simultaneous major regional conflicts', while at the same time 'sustaining the overseas presence of US military forces', and being able to participate in 'peace enforcement operations'. (This in addition to 'maintaining an effective nuclear deterrent' and 'allow[ing] for additional [nuclear] forces to be reconstituted'.)[32] Taken together, this means the willingness to be able to fight two major wars and a couple of smaller ones ('peace enforcement') simultaneously. In almost all possible cases the theatres of combat would be in the Third World. The result is that with the opposing superpower gone, the US will keep most of its military might in place, merely redirecting it southwards. It is no accident that no serious reductions will be made to the tools for Third World interventions. The US will keep not less than eleven aircraft carriers, plus an additional one in reserve and for training purposes (instead of a total of 14 in 1992), and 174,000 Marine Corps troops (instead of 182,000 in late 1992). At the same time, the reduction in size will be compensated for by improvements in quality and fighting power. And again, these improvements will be concentrated in sectors that are most useful for interventions.

The Defense Department states that:

These enhancements ... are especially geared toward buttressing our ability to conduct a successful initial defense in any major regional conflict.

These enhancements include improving: (1) strategic mobility through more prepositioning and enhancements to airlift and sealift; (2) the strike capability of aircraft carriers; (3) the lethality of Army firepower; and (4) the ability of longrange bombers to deliver conventional smart munitions.[33]

Ideological Changes in the South

It is not only in the North that the breakup of the postwar order has made it necessary to rethink future strategies. Progressive forces and freedom movements in the South have also been involved in such debates.

As we have seen, the influence of Soviet ideology in the Third World began to recede in the 1970s, or even in the 1960s, requiring a rethinking of the role of freedom movements and progressive states long before the end of the Cold War. Nonetheless the renunciation of an anticapitalist position vis-à-vis the West by the Soviet Union as a world power, however hollow much of its rhetoric may have been, was a shock for many on the left in the Third World. This loss of an all-embracing frame of reference became total with the disintegration of the USSR. Those who saw world politics in terms of a struggle between imperialism and socialism, and based their own course of action on a predominantly anti-imperialist line, had no firm ground to stand on after the end of the Cold War. Furthermore, in considering the collapse of what had appeared to be the ideological certainties of the bipolar system, while remaining aware that a demystification of the Soviet Union had already been under way for some time and that many of the old assumptions were not based on an unquestioning idealisation of Soviet policies, it must not be forgotten that the historical backwardness of the Stalinist model of socialism made this model credible in parts of the South longer than it was in the North. Its strengths lay precisely in an extremely rigid organisational structure and the ability to impose forced development control at all levels.

Although the collapse of the Soviet Union as an ideological alternative and world power was in principle of more crucial importance to the left in the South than to the left in the North, there is ample evidence that the European and North American left (insofar as it still exists or is even worth talking about) was disorientated to a much greater degree by the end of the Cold War than was the left in the South. Resignation and contraction are obviously affecting far more than the Marxist-Leninist faction alone. This trend is not completely new. It was discernible at the end of the 1970s, when a significant proportion of the left began to move out of sectarian isolation into the 'fashionable alternative' camp. The compromises increasingly made by the 'Green' parties in different countries are clear symptoms of the political dissolution of the left in Europe.[34]

Things looked very different in the Third World. There, any naive hopes of world revolution had already been discredited during the Cold War. Moreover, any expectations that the Soviet Union would or could protect any and every freedom movement against the attacks of imperialism, and help their countries to develop economically, were proved in practice to be without foundation.

As a consequence of this growing realism of the 1970s and 1980s, large sections of the left in the South took the end of bipolarity as an opportunity to jettison ideological ballast which they had carried with them for far too long, without retreating into self-pity and resignation as many of their comrades in the North did. This may be related to the fact that for the left in most countries of the Third World, the need for resistance and political organisation is based on more direct experience than is the case for European leftwing intellectuals, who generally have to rack their brains to find equivalent causes.

Social struggles in the Third World will continue irrespective of the relationships of other states to each other. And there is no indication that the potential for socioeconomic conflicts is likely to be any less in the future.

The left in the South cannot therefore subscribe to the fashionable illusion that the 'end of history'[35] and of social struggle has come, because its material circumstances do not allow it the luxury of such a conclusion. Social upheavals did not fade away with the end of the Cold War, and any suggestion that those problems demanding solutions have become less acute should be ruled out of court as absurd. Nonetheless it has been necessary thoroughly to rethink the strategies of freedom movements and of the left in the South.

Joel Rocamora has described the discussion:

> While some senior national liberation movement leaders hold on to old stalinist ideas, they do so hesitantly. Debate is mostly premised therefore on an acceptance of the critique of the old soviet model and on how to change strategy accordingly. At the center of the debate, the revolutionary strategy of outright military victory is being challenged. Few are calling for dropping armed struggle altogether. The demand is more to reorient armed struggle towards achieving a level of military power necessary to force negotiations. The character of negotiations, in turn, changes from that of negotiating an orderly retreat for the enemy to negotiating a political settlement where the political and economic framework is worked out together with power sharing.[36]

This abandonment of the concept of the armed struggle as a primary way to revolution has been the result of historical experience, not simply of theoretical considerations. Concentration on the armed struggle has had the serious disadvantage in a number of cases of not working. In El Salvador, the Philippines and South Africa, for example, it offered no prospect of success. In other instances which would appear to have been successful, such as Cuba, Nicaragua, the former Portuguese colonies or Vietnam, further reflections reveal that the military victory was due not to military strength and successes, but to the political collapse of the opponent. It was this that made the victory possible, however much military means may also have contributed to the success.

Furthermore, the military path to victory often has the decisive drawback that the duration and intensity of the war, and the scope of the resultant destruction, jeopardise the future of the country whose freedom is sought, or sacrifice it completely. Under very different political conditions, Angola, Afghanistan and Nicaragua/El Salvador are examples of this risk. There are thus situations in which the military victory (before or after a revolution) is indeed possible, but futile. When freedom movements and progressive governments in the Third World began to rethink their attitude towards the armed struggle, such considerations were just as weighty as the altered framework of conditions following the end of the Cold War. Clearly, changes in international politics have necessarily accelerated such reassessments. After all, how could the armed struggle have any prospect of succeeding once the Soviet Union and the socialist camp were no longer there to offer even the hope of military and political assistance?

Rocamora also draws attention to another important point in the internal debates of liberation movements:

> Another Marxist-Leninist formulation, 'smashing the bourgeois state', as a necessary goal of revolution is also being reevaluated. What is at issue here is not just the practical problem of dealing with a pre-revolutionary government apparatus, but the more important one of the legal system and the issue of democratic rights under socialism. There is increasing recognition in national liberation movements, for example, of the need to retain consti-tutionally enshrined democratic rights. These rights are seen not anymore as 'bourgeois rights', but as the result of class struggle throughout the world.[37]

This rethinking of the concepts of the armed struggle and democratic rights was closely linked to other elements in revolutionary theory and practice which also underwent revision. These included revo-lutionary economic and social policy. Few freedom movements or progressive governments in the Third World had been blind to the failures of the Soviet economic model. The idea of centrally planned economies gradually lost its attractiveness to a great extent in most of the Third World and began to be replaced in the 1970s by various 'mixed economy' experiments. Nicaragua is an important example of this. These concepts of a mixed private and state economy in the Third World represented an attempt to find concrete and pragmatic solutions to practical problems. Ideological excesses were generally kept within politically necessary limits.

Closely connected to the question of a mixed economy is that of the position of a national bourgeoisie. Once the private sector is given a legitimate and important role in the development of a country, this presupposes a political arrangement with the national middle class, not only in matters of economic policy, but in the overall management of the economy too. Without political, economic and legal guarantees for the bourgeoisie, a mixed economy cannot function, since the private sector will not function. This also leads to a redefinition of the role of the state in revolutionary theory in the Third World.

There are obviously two sides to the changes in the ideology of leftwing freedom movements in the Third World. On the one hand they draw the necessary conclusions from actual experience in the countries concerned, and from the altered world political situation. Within this process of theoretical rethinking, outmoded ideology can be thrown out if it no longer has anything to do with the social realities as they exist in each country. This discarding of ideological rubbish is naturally a positive process.

At the same time, however, processes of ideological adaptation are also taking place which are more specifically the result of political necessity and its tactical constraints. It is not always easy to say whether these ideological revisions are genuinely aimed at making movements more effective and progressive, or are simply opportunist. For instance, the Democratic People's Party of Afghanistan has abandoned its brutal and blinkered dogmatism of former years, during which it endeavoured to force its country into a Marxist-Leninist straitjacket without any understanding of social realities. It has become the 'party of the fatherland', abandoning practically all its 'revolutionary' aims. But was this a recognition and correction of its own errors, or simply an opportunistic policy designed to enable it to stay in power at the cost of political principle?

In the final analysis it should be remembered that the coordinates for political debates in the Third World over the last generation have already seen considerable shifts. In the Arab world, for example, there is very little talk any more about 'Arab socialism'. This is partly because earlier ideological nationalism has been stifled by the sheer weight of autocratic state apparatuses. But it is also partly the consequence of a return to cultural and religious values made necessary precisely by the disintegration of the old ideologies of the period immediately following independence.

In conclusion, it is not only in the North that the ideological structure defining enemies, threats and risks has become more complicated and heterogeneous. In the South too, models for ideological legitimisation have become increasingly variegated. In many places today religious and ethnic identity is regarded as much more important than it was a generation ago, and secular political concepts such as 'socialism', 'democracy', 'proletarian internationalism' had already lost much of their impact before the collapse of Soviet power. This means, among other things, that to link conflicts in the Third World to Western models of interpretation and legitimisation will remain difficult over the medium term. Ethnic conflicts in Africa or Asia, aspirations inspired by Islam or by Hindu nationalism in the Near East or Southwest Asia, do not fit neatly into the conventional East–West

7

The Ordering of the New World: the Middle East

A New Type of Conflict: the Crisis in the Persian Gulf

The most spectacular conflict following the end of the postwar period was of course the Gulf War of 1991. It suggests a number of interesting conclusions as to the pattern of future conflicts. For instance, there was no hint of former East–West confrontation during this war. Instead there was complete cooperation between the US, its allies and the USSR.

Among the many factors leading up to the crisis was Iraq's own view of its situation. The Soviet Union had continued to reduce its already limited role in the Near and Middle East, and following its withdrawal from Afghanistan (May 1988 to February 1989) was essentially confining itself to improving its diplomatic relations in the region, and to trade initiatives. After its defeat in the first Gulf War (1980–8), Iran was greatly weakened both militarily and economically, and for the moment did not count as a rival in the struggle for regional hegemony in Iraqi eyes. The Palestinian Intifada was presenting Israel with a political problem potentially capable of growing into a military crisis. France was continuing its role as the reliable partner and supplier of the most uptodate military equipment to Iraq, which it had been playing since the late 1960s. The US for some years had been gradually trying to establish closer relations with Iraq, a process which intensified during the first half of 1990, in spite of Saddam's threat in early April to destroy Israel with chemical weapons if Iraq should be attacked by Israel. The US had already indirectly supported Iraq during the final phase of its war with Iran.[1] Iraq thus appeared to have been given a free hand in its foreign policy, particularly after the US ambassador at that time, April Glaspie, assured Saddam Hussein at the end of July on behalf of her secretary of state that the US would not involve itself in 'frontier disputes'. Even when the Iraqi army was known to be on the move to attack Kuwait, a spokeswoman of the US Foreign Ministry was still saying

111

that she could make no judgement on who was responsible for the
troop movements 'on both sides of the frontier'. Only a week before
Kuwait was invaded she added that the US had absolutely no defence
agreement with Kuwait and was 'under no particular defence or
security obligations towards Kuwait'.[2] This official statement from
Washington was not corrected in any way before the Iraqi attack. In
fact it was widely disseminated. In Iraqi eyes therefore the situation
overall seemed favourable for the annexation of Kuwait.

Baghdad had a huge army of 1 million soldiers under arms;
although about half of these were only active reserves and of limited
value in combat, many of these troops had been battle-hardened in
the war against Iran. Their proven strength in defensive warfare was
significant.

Iraq's weaponry was also impressive. It had 5,500 tanks, of which
10 per cent were modern Soviet T-72s, with many of the older types
in modernised versions with improved cannon and armour; artillery
numbering 2,700; modern anti-aircraft and antitank rockets, Roland,
Milan and Hot as well as Russian; and an air force which in addition
to French Mirage F1s included Soviet MiG-29s and other modern
aircraft.[3] Furthermore, it possessed different types of chemical
weapons (mustard and nerve gases) and a whole arsenal of rocket
systems, ranging from artillery rockets through the Al-Hussein and
Al-Abbas (600 and 900 km range) to medium-range rockets capable
of reaching targets 2,000 km away, although the number and readiness
of these was uncertain.[4] Iraq could therefore feel confident that its
military strength was more than enough to withstand a crisis over
Kuwait. After all, international conditions seemed so favourable that
any serious conflict let alone a war, appeared extremely unlikely.

The fact that political and military conditions were favourable for
the annexation of a neighbouring country from Iraq's point of view
does not, however, fully explain why this act of aggression was
regarded as either necessary or in Iraq's interests.

In reality, the invasion was not influenced by outside power rivalry
or similar factors. Its aims were solely to increase Iraqi power. This
was to be achieved first by securing better access to the sea via
Kuwait's port; second, by seizing the Kuwaiti oilfields, which would
almost double Iraq's oil resources, placing about 20 per cent of total
world crude oil reserves in Baghdad's hands; third, by doing this, and
by eliminating an old opponent in matters of oil price policy, Iraq's
influence in OPEC would be increased and thus in the medium term
it would be easier to obtain higher prices for Iraqi oil; fourth, by
conquering Kuwait, Iraq could also wipe out its considerable debts
to that country (approximately US$12 billion). The substantial

Kuwaiti assets abroad were also attractive – certainly not primary reasons for the invasion but nonetheless desirable side benefits.

The Interests of the West

Immediately after the invasion of Kuwait in early August 1990 it became clear that the Iraqi leadership had miscalculated in thinking that although international public opinion might protest, the big powers were hardly likely to intervene with force. This miscalculation was essentially due to an inaccurate assessment of what would be the US and West European reaction to the annexation.

The interests of the various West European countries even during the first Gulf War (Iraq versus Iran) had been far from identical. Throughout the 1980s four aspects had been regarded as important to a varying degree by different countries, although their influence was strongest on French policy.

1. The main concern in the first Gulf War was to prevent a victory by a revolutionary Islamic fundamentalist state in the region. A victory for Iran over Iraq would have threatened the stability of the feudal regimes right along the south coast of the Gulf, including Saudi Arabia. Any overthrowing of these regimes would have meant a reduction in scope for political influence and a rise in oil prices.
2. Furthermore, neither the US, the Soviet Union nor the West European countries had any interest in seeing either of the two warring parties achieving a clear military victory. A victorious Iran or Iraq would become so powerful in the Gulf as necessarily to reduce Western influence. The best solution therefore was for both countries to weaken each other until their mutual exhaustion brought an end to the war. Maximum influence could then be exerted on both sides in the period following the war. Both would then need time and aid to recuperate, offering a chance to force a more moderate policy on Iran and establish greater control over Iraq.
3. Another not insignificant factor was that the war offered valuable sales opportunities for weapon systems, particularly to the French.
4. Also important for West European countries was the desire to prevent the US from assuming too powerful a position in the Gulf, making sure that West European voices, especially French and British, were taken into account through participation in political, economic and military measures. Without such participation there could be no hope of influencing US policy.

'Protection of the oil supplies', on the other hand, was a hollow argument in relation to the West's position. Oil supplies were never seriously threatened during this war. If they were, then it was precisely the militarisation of the region by outside powers which would initiate the threat. Iraq was after all not exporting its oil supplies through the Gulf but through Turkish and Saudi Arabian pipelines, while Iran (against whom naval operations were mounted) was having to sell its crude oil and ship it out through the Gulf in order to finance the war.

The structure of interests outlined above was one reason for the informal division of tasks within the alliance. France supplied Iraq with weapons on a massive scale (recently valued at US$5 billion but probably worth $8–9 billion) and with loans, while West Germany did its best to maintain good working and economic relations with Iran. This was agreed both in the EC and with Washington. It was feared that any complete isolation of Iran would force it into the Soviet camp.

The policy of the West European states in the 1990–1 Gulf crisis adapted the structure of interests prevailing in 1987–8 to the new situation in which one country (Iraq) had emerged as the clear victor, although this had passed unnoticed by European public opinion. This was an unwanted result of the first Gulf War which promptly led to an undesirable consequence. Iraq wanted to harvest the fruits of its victory and establish itself clearly as the major power in the Gulf. The destabilisation of already very unstable regimes in the region was an aspect positively welcomed by Iraq.

France, Great Britain and Western Europe as a whole, via the WEU, again demonstrated in the second Gulf War their determination to play a leading political and military role in tandem with the US in stabilising the status quo in the area. It would hardly be possible to maintain this stability over the longer term. Other factors, such as the implementation of the decisions of the UN Security Council, were useful as legitimisations for these actions, but exerted no fundamental influence. In all this, West European interests in practice coincided with those of the US, although they were not always completely identical.

The reasons for the massive deployment of US troops in Saudi Arabia and the Gulf in Operation Desert Shield, and for the launching of the air and ground war against Iraq in Desert Storm, were complex. Officially the aim was to demonstrate that no country can be allowed to 'rape, pillage and brutalize its neighbour'.[5]

This needs to be taken with a pinch of salt, because a country which only a short time before had invaded the small country of Panama, on the pretext of going in to arrest a criminal, was itself obviously highly flexible in the way in which it interpreted the principles of national sovereignty and territorial integrity, despite the fine-sounding words. And neither Kuwait nor Saudi Arabia were exactly democracies.[6]

Moreover, we have already seen that large-scale military action was not necessary to protect oil supplies. An escalation of such action could in fact have put the oil flow at risk. After all, Iraq did not seize Kuwait in order to stop exports of oil, but quite the opposite – 95 per cent of its earnings from currency came from this source. Nor did concern about oil prices provide an indisputable ground for military action. It is true that at the start of the crisis there was discussion in Washington as to whether the fragile US economy might not slide into a recession if oil prices reached US$25 a barrel. Iraqi control of Kuwaiti oil, giving it a hold over one-fifth of the world's oil reserves, would presumably have meant higher prices over the medium-term. At the May 1990 OPEC conference Iraq had indeed tried to exact a price of $25 a barrel, an attempt foiled by Kuwait among others.

On the other hand, to mount a big US military operation was not without economic risk in itself. It was estimated, that any escalation into a land war against Iraq would cost the US$1 billion a day. This would indeed have been catastrophic, considering the state of the US national budget, if in the event the war had lasted for more than a short time and if it had not been paid for by the allies. How long the war would last, and its precise consequences, could not be foreseen when the Desert Shield troops were deployed. In fact, if there was one event which could have physically threatened the supply of oil to the world market, this would have been a long war in the Gulf involving Saudi Arabian territory. Such a scenario, more for psychological than for material reasons, would have meant a dramatic rise in oil prices. Quite simply, to deploy more than half a million soldiers and wage a war at enormous cost would scarcely have been logical if its only purpose was to keep oil prices a few dollars lower. The strategic importance of the region in relation to oil supplies thus had something to do with the huge military action against Iraq, but not in any direct and clearly obvious way.

The main interest of the US in the Persian Gulf, and thus in Iraq and Kuwait, lay and lies in securing the stability of the whole area, as defined by the US. Saudi Arabia, Kuwait and the other Gulf states have since the Second World War served several useful purposes for the US and the countries of Western Europe. Among other functions, they have:

- ensured continuity of the oil supply;
- maintained a consistent low-price policy, giving priority to the interests of the West-dominated world economy over their own financial interests, or at least giving them equal priority;
- controlled and combated nationalistic or revolutionary movements or trends.

What the West wanted was to keep the various reactionary sultanates and kingdoms in the Gulf, including Saudi Arabia, firmly in the Western camp and policing the region for the West, whatever their decadence and/or fundamentalism. Iraq, and Iran since the fall of the Shah, represented a threat to this position. Both these countries, highly repressive themselves, were nonetheless aiming at the overthrow or incorporation of the feudal Gulf states and thus constituted a threat to stability as defined by the US. At the same time both countries were pushing hard for a high-price policy for crude oil, made even more necessary for them by the high costs of the first Gulf War. Iran also constituted an ideologically subversive power. The US and France had after all supported Iraq in the first Gulf War in order to try to insulate the Arabian peninsula from the Islamic revolutionary threat constituted by Iran.

Therefore if the US had not intervened massively on the side of the sheikhs and Saudi Arabia after the Iraqi invasion of Kuwait, all these countries would necessarily have had to conform politically to Iraq in oil-price policy as in other matters. They would have been left with the impression that the promises of the US to offer them protection were empty, and they would have had no other choice but to come to an arrangement with Baghdad. Iraq would then have become the undisputed great power in the Gulf region, and the US would only have been able to control or even influence the area with difficulty.

One final factor was that the US thought to protect its own interests by protecting the interests of other industrialised nations. Even though the US could do without the oil from the Gulf region, since it took only 3.6 per cent of all the oil it used from Kuwait and Iraq combined and 7.1 per cent from Saudi Arabia, other countries could not. France imported 35 per cent of its oil from the Gulf, Japan a high 64 per cent. If these and other countries were to be completely deprived of Gulf oil, extremely deep and wide-reaching economic crises would become unavoidable. Such crises in the European countries or Japan, in Washington's opinion, could easily topple the US economy into the abyss.

Two years after the war an American observer stated the US pattern of interest:

> If a single indigenous power – Iraq, Egypt, or Syria – were able to dominate the oil fields, that country would quickly become a great power. It would be less susceptible to US influence; it might well keep a smaller proportion of its revenues in US assets and in dollars; it would charge a higher price for oil and, militarily secure, it might make Europe, rather than the United States, the pivot of its policy. If this power were to demand payment in marks or yen for its oil, the consequences for the United States might be little short of catastrophic, and even the potential to make such a decision would give the dominant Middle Eastern country enormous leverage over the United States.[7]

Aims of US Policy

One of the main reasons why a political solution to the Gulf crisis was so extraordinarily difficult was, quite apart from Saddam Hussein's own intransigence, the fluctuating and contradictory official proclamations of the Bush administration, which concealed its conceptual rigidity.

At the start of the crisis the deployment of US troops was justified principally on the ground of defending Saudi Arabia. It was presented as purely and simply a defensive move to prevent any further Iraqi expansion, although whether Iraq would have had any interest at all in attacking Saudi Arabia once it had seized Kuwait is doubtful.

The second declared aim which was soon added was that of freeing Kuwait from Iraqi occupation and restoring the Kuwaiti royal family. Combined with these two points was the argument of protecting Western oil supplies.

Then came the stated political goal of eliminating Iraq's weapons of mass destruction and weakening its powerful military machine, sometimes associated by some members of the US administration with the aim of toppling Saddam Hussein himself. The two latter points were of course handled with a certain amount of discretion, particularly in the initial stages of the conflict, since they were not covered by the UN resolutions and were not part of the aims of the international coalition, so their enunciation entailed a risk of weakening the unity of the alliance against Iraq.

These objectives were contradictory because a simple declaration of support, and perhaps a limited military presence, would have been more than enough to protect Saudi Arabia from attack. The liberation of Kuwait could have been effected within a set period of time, without any war, by a combination of economic pressure (perhaps with some military pressure) and face-saving offers to Saddam Hussein. To liberate Kuwait militarily was conceivable, but included the risk of destroying the country it was designed to liberate. However, the destruction of the Iraqi military machine and the elimination of its nuclear, biological and chemical warfare potential, together with related research and production facilities, were not possible without a major war.

It is significant that the shift of emphasis from economic sanctions to threat of war occurred at a time before economic pressure could even begin to have its full effect. This crucial change of emphasis was due to a shift in American political objectives. These were no longer simply aimed at the liberation of Kuwait but also at eliminating Iraq once and for all as a major power in the Gulf region.

It has become clear since that time, from the evidence which is now available, that a preference for the war option became the dominant view in the US administration by October at the latest, although the second and offensive phase of troop deployment in Saudi Arabia only began after the Congressional elections early in November. It was at this time, if not before, that the objective of destroying or at least significantly weakening the Iraqi military potential became the driving force within American Persian Gulf policy. This meant that from now on a war, a successful war, was the form of conflict solution to which Washington was giving priority. From then on too, the Iraqi leadership could only avoid its military defeat by a more or less unconditional withdrawal from Kuwait. Such a withdrawal would not of course have made the US government any the less enthusiastic for the war option, but it would have made an American attack impossible to legitimise and would have meant the breakup of the international coalition.

The Role of the Soviet Union and the United Nations

During the regional crisis in the Gulf the United Nations and its Security Council assumed a new role, one which was only made possible by the attitude of the Soviet Union. The Soviet Union was after all closely linked to Iraq by its 1972 treaty of friendship with that country. It had supplied the Iraqi armed forces with more than half their equipment. It was this policy which had enabled the USSR in the 1970s to establish another partner besides Syria in a strategic position between the pro-Western countries – Turkey, Iran, Saudi Arabia and Israel. Although this relationship was never without its problems, partly because of the tension between Syria and Iraq, nonetheless Iraq gave the Soviets an important base for influencing the Near East, and constituted a potential source of trouble for the US, in particular because Moscow also had close links with the PLO. US policy was therefore one of excluding the Soviet Union from the whole region as far as possible, or at least limiting it to the positions it had already secured and which were to be kept as politically isolated as was feasible. The long and successful exclusion of the Soviet Union from any role in the peace process in the Near East is proof of this policy, although the US and above all the region itself paid a high price for this success, because a political solution to the Palestine conflict and the civil war in Lebanon consequently became an even more remote possibility.

In the conflict over Kuwait this background did not even play a vestigial role. From the start, US policy was aimed at building up a coalition of nations to oppose the Iraqi invasion which would be as broad and all-embracing as possible, based on the principle of international law according to which the territorial integrity of nations must be respected. This policy had two aspects. First, there was the practical objective of making sanctions effective, which meant all countries participating in the boycott; and second, it provided a cover of legitimacy, lent by the international community, for America's policy. Iraq was to be branded an aggressor and isolated from the rest of the world. The Soviet Union played a key role in this policy. It would have been possible for Moscow to break the economic or military cordon round Baghdad, and it could have constituted an obstacle to the united international front being formed. But instead, the Soviet Union adopted a position of clear support for US policy.[8] Indeed the US was even able to ask Moscow for secret information about the Iraqi military, obviously with some success.

It is not difficult to unravel the various reasons for this. In the course of rethinking its foreign policy, the USSR was attaching particular importance to the upholding of international law, the peaceful settlement of conflicts and international cooperation if possible within the framework of the UN and other international organisations. All these criteria applied in the case of Kuwait. By definition the Iraqi aggression was neither peaceful nor lawful, and the United Nations was fulfilling the role of coordinating agency for international reaction to the aggression. The Soviet Union also had an even stronger motive for its policy of cooperation. The Kuwait crisis gave it the opportunity, at no special material or political cost to itself, to demonstrate to the West and above all to the US that this was the beginning of a period of real cooperation over the Third World. It thus hoped to benefit in return from cooperation in other areas, such as economic aid to the Soviet Union and American tolerance of the situation in Afghanistan.

This in fact was how the US understood the Soviet position, with James Baker hastening to declare:

> From the outset of this conflict let me say that the Soviets have been very reliable partners in the worldwide coalition that has successfully isolated Saddam Hussein ... There were really no major substantive differences between the two leaders as to how the conflict in the Gulf should be managed.[9]

Only a week before this statement, Secretary of State Baker had spoken of the Soviet Union as 'a responsible partner', and of 'new possibilities for active cooperation by the superpowers in the solution of regional conflicts'.[10] A month later the US was already modifying its policy on Afghanistan and coming closer to Soviet thinking, although up to that moment Washington had always tried to use that country as a stick with which to beat Moscow.

President Bush himself, after his Helsinki meeting with President Gorbachev in September 1990, related cooperation in the Gulf to other aspects of policy, declaring that 'against the background of our common position at the United Nations, we should cooperate economically as closely as possible, and this is my intention'.[11] And in December the Soviet Union received, for the first time for quite a long period, an American credit for wheat imports amounting to US$1 billion.

Although Gorbachev had felt compelled to state a few months before this that it 'would be very oversimplified and superficial to assume that the Soviet Union could be bought for dollars',[12] it was in the Soviet interest to obtain favourable deals from the US and the other NATO states by giving its full cooperation in the Gulf crisis. Thus on the one hand the crisis resulted in the US for the first time allowing the Soviet Union to play a more active role in the Persian Gulf region, with possibly even a military presence to come, while on the other the Gulf crisis and Moscow's cooperation enabled the latter to limit the damage done to its international reputation by its intervention in the Baltic states. If the Soviet Union had acted differently over events in the Gulf, the US and some of its allies would undoubtedly have mounted a massive campaign against the Soviet leadership, which might have gone as far as economic sanctions.[13]

As the crisis evolved so the Soviet role diminished, until during the weeks just before the war it was afforded very little weight. It had been of significance while the US was concerned to avoid a Soviet veto in the Security Council, but this worry was over by the end of November. Any differences behind the façade of unity, in that the Soviet Union wanted to prevent the war and the US to start it, therefore amounted to nothing in practice. Washington informed the Soviet Union that it was going to war just one hour before hostilities began.

Similarly with the UN. For as long as the United Nations could be used to isolate Iraq and give international legitimacy to the US position, it was kept in the centre of political activity. From the moment it gave the US and the latter's close allies carte blanche for a military attack after 15 January 1991, its role became purely ceremonial. The UN secretary-general was not informed by the US government that hostilities were about to commence.

The Results of the War: a Regional Peace?

At least in the official rhetoric the Gulf War was the first loud drumbeat announcing the coming into being of the New World Order. Officially the war was fought to give reality to the principles of the peaceful solution of conflicts, international law in general and territorial integrity in particular. In terms of power politics, it was fought to prevent Iraq from becoming too powerful in the Persian Gulf and thus to maintain a regional stability in the area that was favourable to the West. As the conflict progressed there was a tendency in Washington to link the two aims in a single concept of a 'regional peace for the Middle East'. This prescription was bound up with America's leadership role as demonstrated by the Gulf War and applied to the solution of some of the more vital problems of the region. This was desirable in order to achieve regional stability, but also further to reinforce the overall US role as world leader following the end of the Cold War.

What kind of a regional order for peace was established by the Gulf War and how is the situation in the Near and Middle East likely to evolve as a result, as far as can be foreseen?

In answering this question the key point is that the main war objective of the US and its closest allies – that is the foiling of Iraqi hegemonical aims in the region by the destruction or reduction of its military apparatus – was successfully achieved. It is true that Iraq was weakened militarily as a result of the war less than was initially assumed, in that it remained capable of substantial military action and its Republican Guard in particular was essentially intact, but it no longer constituted a serious threat to the area either militarily, economically or politically. It is difficult to see how this can change over the next decade.

However, this very success threatened to make the establishment of a Pax Americana in the Gulf more difficult in the aftermath of the war. In no way was it in the interests of the US to remove the threat to regional stability posed by a powerful Iraq, only to be faced with the destabilising effects of a weak or disintegrating Iraq. Yet the war did not simply result in 'cutting Iraq down to size' while leaving it stable and as far as possible under Western influence. Rather, the conflict threatened Iraq's very existence and thus the whole stability of the Gulf region. As a senior White House official with responsibility for the Middle East stated: 'our policy is not to overthrow the regime, but to get rid of Saddam Hussein'.[14] The hoped-for coup against Saddam, which would have left the Ba'ath regime intact with a more amenable person at its head, did not take place. Instead the war led to popular uprisings by the Kurds in the north and by the Shi'ite majority in the south of Iraq. This considerably reduced the likelihood of a coup, since no nationalist officer in Iraq would involve himself in a putsch at a time when the existence of the state was under such a threat. The uprisings in fact united the military behind Saddam Hussein, and in this sense they may be said to have saved him at least temporarily. In the US view, they also in themselves directly threatened regional stability. It was feared that a successful Kurdish revolt might lead to an independent Kurdish state, or at least to an autonomous Kurdistan within Iraq. This would not only give the equally oppressed Kurdish minorities in Turkey and Iran a political model to aim at, thus spurring them on to try and win their own autonomy, but also for the first time provide them with a secure base and sanctuary from which to operate. The effects on the internal stability of Turkey, a member of NATO, as well as the consequences for the region as a whole, would be incalculable. Furthermore, an independent or autonomous Kurdistan, as a consequence of its partial or full cessation from the Iraqi state, would greatly increase the political weight of the Shi'ites in Iraq. It was this that the US and most of its allies feared more than a Kurdistan, and more than Saddam's rule. A Shi'ite south Iraq that was to all intents and purposes independent, would have control over two thirds of Iraqi oil production, while the Kurds could at most control one-third. Moreover, a Shi'ite regime in south Iraq would possibly ally itself closely with the Shi'ite government and clerics ruling Iran – that is, those forces which the US had feared the most in the Gulf throughout the 1980s. If the Shi'ites took power in Baghdad the threat would be even worse. The Shi'ite clerics would then presumably exert great influence over the whole of Iraq and the fulfilment of the Ayatollah Khomeini's war aim, an 'Islamic republic of Iraq', would be very much on the cards.

It was the latter nightmare which frightened the US and its allies most. But even an Iraq split into three, with an Islamic republic in the south, an autonomous Kurdistan in the north and a Sunni rump still centred around Baghdad, would have meant unavoidable conflicts.

For all these reasons, therefore, despite the revolts following the end of hostilities, no significant support was given to the Iraqi opposition during or shortly after the war, nor was any further attempt made to topple Saddam. Once the popular uprisings began in Iraq, the dictator shifted from being the greater evil to being the lesser, since without him the Kurds and the Shi'ites would triumph. American strategy was now to leave Saddam Hussein in power, while keeping him on a short lead, to enable him to put down the revolts. The economic embargo was not lifted, Baghdad was kept isolated, reparation claims were pushed so high as to make any recovery by the Iraqi economy and infrastructure impossible for the time being at least. The double objective here was to punish Saddam but at the same time leave the doors open for a palace revolt or coup at a later date. This possibility too must put pressure on Saddam. Those who paid the price for all this, however, were the people of Iraq, the Kurds, Sunnis and Shi'ites, not the political leaders of the country. This led UN Secretary-General Perez de Cuellar to say: 'It is not right that the Iraqi people should suffer. It isn't the Iraqi leadership which is being affected, it's the people who stand on the brink of starvation'.[15]

In Iraq the war led to the widespread destruction of the infrastructure, to civil war, population displacements, and tens of thousands of deaths even after the end of the fighting. A political solution to the Iraqi problem is not yet in sight, either from within the country itself or from the US. There can be no talk of a new regional order for peace being established as a result of the war. There are not even any signs of this.

Regional Democracy; Lebanon, Palestine

The situation is no different with respect to a number of other problems in the region. Kuwait, having been freed by force from the Iraqi occupation at high human and material cost, was handed back to the Sabah family dictatorship. Martial law and torture became the rule. Any democratisation of Kuwaiti society or implementation of the constitution seem as improbable after the war as before. Even the elections of 1992 did not fundamentally change this. The Saudi royal family plays an important part in this, as it is determined to prevent any democratisation of Kuwait, fearing the example of a democratic neighbour. Saudi Arabia itself has no constitution and no parliament. Political parties are prohibited. In fact, despite diplomatic contacts and fine rhetoric about obligations and rights, the question of democracy as part of a regional peace settlement for the Near East has been regarded as being of only third-rate importance. While the torture taking place under the Sabah dynasty in Kuwait does constitute a public relations problem for the allies, and this requires them to express at least a minimum level of criticism, the theocratic dictatorship exercised by the Saudi royal family is passed over in silence.

A further hotbed of conflict in the Near East, and a necessary element in any peaceful regional order worthy of the name, is the Lebanon. It has suffered from domestic conflicts amounting to the disintegration of its society and state, under the anarchy of bitter rivalry between armed militias. It is also entangled in the Palestinian problem and has been subject to continuous military interventions by Syria and Israel, as well as to the destructive influence of other outside powers such as Iran and Iraq and to the involvement of the US and three of its European allies in 1982–4. In the regional order following the Gulf War the Lebanon has become to all intents and purposes a protectorate of the Ba'ath dictatorship of Syria, although this has had a positive side in the disarming of some of the militias. In the past Washington had criticised the Syrian policy of continuing its occupation of the Lebanon and increasingly tightening its hold, but during the war Damascus was given the green light to continue with this. The US now grants that the Lebanon is a zone of Syrian influence controlled by Syrian military forces. The fact that the Syrian dictatorship is just as brutal as the Iraqi regime, and is constantly violating the territorial integrity of its neighbour Lebanon, is disregarded despite all the talk about a New World Order, as of course are the frequent Israeli air or ground attacks on the country. The Lebanon was the price for Syrian cooperation in the Gulf War.

By now very little is left of the peaceful regional settlement for the Middle East which was announced and worked for as a fruit of the Gulf War and the New World Order. Iraq, defeated militarily, has become a source of regional instability with no prospect of recovery in the foreseeable future.

If a 'regional order for peace in the Near East' is supposed to be part of the New Order, the situation is not very promising. Saudi Arabia, Kuwait and other Gulf states are governed by semi-feudal repressive dictatorships whose internal stability is also doubtful over the long term. The whole question of Kurdistan, with its possible ideological and political impact on Turkey, is another problem. And the Lebanon has emerged from civil war at the cost of dependence on the Syrian dictatorship. It is under partial military occupation and is bombarded at regular intervals by Israeli war planes. Finally, there are the uncertainties in the whole area resulting from the rise of Islamic 'fundamentalist' movements in various countries of the region.

When all these issues are taken into account, it is clear that the stability of the Near and Middle East has not been strengthened by the Gulf War. The US position today looks stronger than it actually is. Walter Russell Mead has made the dilemma clear:

> This is a place where the United States does not know how to succeed and where it cannot afford to fail. These situations do rarely turn out well ... American diplomats and strategists must understand that our need to be dominant in the Middle East is a sign and a source of national weakness, not strength ... With all its power, and with the laurels of military victory fresh on its brow, the United States has lost the initiative in the postwar Gulf.[16]

If such a dubious result has been achieved precisely in that region selected for the establishment of the New World Order, and in which US influence has been considerably increased by its military victory in the Gulf War, there cannot be much expectation that this Order can become a Pax Americana in the true sense of the term.

Any truly regional peace settlement depends on a solution being found for the Palestinian problem. This was made even clearer to the US government by its difficulties, during the Gulf crisis, in preventing the coalition of Arab states against Iraq from falling apart over close American links with Israel. Saddam Hussein endeavoured to use the Palestinian question as a wedge to split the coalition, while Israeli actions such as the massacre of Palestinians on the Temple Mount threatened to bring about the same result.

After the war Washington hoped that increased US prestige due to its victory, together with stronger links with a number of states in the region such as Syria, would facilitate a solution to the problem. However, the Gulf War not only had the effect of increasing American influence in the region, it also in some respects made a solution to the problem more difficult to achieve. Many Palestinians supported Saddam Hussein in the war, although they were under no illusions as to his dictatorial character. It was above all the lack of a political alternative of any kind which drove them into this allegiance. As a result of their attitude, the Palestinians in general and the PLO in particular became discredited in the eyes of many governments.

This was particularly painful for the Palestinians when it meant the loss of support from Arab states such as Saudi Arabia, which cut off the supply of funds to the PLO.[17]Moreover, the Palestinian enthusiasm for Saddam during the Iraqi Scud attacks on Israel further worsened the climate between Israelis and Palestinians, making any dialogue between them more difficult.

Another result of the Gulf War was that it left the king of Jordan even less able to play a constructive role in solving the problems of the Near East than before. His difficult balancing act during the conflict, when he was compelled by domestic public opinion to support Iraq, but because of foreign policy necessities did not want to offend the West and the anti-Iraqi Arab states too much, had the effect of further reducing his already limited room for manoeuvre after the war. His position in Jordan has not been secure enough to enable him to make any special concessions to Israel or the US even if he wanted to do so.

A further short-term consequence of the Iraqi defeat was that Israel under the Likud government felt even less politically compelled to make any concessions to the Arab states or to the Palestinians, for example by returning the occupied territories or by agreeing to the establishment of a Palestinian state. Purely in terms of power politics, Israel's position after the Gulf conflict was considerably strengthened. The Palestinian Intifada movement in the occupied territories was weakened and the PLO internationally discredited. The anti-Israeli front of the Arab states had become less hostile, due to the informal cooperation between them during the Gulf War mediated by the US, and was in any case split by the maverick action of Iraq. Above all the only potential enemy with real military strength, Iraq itself, had been put out of action without Israel having had to contribute much to this desirable result. Thus although it was true that the possibility of Israeli concessions was greater after the war than it had been for a long time, the necessity or even the attractiveness of concessions was reduced. Israel's interest in a political compromise to solve the region's problems, by giving up the occupied territories as part of a solution, would only be engaged if it felt such a course could ensure its security in a more stable and permanent way than military means could achieve. The American victory in the Gulf reduced any such need. It left Israel's security position better than before, both militarily and politically. Why then should it make any substantial concessions?

This was the background for Prime Minister Yitzhak Shamir's open obstruction of the negotiations with the Arab states which the US subsequently attempted to broker.

The American secretary of state, James Baker, in the course of his hectic shuttle diplomacy after the war, found to his surprise that the Israeli government had no intention whatsoever of making any sub-stantial compromise in the interests of reaching a political solution to the Palestine conflict. This was despite the American design for a solution that would take very great account of Israel's interests, or at least would be worked out in accordance with Washington's view of those interests. Baker's diplomacy in essence was not aimed at bringing about a compromise between the Israelis and Palestinians, that is between Israel and the PLO, and thus tackling the core problem of the conflict. His objective was rather to achieve bilateral partial understandings at government level, for instance between Israel and Syria and between Israel and Jordan. This was very much in conformity with Israeli government policy, but nonetheless Tel Aviv strongly resisted Baker's initiatives. In order to get the agreement of the Arab states, the US government had to garnish its pro-Israeli proposals so as to make them acceptable to the Arab side, giving the bilateral talks the multilateral framework of an international Middle East conference. In return Israel would have to make substantial concessions in terms of 'land for peace'. Without such a signal the Arab states would have no interest in participating in talks, whether bilateral or multilateral. There was also the constant problem of whether and how the Pales-tinians should be brought into the Middle East conference. A PLO presence was not acceptable to Israel or the US, and after the Gulf War the Arab states no longer insisted on it. The US government did, however, consider that the Palestinian population in the territories occupied by Israel should have the right to be able to choose their own representative, presumably within the Jordanian delegation. This would have amounted to an indirect PLO representation in the talks. Israel rejected this. Furthermore, Israel showed no sign of wanting or permitting any solution along the lines of 'land for peace'. Quite the opposite. Even during a visit of the US secretary of state to Israel, new Israeli settlements were established in the occupied territories in obvious demonstration of Tel Aviv's intent.

The Middle East conferences which followed proved to be difficult. Israel had accepted a leading American and Soviet Russian role in the talks, and after long hesitation and opposition had accepted EC participation at least in an observer role. But Tel Aviv absolutely refused to accept any participation by the United Nations, which was an affront to international opinion after the role played by the UN in the recent war. These disputes over what appeared to be mere for-malities reflected fundamentally opposed interests. Israel was only interested in a Near East conference if it was purely of a ceremonial nature, constituting recognition of Israel by the Arab states, without their being able to exert any pressure on Tel Aviv. It wanted serious negotiations to take place at bilateral governmental talks, in which the overall Arab context and the Palestinian question would be of less significance, and in which Israel would be in a considerably better negotiating position since it would be face-to-face with the weaker Arab governments. The Arab states, on the other hand, wanted a substantial Near East conference, at which the EC would be represented and the United Nations would play an important role. Only within such a multinational framework and on the basis of the various UN resolutions concerning the Middle East conflict would there be any chance of persuading Israel to compromise. In the summer of 1991, Syria and Israel nonetheless declared themselves ready to take part in a Near East conference organised by the US and the Soviet Union. At the same time, the Israeli government stated that any agreement on the basis of 'land for peace' continued to be unacceptable. This declaration doomed the process of negotiation to failure before it started, even if it did not fail for other reasons, because it was limited to seeking diplomatic agreements between governments, without touching on the need for an agreement between the Israelis and Palestinians.

When Shamir and his Likud Party were defeated in the Israeli elections of 1992, the way was opened for serious negotiations for the first time.[18] The new prime minister, Itzhak Rabin, lost no time in sending out a series of positive signals, which at least improved the atmosphere, particularly a striking readiness on the Israeli side to give up sections of the Golan Heights, which brought a positive reaction from Syria.

But there also were negative signals. The massacre on the Temple Mount, the illegal deportation of alleged Hamas activists from the occupied West Bank into Lebanon, the cutting off of the Gaza Strip and the repeated Israeli air and ground attacks on Lebanese territory were hardening the positions of the opposing sides. Still, the series of conferences between Israel and its Arab counterparts made progress. This was chiefly due to the PLO's desperation to reach any compromise. Yasser Arafat was even prepared to exclude the future status of East Jerusalem from the talks, a very touchy emotional issue with Palestinians. On the other hand Israel's Labor government was trying to keep the diplomatic process on track and to find a modus vivendi with the Palestinians, in response to public opinion at home. So Prime Minister Rabin was trying simultaneously to demonstrate strength and to make progress on the talks. These contradictions, together with the fact that the interests of the PLO leadership in Tunis differed from those of the Palestinians in the occupied territories, led to splits in the Palestinian ranks, which made the talks even more difficult.

Suddenly, in September 1993, there was a breakthrough. In one stroke the Tunis-based PLO leadership which had been gradually shifted to the sidelines moved back centre stage. Yasser Arafat and his colleagues had undertaken a secret round of direct negotiations with Israel, parallel to the official Middle East talks, basically outflanking the newly strengthened Palestinian leadership inside the occupied territories. Israel and the PLO reached agreement on partial autonomy for the Palestinians, starting with the Gaza Strip and the Jericho area in the West Bank. It is quite remarkable that it was not Washington which brokered this compromise: it was the government of Norway which was instrumental in getting the secret process going.

If Israel considers the agreement to be a first move towards meaningful Palestinian self-determination and statehood, and if both parties can deliver their promises to the other side, this might really be the first step to peace. It now it depends on the ability of the Israeli and the PLO leaderships to move ahead against the resistance to the proposals from within their respective sides, to achieve the setting up of the new Palestinian state and to make it economically sustainable. In any case, the direct bilateral talks have been much more effective than the US-Russian sponsored Middle East talks.

8

The New Order of World Power

The New World Order, as a concept engendered by the transformation of East–West relations and the related radical restructuring of Europe, was made possible by the Soviet Union's relinquishment of its claims to world power and its subsequent dissolution. Although other significant international developments played a role, such as the slowly altering relationships between the US, Western Europe and Japan, and between a changing Third World and the centres of world economic power, these alone were not sufficient to create a new international system. It was the combination of these political and economic trends with the complete transformation of Europe that justifies the claim that a new international order is coming into being.

This transformation took place in four stages. The first comprised the internal changes within the former Eastern bloc, culminating in the disintegration of the Soviet Union and subsequent further fragmentation; second was German reunification and its impact on European politics; third came the process of European integration within the EC; and fourth there was especially with the US the changing relationship of Europe to powers and regions outside Europe, but also involving the Near and Middle East. These four phases are closely interlinked.

Germany within Europe

Reunification
German reunification was unexpected and took place with astonishing speed. After 1945 the division of Germany had become accepted as a stable and indisputable part of the status quo, for more than 40 years, in spite of Bonn's occasional dutiful rhetoric to the contrary, which itself was heard less and less often as time went on. Then suddenly within a year at the end of the 1980s the political and economic system of East Germany fell apart. East Berlin's leadership had been gradually losing its political legitimacy for some time, due to economic stagnation and decay, political repression and an increasing lack of ideological credibility. Perestroika in the Soviet Union

then provided a model for possible change and at the same time offered a political framework permitting this change to take place. Once the East German leadership set its face against this historical opportunity, its rule was doomed. It was like a house of cards which would tumble at the slightest push, and this push came with the illegal mass emigration of East Germans via Hungary to the West. As Gorbachev himself said in East Berlin in October 1989, 'life punishes the latecomer'.

By the time this collapse occurred, the German Democratic Republic had lost all its legitimacy as an independent, let alone a socialist state. Nowhere was there any serious political thought about a way forward which would justify the continuation of East Germany as a separate entity allowed to evolve in its own way. There was therefore no political or ideological alternative to the discredited system other than identification with the system in the Federal Republic, which had for so many years been its opposite pole. This meant that the aspirations of the GDR's citizens and movements became concentrated on national unity.

Then came the opening of the Berlin Wall early in November 1989, with East Germans able to travel to the West to see for themselves just how affluent the West Germans were, how low their own living standards were in comparison and how materially backward their country was. Such personal experience radically changed the political mood within a few weeks. In the elections of March 1990 the Christian Democrats (CDU) won a substantial victory, in contrast with the massive support given to the Social Democrats (SDP) in November/December 1989. East Germans saw the rapid adoption of the Western economic model as the only way of solving all their problems, and national unity was a necessary part of this. It was this combination of ideological and material factors which gave such a dynamic impetus to reunification. The rightwing nationalists among the West German conservatives had no need to persuade or exhort.

The result of the 'unification' process – partly voluntary and partly takeover – was a Federal Republic, with 16.6 million more inhabitants than the old FRG and larger by 108,000 square kilometres. The Republic also acquired very serious economic and social problems.

At the time of unification the Federal Republic was already the strongest country in Europe economically, occupying a key position in the EC. Reservations about this were generally expressed discreetly but were nonetheless real, as indicated by the former Italian Prime Minister Andreotti's well-known bon mot that he liked Germany so much he was glad to have two of them, or by the 'scandal' of British minister Nicholas Ridley, who warned of a 'German threat' and expressed his misgivings over the 'German character', thus bringing about his forced resignation from the cabinet .

The creation of a unified German state was regarded in the rest of Europe as a further strengthening of the Federal Republic, and as a further expansion of its economic and political power.

What reinforced the concern was the speed and highhanded manner with which German Chancellor Helmut Kohl pushed reunification through against the wishes of most of Germany's neighbours. Stanley Hoffmann has described the proceeding of the reunification in the journal *Foreign Policy*:

> What is striking about Kohl's leadership is his decision to make German unity an issue for the Germans alone. All the key initiatives have come from Bonn. The European Community (EC) was not consulted, even though the absorption of the German Democratic Republic (GDR) amounts to the entry of a 13th member into the Community; Brussels was not always even informed. Both political unification and economic aid have been shaped on Bonn's terms. To be sure, the FRG had to accept the Two plus Four formula; but it was directly with Gorbachev that Kohl negotiated Moscow's acceptance of German membership in NATO, the limitation on the size and nature of German armed forces, and the departure of Soviet forces from East Germany and of the occupying forces from Berlin. Like Adenauer, Kohl proclaims his intention to work for West European monetary and political union and to keep Germany in NATO. But he has in effect presented these courses as sovereign German choices, not as constraints imposed, or even collective options adopted, by a coalition of countries. At every turn, including in NATO summit meetings, he has preempted or evaded external control, while providing what might be called sovereign reassurance about his intentions and destination.[1]

Only in London, where German reunification coincided with the last phase of the Thatcher regime and the associated 'Europhobia' of the Conservative Bruges Group, was there a note of loud panic. The British government was even supporting a 'continuing Soviet military presence in East Germany', since this give a raison d'être to NATO and the presence of both NATO and Soviet troops would permit some level of control over Germany.

The French government adopted an opposite position. It shared the general discomfort at having this new giant established in the middle of Europe, a Germany not only economically the strongest country in Europe but also no longer kept in its place by a subordinate position within NATO now that the Warsaw Pact no longer existed. Paris took the view that the 'German threat' could only be controlled over the long term by integrating Germany more and more closely into common political and economic institutions. The British saw an emphasis on their own sovereignty and role as a nuclear power, within the context of their 'special relationship' with the US, as being the best way of containing the economic and political threat from a united Germany. The French regarded the real danger as emanating not primarily from Germany itself as an economic or military power, but from the possibility of a military 'power vacuum' in Central and Eastern Europe, leading to an informal economically based domination of the countries of Eastern Europe, and particularly of Russia, by Germany.

A combination of western German financial strength and technology with raw materials from the eastern region, associated with a potentially huge market for German products, was regarded as dangerous, not only in Paris but also in the other EC countries and the US. The shrewdness of Chancellor Kohl in engineering reunification was particularly evident in the way in which he kept all the options for such an economic scenario open, while at the same time presenting himself in the West as an absolutely wholehearted NATO supporter and prime mover towards European integration. Peter Ludlow has summarised the French position: 'the surest way to lock the Federal Republic into the Western system lies in a strengthening and deepening of the EC's identity. Excessive dependence on bilateral pressure can only undermine the longer-term objectives.'[2]

The European Community, the WEU and NATO, however are not simply institutions which integrate Germany and in this way limit Germany's freedom for independent action, they are also a means of strengthening Germany internally, that is economically and ideologically, and externally vis-à-vis the US or Russia and the CIS. This is why the Federal Republic finds little difficulty in accepting the constraints imposed on it by integration. In return for a modest loss of freedom for independent action, it gains substantially in economic and political weight, and avoids numerous conflicts which are bound to be disadvantageous to a country depending heavily on foreign trade, with imports and exports combined making up half of its GNP. Cooperation with France and the other EC countries represents for Germany the simplest way of influencing the future evolution of the EC, without at the same time feeding the widespread suspicion of a reborn German ambition for mastery over Europe.[3]

Thus Germany's self-interest in integration dovetails with French policy and this coming together of mutual interests constitutes the basis for the particularly close German-French relationship. This does not mean of course that the new Germany will not seek to look after its own interests within a European Community.

An example of this is the issue of a common European currency and a common central bank. In this case, what is at stake is not seemingly trivial disputes over the distribution of resources, as for example with farm prices, but the economic and political domination of the Community. Western Europe in reality already has a central bank in the German Bundesbank. This has never been formally agreed or established by law, but the economic power of Germany, and particularly the special role played by the deutschmark, have naturally led to the Bundesbank assuming a leading role in European monetary policy and thus exercising considerable influence over the economic policies of a number of European states, including France. Some currencies are in practice linked to the deutschmark, so that monetary policy decisions made in Frankfurt have a direct effect on such countries, for example on Denmark, or even on France. This influence has weakened somewhat because of the monetary chaos in the EC in 1993, but it has not fundamentally changed.

Within the EC context, the moves towards a common European central bank can be looked at in two ways. On the one hand, such a bank would symbolise a further important step in EC integration and the evolution of common European institutions, which are regarded sceptically by the British, while Bonn makes supportive statements. On the other, the establishment of such a bank would weaken the Bundesbank and thus the role played by Germany in determining European monetary policy. A European central bank would give France, Great Britain and the other EC countries an equal voice, which is not the case today. The Bundesbank therefore, and to a lesser extent the German government, despite all its declarations of support for European unity and the establishment of the common internal market, which would have to include a common monetary policy, repeatedly endeavour to delay the establishment of the European central bank. It is constantly thinking up new conditions which must be fulfilled beforehand, obviously wanting to see such a bank located in Frankfurt and modelled on the Bundesbank.

Even before the process of unification, in May 1989 George Bush was speaking of the US and Germany as 'partners in leadership.'[4] This may have been a somewhat exaggerated description of the real relationship, but nonetheless 20 years previously no American president would have dreamed of saying anything like it. The weight of a united Germany compared with that of the US, in relation to Russia and the CIS as well as within the EC, has continued to grow in importance. A sign of this is the discussion over a permanent German seat on the UN Security Council. It must not be forgotten, however, that the reconstruction of the bankrupt economy of the former German Democratic Republic, together with other costs relating to the end of the Cold War such as assistance to the countries of the former Soviet Union, will require all the financial and economic resources of the new Germany for some time and will determine its margin for action in terms of fiscal and foreign trade policies. The West German economy had experienced a boom, and will now probably experience a period of crisis until the economy of the former East Germany can be revitalised. During the early 1990s between about US$80 billion and US$100 billion per annum had to be transferred from western Germany to the eastern area.

The claim has frequently been made in the context of reunification that Germany is now a 'world power'. This has been echoed by both the political right and the left. But even a united Germany, despite all its strengths, cannot become a power in the same league as the US within the foreseeable future. Nor does it want to. The new Germany does have efficient and highly modern armed forces, but it remains a second-rank military power. It has officially renounced the possession of nuclear, biological and chemical weapons, despite repeated murmurs about possible 'back doors', and has consented to a limitation of troop numbers to 370,000.

An economic big power it may be, therefore, but Germany lacks the military resources to play a role as a world power, a fact which the US may have regretted when Bonn seemed reluctant to participate fully in the Gulf War and other military interventions. Strategically, however, this is in the American interest. To some extent too, a reluctance to assume a global role can be detected in Germany's policy towards the Third World, where it clearly does not exert the political influence of which it is potentially capable.

The Federal Republic has never seriously tried to establish zones of influence in the Third World in the conventional sense, although for France and Great Britain, as well as for the US and the former Soviet Union, this was until recently regarded as a natural option. In general, Germany has limited itself to supporting the policy followed by its allies in the Third World, and to offering sufficient political, economic and infrastructural backing to show 'solidarity' without exposing itself too much in practice. Vis-à-vis the Third World priority has been given to an offensive foreign trade policy as opposed to 'empire-building'. The latter distinction was evident during the war between Iran and Iraq, in that while for strategic reasons France staked everything on the Iraqi card, the Federal Republic continued to do business with both warring parties, supplying weapons or military knowhow to both sides. This political and military low profile in the Third World, however aggressive the export policy of Germany, will continue in modified form now that the GDR has been absorbed, because it best serves German economic and political interests. The term 'aggressive export policy' includes the export of knowhow or components relating to weapons of mass destruction or missile technology.

At the top of the economic and political agenda in Germany today is the integration of the former GDR within the Federal Republic. This is proving difficult and costly. Next on the agenda will come, the adoption of West European models and structures by the economies and political systems of Hungary, the Czech Republic, Slovakia, and Poland – a process that will reinforce German hegemony. This process might then, to a lesser degree, be extended as far as possible to Russia and other countries of the former Soviet Union, which by then, it is hoped, will have undergone reforms and have established market economies. In any case no other attractive option is open to the former Eastern bloc countries. This ambitious agenda will keep the German Federal Republic in the form of the new united Germany so busy that it will have little energy left over for any flights of fancy about a role as a 'world power'.

The discussion on the possible use of the Bundeswehr in operations outside the NATO area is relevant here. Only a minority in the German government, and in the parties they represent, are eager to extend the military role of the German armed forces to carrying out such operations independently and unilaterally. The German government is in the main interested in the political and legal possibilities of out-of-area operations by the Bundeswehr for tactical reasons – that is, it is primarily interested in avoiding such setbacks with its partners as it experienced in the criticism of the lack of German support in the Gulf War. Nonetheless, a full deployment capacity for the Bundeswehr is regarded as a precondition for the establishment of a European Defence Force. Any close military cooperation with France and Great Britain will only become possible if the Bundeswehr can take part in out-of-area operations. On the other hand the German government has little interest in embarking on military adventures of its own in the Third World, at least for the time being. However, these views began to change in 1992 and 1993. The argument that out-of-area capabilities are not just a price to be paid to the allies, but a goal in itself, is gathering strength. To make Germany a 'normal' country again, that is, to forget the world wars and the Holocaust as defining points of German foreign policy, the country must be able to pursue normal imperial policies, as Britain and France do.

Two aspects of the Eurocentricity of German foreign policy, with its emphasis on trade, are important here. First, there is a kind of division of labour between Germany and its EC partners. France and Great Britain will continue to pursue their own political, economic and military interests and the interests of Europe as a whole in the Third World, principally in Africa and the Near East. Furthermore France will play the role of junior partner, and competitor, in the economic penetration of Eastern Europe. Second, Eurocentricity will mean that the principal energies of Germany will for the foreseeable future be directed at areas which the US will not regard as objectionable but rather as legitimate and useful. The US has still difficulties in drawing up any serious aid programmes for Eastern Europe, where Washington has shown no signs of wishing to compete seriously with the EC, because of its own lack of resources. To be precise: the US has avoided competing in regard to the amounts of funds made available for assistance, and has concentrated on advising and influencing the course of economic restructuring in Russia, and on the cultural 'Americanisation' of sectors of the Russian elite. The US government thus looks favourably on Germany as its 'partner in leadership' in the region.

The United States and countries outside Europe are therefore confronted not with Germany as a world power, but with the coming into being of the internally heterogenous European Community, containing interests which are contradictory but which nonetheless are increasingly organised to work together. However, Western Europe will not qualify as a world power in the true sense of the term. A world power is not the same as a big power; the worldwide economic interests of a Switzerland do not make it a world power. When correctly used the term implies not just having worldwide interests but also the capacity to safeguard those interests by force if necessary. It is precisely this capacity which Western Europe will not have for the foreseeable future, except to a very limited extent. French interventions in Chad or Central Africa, British manoeuvres in Oman, German minesweepers in the Gulf or European troops in Somalia, all operations involving small numbers of troops, are the type of military operations which have taken place in the past and may occur in the future. A serious war of medium or high intensity waged thousands of kilometres away from home bases, as was the case with the war against Iraq, will be completely beyond Western Europe's real capability, at least over the next ten or 20 years, without support from the US.

Within this restricted West European role, France and Great Britain will tend to embody the military dimension, while Germany will guarantee the economic basis for global importance within the framework. A united Germany, though by no means militarily negligible, will thus be the strongest country within Europe without ever being able to become completely dominant in any global European role. In any event, for at least another generation Western Europe's main interests will continue to be regional rather than global, concentrating on Eastern Europe, including the countries of the former Soviet Union, the Mediterranean and adjacent areas.

The US is bound to try to build up its own special relationship with a united Germany, as well as retaining that with London, so that it does not further weaken its already reduced influence over Western Europe. Nonetheless, whatever the rhetoric, which will probably be loud and inflated, in reality this US aim is doomed to failure.

Apart from the future role of Germany, a decisive question for the future of Europe after the Cold War is that of designing a practical, political and security structure for the continent. This is a complicated problem involving a whole range of very different questions:

- How should the countries of Eastern Europe be drawn into an overall European structure and be economically strengthened and stabilised?
- What role can and should Russia and the CIS play in Europe?
- How can Germany's potential for Europe be used without allowing the country to assume too much power?
- How can EC integration be both deepened and expanded, or must a choice be made between the two processes when new applications for membership are received?
- How can the capitalist non-EC states of North and Central Europe (that is, the EFTA countries Sweden, Switzerland, Austria, Norway, Finland, Iceland and Liechtenstein) be taken into account?
- What is to be the future relationship of Europe with the United States now that the common enemy of the past has gone?
- How is the future Europe to deal with conflicts on or within its immediate borders, such as the tragedy in former Yugoslavia, let alone conflicts affecting the South and East Mediterranean and the Middle East?
- What is to be the future role of the military alliances, NATO and the WEU?

EFTA and the CSCE

Almost the only remaining functional frame of reference for the future architecture of Europe in the period following the dissolution of the Warsaw Pact and Comecon is the combination of the EC, the WEU and NATO. Neither EFTA nor the Council of Europe have or will have in the foreseeable future the political or economic weight to constitute an alternative. EFTA continues to be increasingly dwarfed by the economically much more powerful EC and its members are looking for different ways of achieving closer cooperation with the EC, including actual entry. EFTA has negotiated with the EC over the setting up of a European Economic Area, and over plans which seem to be a preparatory stage for EFTA members joining the EC.

Perhaps the only conceivable structure outside the EC/WEU/NATO context for an overall European order might be provided by the Conference for Security and Cooperation in Europe (CSCE). This includes not only all the European countries, and Russia, but also the non-European CIS countries, the United States and Canada. The CSCE will probably continue to gain in political and organisational importance, because it constitutes a forum within which the states of the former Eastern bloc can cooperate with the neutral and NATO states and coordinate policies, without being bound up in existing fixed structures. Its importance is growing, particularly for Eastern and Southern Europe. The task of the CSCE at present is to equip itself with the means of conflict prevention and control, especially in relation to nationalist conflicts in Eastern and Southeastern Europe. A second function is to provide a meeting place where the countries of Eastern and Southeastern Europe which are at present excluded from the EC and NATO can meet to discuss cooperation with Western Europe and the United States, without excluding the countries of the former Soviet Union. The further development of the CSCE, however, depends on finding solutions to at least two principal difficulties. First, it is only equipped to negotiate, mediate and observe conflicts, having no means by which it can enforce solutions. Even if it became sufficiently developed to undertake the settlement of a conflict in Europe, the CSCE would still have to apply to NATO or individual states for the material and human resources required (including troops). Such a role would be like that of the United Nations in the Gulf War, inviting powerful states to use the institution to act in their own interests. Second, there is the difficulty of the freedom with which NATO, the EC and the WEU will allow the CSCE to act, for these groups will not want any encroachment on their own functions and will thus presumably permit the CSCE to act merely in an auxiliary role. It therefore may find itself landed with only those tasks which the other bodies do not want to handle. Nonetheless this may still give it a more important function within an overall European framework, even though it will be unable to evolve into a security system within a complete European architecture. The experience of the last few years, however, does not provide ground for optimism. The helplessness of the CSCE in former Yugoslavia or in Tadzhikistan was even worse than that of NATO, the EC and the UN.

Eastern Europe

The smaller countries of Eastern Europe, after the abandonment of the Soviet model and their release from Moscow's control, are faced by three related sets of problems: how to restructure and revitalise their economies; how to achieve internal political stability; and how to achieve national security within the overall European framework. In general, throughout the region the tendency is to believe that these three aims can only be achieved by heavy reliance on Western Europe, with entry into the EC and NATO as the final objective. There appear to be no alternative economic, political or military ideas. Close regional cooperation between Poland, the Czech Republic, Slovakia and Hungary is being worked on in order to solve practical problems, because there is no alternative. This will not solve the basic foreign policy problems of these countries, however. Reliance on the Soviet Union, or Russia, is no longer an option, and to hope for much cooperation from the US is unrealistic. It was only with the final breakup of the Soviet Union that the American budget allocation for aid to the whole of Eastern and Central Europe increased significantly. In mid-1992, within the context of an international aid programme, the US made US$8.5 billion available. American private investments are also thin on the ground. For example, by March 1991 US companies had invested barely $30 million in Poland.[5]

The EC must therefore play a key role in Eastern Europe. But it cannot take in all comers. Austria, Sweden, Switzerland, Cyprus, Malta and Turkey are all already pressing for entry, with varying degrees of urgency. Even Morocco has made tentative approaches. If Poland, Hungary, the Czech Republic and Slovakia, quite apart from any surviving republics of the former Yugoslavia, Bulgaria, Romania or the three Baltic states, all crowd into the EC in the near future, the political and economic consequences for that organisation, and its ability to act as a community, would be greatly impaired. Instead of being deepened it would be widened to such an extent that its very existence would be in danger. In any event, the serious problems which have arisen throughout the EC over ratification of the Maastricht treaty have already make clear the fragile state of the Community, even without additional members.

Any close cooperation with the EFTA countries is also no alternative for the East Europeans, particularly since the EFTA countries increasingly want full EC membership for themselves. The former allies of the Soviet Union would thus find themselves in the difficult situation of being dependent on the cooperation of Western Europe without, for the foreseeable future, having the opportunity to cooperate as EC members with equal rights. The most they can hope for in the next few years is associate membership, which Poland, Bulgaria, Hungary and Romania have already achieved.

This situation reinforces bilateral political forms and strengthens Germany's position as the central dominant European power, economically, geographically and increasingly politically as well. The then Polish prime minister, Mr Bielecki, in signing the German-Polish Treaty of Friendship in Bonn in June 1991, was stating the literal truth when he said, 'Poland's roads to Europe lead through Germany.' Chancellor Kohl indicated that he wanted to see German support for Poland's future entry into the EC, 'as far as is possible' and 'as soon as the conditions permit.'[6]

In terms of security policy, the future for the region is even more difficult to fathom, after the disintegration of the Soviet Union into the increasingly chaotic Commonwealth of Independent States, with the civil war in former Yugoslavia threatening to destabilise the whole of the Balkans, and with a host of associated problems leaving a vacuum which only NATO, Germany and the European Community can fill.

The basic question, once again, is how to integrate the post-communist states of Eastern Europe into a European framework to help stabilise them, without too openly cutting off, threatening or destabilising Russia and the other CIS countries.

From the first it was quite clear that membership of NATO was out of the question. This would have been perceived as a threat by the Soviet Union, and later by Russia. Instead, NATO offered the Eastern European countries different forms of cooperation, common discussions and a network of bilateral cooperation. But with the disintegration of the Soviet Union, the proliferation of regional conflicts in former Soviet republics, and Ukraine and Kazakhstan becoming de facto nuclear powers potentially threatening their Russian neighbour, Moscow began to perceive NATO as a stabilising factor in Europe. Russia also started to approach NATO for different forms of cooperation, and finally dropped its opposition to Poland becoming a member of the Western alliance at some point. This strengthened a debate in the West ultimately to extend NATO into Eastern Europe.

The influential US Senator Richard Lugar pushed this point forcefully: 'NATO membership must be extended to East-Central European countries. But who should be in, and when? Poland, Hungary, and the Czech Republic are currently staunch Atlanticists; bringing them in would strengthen the Alliance and Western interests.'[7]

This was somewhat ahead of official policy, but illustrative of a trend of debate which two or three years previously was much more cautious. The US government's and NATO's official position was summarised by Walter Slocombe, principal deputy under-secretary of defense for policy, before the US Senate's Defense Committee. He stated that membership of Eastern European countries in NATO was:

> by no means ruled out, but at this time membership is not the immediate issue, and there is much to be done before the decisions on membership are reached. The United States has, therefore, urged that the Alliance move immediately to innovate ways to draw our Eastern European partners closer to the Alliance, developing a range of relationships between NATO's central structures and the defense ministries of the new democracies of the East.[8]

This process is deemed necessary for the creation of a common framework to integrate Eastern Europe and help stabilise it. But in the long run it will also be interesting to follow the ways in which the strategy to draw Eastern European countries closer to NATO, or even to make them full members, will influence the balance between European members and the US. Very probably this will have the effect of strengthening the part played by Europe in NATO, and thus the identity of the European defence machine.

Europe and NATO

After the end of the Cold War, and with the Soviet threat removed, questions were asked on both sides of the Atlantic about the presence of the US in Europe and the usefulness of NATO. These questions may seem even more pertinent now that the Soviet Union has ceased even to exist. Nonetheless, it would be wrong to link the US presence in Europe and the existence of NATO solely or predominantly with the existence of a 'Soviet threat' in particular or with 'military security' in general. Although of course the Atlantic alliance owes its very existence to the Cold War, and its purpose has been aptly summarised as being to 'keep the Germans down, the Americans in and the Russians out', this formula in itself indicates that for decades the aims of the alliance were as much to do with relations between the Western powers themselves as with a Soviet threat. In the view of most European governments, the loss of the former military enemy has made the other functions of NATO even more crucial.

Representative of this view was a lecture given at the end of 1990 by Admiral Sir James Eberle, a former director of the British Royal Institute of International Affairs. In his speech Sir James maintained that the strategic importance of a continued US involvement in European security was based partly on the relative positions of the newly reunified Germany and the dissolving Soviet Union. It could no longer be assumed that France and Great Britain would constitute a sufficiently powerful counterweight to balance the pull of the East on Germany, something which was already making itself felt in many barely perceptible but significant ways. Germany was not to be blamed for this. According to Sir James, it was obvious that no stable European security system can exist without some involvement of the Soviet Union, whatever its future form may be. In order to balance this pull towards the East, Europe needs the United States to be involved in its security. A second reason for continued US involvement concerned different European interests:

> On the other hand, Europe must recognise the pull exerted by Asia and the Pacific Ocean on the United States. Whilst the emotional ties of most Americans, even those living on the West Coast, remain attached to Europe, American trade is increasingly turning to the Asiatic markets. Europe must take positive steps in order to bind the United States to Europe, if it does not want to run the risk of seeing it drift away into the Pacific. The American involvement in Europe is a fundamental security interest of Western Europe.[9]

These views are basically common to London, Paris and Bonn. Since they were expressed the Soviet Union has, of course, disintegrated completely. Thus as Europe moves further into the 1990s its situation is increasingly one of uncertainty. The old postwar order at least was stable, but now one of the blocs in this balance has become fragmented into a shifting mosaic of states characterised by economic problems and by ethnic and nationalist conflicts which in some places amount to civil war, with the threat of possible escalation into warfare between nations. From East Germany to the other side of the Urals, there is economic catastrophe everywhere, due partly to the bankrupt late-Stalinist systems which ruled until recently, partly to the difficulties of making a transition from a state-controlled to a capitalist economy, and partly also to the existence even at this early stage of the worst forms of predatory capitalism. Whether or not all these problems can be resolved or even kept under control remains to be seen. The immense costs involved in the revitalisation of the former German Democratic Republic and its transformation into a capitalist society must raise doubts as to whether Europe, let alone the US, has the resources to transform the whole of Eastern Europe and the countries of the former Soviet Union to any significant extent. It is very possible that the whole of Central, Eastern and Southeastern Europe stand on the brink of a long period of social, economic, political, demographic and even military insecurity.

Jane's Soviet Intelligence Review has summarised the situation thus:

the German government is aware that in the wake of German unification and the German stance during the Gulf conflict it could easily be accused of neglecting its western ties in favour of a more Central European orientation. Already, the decision by the Czech Skoda industrial concern to seek close cooperation with Volkswagen rather than Renault, despite strong French lobbying, has been regarded as an economic decision of major strategic relevance. All three countries seek closer military ties with Germany. On the other hand, military hardware from the former East German armed forces (NVA), like T-72 MBTs [main battle tanks], artillery pieces, infantry weapons, combat aircraft, and naval vessels, could easily be incorporated into the arsenals of the Polish and Hungarian forces. Hungary has already detailed its request: 360 T-72 MBTs, 350 BMP armoured infantry fighting vehicles, over 1000 trucks, some 72 2S1 122 mm self-propelled artillery pieces, 50 000 AK 74 automatic rifles with 50 million rounds of ammunition, 100 000 anti-tank guided missiles and 200 000 grenades of various sizes. Poland has also suggested that it would be ready to take arms and equipment of Soviet origin from Germany. Apparently, Poland is interested in the 24 MiG-29 'Fulcrum' fighter aircraft currently operated by the Luftwaffe. In contrast, Czechoslovakia has indicated that it does not require surplus NVA arms for its forces, which are to be reduced considerably. The dismantling of the WTO integrated air defence system means that the three countries will be virtually without a coordinated national air defence. The author understands that cooperation in the field of air defence has been the subject of talks between Czechoslovak and Hungarian military officers and their German counterparts. Apparently, the German side rejected close military cooperation at this stage since it could be misinterpreted by Germany's NATO allies. Yet, informal contacts between the parties involved, in the spirit of good neighbourly relations, should not be ruled out, a senior German officer has told *JSIR*.[10]

Political planners in Western Europe cannot exclude crisis scenarios – and this is the case at exactly the time when they have their hands full with the difficult and intricate problems of bringing the single market into being, are faced by a flood of applications for entry, and are having to fight hard to maintain European competitiveness on the world market in strategically decisive sectors, particularly against the US, Japan and the 'four small dragons' of Southeast Asia.

Against this background, no European country wants any increase in the number of factors that create insecurity. This is why drawing the US into a European structure is welcomed. A breakup of the Atlantic alliance at this time would greatly increase the level of instability; and any expulsion of the US, or its withdrawal from Europe, would furthermore bring to the surface the many latent conflicts between the US and Europe. These conflicts relate to trade, strategic differences, and technological, monetary and financial policy disagreements, some of which are of considerable magnitude. In addition there are fears even among the foreign policy elite that the US and Japan could form a common Pacific economic front against Europe.[11] Any break with the US and a winding up of NATO would presuppose Europe's ability economically and politically to withstand the resultant conflicts. Not only is there no new stable and functioning political and economic system in Eastern and Central Europe, including the CIS, that could constitute a strategic hinterland, but conditions are not ripe for any severing of ties between Western Europe and the US either.

NATO will therefore continue to exist for the foreseeable future. This does not mean that it will remain unchanged, nor that the Alliance and transatlantic relations in general may not undergo a process of erosion and transformation.

For some time already, NATO has been seeking to define potential new enemies, new tasks, a new strategy and a new structure for its armed forces. As early as the end of 1990 US Secretary of State James Baker was formulating five essential NATO tasks for the future:

1.   The continuing protection of the member states against a Soviet threat which, however much it might be changing, still existed and might conceivably come from Russia.
2.   The creation of a stable security structure in Europe, in particular involving Eastern and Southeastern Europe.
3.   The fending-off of threats to member states from outside the Alliance, as in the case of Turkey being perceived as threatened by instability in Iraq and the Caucasus.
4.   Adjustment to new and additional threats arising in geographical regions outside the NATO area.
5.   The establishment of a 'transatlantic forum' for consultations between the allies over any matter 'affecting our vital interests.'[12]

In relation to the third and fourth points on Baker's list, the war against Iraq has already supplied much important experience which has been intensively discussed in NATO. What was striking in the Gulf War in fact was that NATO as an institution legally had no role in the war, but that without the intensive use made of NATO infrastructures for logistics, lines of communication and so on, the allies would not have been able to resolve the conflict with the same efficiency and speed. The US ambassador to NATO, William Taft, paid tribute to this, saying that the Alliance had proved to be an invaluable forum for consultations and agreements in this situation and that continuous and detailed military consultations with NATO had led to exceptional bilateral and Alliance-wide support in the preparation of logistical infrastructures and bases for the armed forces on their way to the Gulf, (including transport, landing rights, refuelling, land transport, harbour and port facilities, ammunition supplies from one ally to another, flight safety, spare parts, expertise in minimizing damage to the environment and medical supplies).

> Without the military support from NATO allies in the Gulf theater and the logistical support from NATO allies in the European theater, the United States and the Gulf coalition could not have accomplished what they did. NATO's consultative machinery, designed to preserve European security, also worked in dealing with this 'out-of-area' crisis.[13]

This experience further reinforced NATO's tendency to be increasingly South-orientated, and strengthened the argument that in future the mobility and flexibility of the NATO forces should be substantially increased. There had been no formal extension of the NATO area by treaty agreement nor any official redefining of NATO's treaty obligations. The smooth coordination between the allies in the Gulf War has of course now proved that such large-scale operations by NATO member states outside the NATO area will not need any such formal sanctioning. NATO flexibility is to be related not just to military operations but to the political framework too. To be able to make use of NATO infrastructures without having to obtain the unanimous agreement of the 16 NATO member states before operations can be carried out will clearly prove advantageous in the future.

As early as June 1991 NATO was outlining a new structure for its armed forces, designed to take into account the changed situation both in Western and Eastern Europe and out-of-area. These structural modifications were decided on without evolving a new military strategy for NATO, which was to be drawn up by the end of the year. However, to outline a new military structure without a strategy on which it is based demonstrates both the necessity for NATO to adapt to new realities, and the difficulties it experiences in doing so. Such a strategy was formally adopted in the autumn of 1992.

The June 1991 decisions were aimed at reducing the size of NATO forces in Europe to about 1 million, while making them more powerful and mobile, with the US presence in Europe to be reduced from 320,000 to between 100,000 and 150,000 troops. This stream-lining of the 'Main Defence Forces' to increase their efficiency, together with that of the 'Augmentation Forces', was to be accompanied by the setting up of a 'Rapid Reaction Force' of between 70,000 and 100,000 troops. An important feature was the multinational composition of the Main Defence Forces, with one corps under US command and one under German command, and of the Rapid Reaction Force under British command but with German participation. The latter was officially intended for the defence of Turkey and Arctic Norway. Many of the most important decisions, however, were postponed and much detail was left vague.[14]

Essentially the decisions were of a political rather than a military nature. The planned reduction in the size of its armed forces was intended to be a signal that NATO really was taking the end of the Cold War seriously, while the multinational composition of the Main Defence Forces was aimed at facilitating the integration of the reduced US contingent, thus attaching it more permanently to Europe. The Rapid Reaction Force, which was officially only to be available for operations within the NATO area, had the purpose of creating the kind of infrastructure and mechanisms which would make it capable of deployment out-of-area, such as in the Near and Middle East. NATO representatives in Brussels at the time were already emphasising that 'ethnic violence in Eastern Europe, most likely in Yugoslavia, might be interpreted as a direct threat to the alliance requiring a military response.'[15]

Newsweek commented: 'None of these quite justifies the retention of vast military force, including about 100,000 American troops. Ever since November 9th, 1989, when the Berlin Wall was first breached, NATO had been looking for a mission.' No NATO decisions had touched 'the central question: what does a military alliance do when peace breaks out?'[16]

After the Soviet breakup the Clinton administration translated Baker's late-1990 five tasks for NATO into four 'new dangers'. A high-ranking Defense Department official listed these new threats in the summer of 1993:

- Regional threats and ethnic conflicts;
- Risks of proliferation of nuclear weapons and other weapons of mass destruction;
- Economic rivalries producing security challenges; and
- The prospect that fragile new democracies could revert to imperialistic tyranny once again.[17]

These are the main 'dangers' as perceived from Washington. But NATO might very well also be threatened from a different side, from within. Its internal dynamics – the relationship between the US and the West European nations within the Alliance – remain extremely complex. Political differences between the European nations themselves, as well as between Europe and the US, the global shifts in economic and political power, all in the context of the end of the Cold War, have led to a tangled thicket of contradictions in which US-European relations remain for the moment helplessly entangled.

The real core of this problem is evident in the debate over a future 'European defence identity' in military policy. NATO was and is structurally designed, in terms of political symbolism as much as anything else, in such a way as to make military and defence policy primarily a matter for the West as a whole under US leadership. The US military presence in Europe and the nuclear domination of NATO by Washington have ensured this. It is true that the larger European states have always endeavoured to maintain their own specific interests within NATO, but in the final analysis NATO has always been an alliance which functions according to the way in which the US exercises its leadership. 'European security', even for those European governments critical of the US, has been inconceivable without NATO and thus without the US.

This one-sided distribution of power within the Atlantic partnership has become less and less marked, at first in economic terms and then increasingly in military terms as well. These shifts in military weight have led to a discussion of the two alternative policies of either reinforcing the European pillar of NATO – that is, creating a stronger European role within the Alliance – or evolving a stronger independent European defence policy. Naturally, for political and rhetorical reasons these two possibilities are rarely presented as stark contrast.

Karl Feldmeyer, a commentator for the *Frankfurter Allgemeine Zeitung*, has got to the heart of the debate with great clarity. In the run-up to the above-mentioned conference of the NATO Council of Ministers in June 1991, he wrote:

> The question is once again about whether or not America should retain its decisive influence. Technically speaking, it is about whether or not the Western European Union (WEU) should be changed into a division of the EC, and be equipped with its own military apparatus like NATO.

This would be a variation of the 'European defence identity'. Feldmeyer continues:

> Related to this is the intention to establish a joint stand on security policies within the circle of the nine WEU countries[18] (that means, above all, outside NATO), and then to have them represented as a closed bloc within NATO. [This, then includes the possibility of justifying the arrangement as a 'European pillar of NATO'.] Then the other allies, notably America, would stand outside this pre-formed position.
>
> The aim of all this is to reduce Washington's influence over European affairs. As yet, this conflict is only discussed internally, but the tone has become rough. France, which has represented the WEU position most strongly, must in the meantime come to terms with the accusation of wanting to supersede NATO with a competing alliance.[19]

In Europe this discussion is conducted more privately, and the openness of Feldmeyer's comments is rare among government officials. Alarm bells have nonetheless already rung frequently in America. The fact that these developments in Western Europe coincided with President Gorbachev's well-known formulation of a 'common European home' was particularly disturbing. As early as May 1989, US Secretary of State Baker was at pains to counter this, emphasising that NATO was not simply a community of interests but also a community of values. Against this background, he went on to argue:

> Some have suggested that Europe's future depends on a narrow territorial vision, on an idea within geographical boundaries and without a specially solid content – naturally, I refer here to calls for a common European home.
>
> In contrast to this is our vision, where the future of Europe depends on common Western values. We regard this as a fundamental core that has formed as a result of centuries of struggle for the principles of the Enlightenment – one that will not be inhibited by geographical boundaries.[20]

In the first of the two 'visions' the US would be excluded from Europe, while in the second the 'outsider' would of course be the Soviet Union, even if milder variations of the two scenarios were possible. Following the rather 'philosophical' objection of the secretary of state quoted here, the NATO ambassador William Taft was clearer in February 1991 – after the Cold War had come to an end both officially and in practice:

> We support a European Pillar, but only if it does not double the Alliance, if it operates within the Alliance and fulfils the tasks of the Alliance and only appears outside the Alliance when it wants to fulfil supplementary missions...
>
> Every new venture should also ensure that all 16 [member states] are able to take full part in them. It should not weaken the decisive transatlantic ties or marginalise any member in matters of security. Frankly speaking, this means: that those members who do not belong to the EC or WEU should not stay out of decision making processes... The USA believes that NATO must remain the most important organisation for Europe's security. NATO and only NATO can match the Soviet Union's size and military capabilities both in times of cooperation and in times of conflict.[21]

The US worries about being excluded from Europe call for two comments. First, they are not the words of a superpower, nor those of a power in a position of complete dominance, which has its allies properly under control. Washington's sometimes shrill declarations – which were something of a démarche to all EC governments in March 1991 – give the impression that the US feels and fears it will be pushed to the margins of events. This fear was masked by the Gulf War for a few weeks but did not disappear completely.

On the other side, Washington is following a strategy to limit Western European independent action. Christopher Layne has described the US approach:

> American alliances with Japan and Germany are viewed as an integral part of a strategy that seeks: (1) to prevent multipolar rivalries; (2) to discourage the rise of global hegemonies; and (3) to preserve a cooperative and healthy world economy. The forward deployment of U.S. military forces abroad is now viewed primarily as a means of preserving unipolarity. If the United States continues to extend security guarantees to Japan and Germany, it is reasoned, they will have no incentive to develop great power capabilities. Indeed, fear that Japan and Germany [or Western Europe] will acquire independent capabilities – that is, that they will become great powers – pervades the thinking of American strategists.[23]

Second, however, these American fears are greatly exaggerated. The WEU will not develop into an alternative to NATO in the foreseeable future, and it is even less likely that the European countries will drive the US out of Europe. Even France has no interest whatsoever in this, for it sees the US as a stabilising element against Germany and crumbling Soviet power. It is not exactly a question about uncoupling Europe from the US. The aim of 'Europeanising security policies' is rather more to undermine the tried-and-tested American strategy of 'divide and rule' within the Alliance and to be able to negotiate with the US not only on a formal basis but also from an equal power-political base. Furthermore, this Europeanisation should open up specific options for Europe – although it is not always clear what exactly those will comprise – to create, in principle, the possibility of defining security policies independently and by itself: a possibility that the US has always had at its disposal in the Alliance. Finally, the Europeanisation of security policy should serve to create compensatory advantages in military matters for France (but also for other countries) to counter economically-dominant Germany. For Germany will not play the main role in the defence of Europe commensurate with its economic position, for political, historical and military reasons. Thus the atomic powers of Great Britain and France will have the opportunity to gain a few points in the struggle for the balance of power in Europe. This is far more difficult in NATO, where the US will naturally continue to set the tone, at least for as long as Europe does not speak with one voice (under Franco-British command).

We will see an increase both in the significance of the European countries within the North Atlantic Alliance, and in the independence of West European military policy. This trend can no longer be reversed, for rather than an isolated phenomenon it is an expression of a decisive shift in the balance of power, which has an economic basis. In the long term, this will give rise to a tendency that will increasingly rob NATO of its former importance. This process will evolve slowly and inconsistently, and it will not be till the beginning of the next century, at the earliest, that these developments will threaten NATO's existence. This outcome will only be avoided if extraordinary circumstances arise – in particular, the emergence of a new, concrete threat to both Western Europe and the US. It is very unlikely that NATO will be destroyed by sensational and spectacular developments, the foundation of explicitly European counterorganisations or the departure of individual members; rather, it will be eroded by a creeping loss of importance. NATO never was simply a military alliance, it has also always been an amalgam of the capitalist economic powers of the Atlantic. And it was – they have been at pains to say so – a community of values, an alliance of states on the basis of a common ideology. The economic, ideological and military trends of the next generation are undermining NATO's foundations even if there are desperate attempts on both sides of the Atlantic to stop this. In 20 or 30 years' time it will probably be what the WEU is (still) today – a hollow shell.

Japan and the US

The 1970s and 1980s saw a shift in power relationships within the West almost as spectacular as that caused in East–West relations by the gradual collapse of the Soviet Union as a world power. But the real winner of the Cold War was Japan.

At first glance, some indicators suggest that the US was substantially improving its position during this period in relation to its most important competitors. The unfavourable growth rate of the US economy was corrected. During the years 1982–7, the average real growth in US GNP per annum was a substantial 4.4 per cent. Japanese growth was the same, while West Germany could manage only 2.5 per cent, and France lagged even further behind.[24] Unemployment figures improved and other criteria also evolved more positively in the US economy than in other countries. Even productivity improved considerably. The growth in US productivity may have been a little behind that of Japan, but it was significantly ahead of the figures for Europe. Behind this apparently positive picture of the 'Reagan boom', however, there lay important weaknesses. One of these was the increasingly unfavourable balance of trade throughout the 1980s, particularly in comparison with West Germany and Japan.

Table 8.1 Balance of Trade (in billion ecu)

Year	USA	West Germany	Japan
1980	– 14.7	+ 3.5	– 8.3
1981	– 33.4	+ 11.0	+ 8.1
1982	– 32.3	+ 21.6	+ 7.3
1983	– 64.6	+ 18.5	+ 23.1
1984	– 136.7	+ 24.1	+ 43.1
1985	– 173.2	+ 33.0	+ 60.1
1986	– 155.2	+ 53.1	+ 84.5
1987	– 132.6	+ 57.0	+ 69.0
1988	– 102.2	+ 61.0	+ 65.6
1989	– 99.5	+ 64.0	+ 58.4
1990	– 80.3	+ 44.0	+ 41.0
1991	– 53.5	+ 9.2	+ 63.1

Source: *Eurostat Revue 1977–86* p.189.

As Table 8.1 shows, during the first half of the 1980s the United States' balance-of-trade deficit increased by a factor of almost 12. It subsequently remained at a dizzying level. In contrast, the surpluses of Japan and West Germany rose rapidly during the same period, from a combined slight deficit in 1980 to combined surpluses of 120 billion ecu per annum in 1988. (One ecu in 1988 was valued at US$1.18 , or DM2.07.)

The US budget deficit rose from US$78.9 billion in 1981 to $212.3 billion in 1985. The total national debt of the US in 1988 rose to over $2,700 billion. In 1992 the total national debt amounted to about $4,000 billion, and the budget deficit to some $290.2 billion, or 5 per cent of GNP. To pay the interest alone the US government must spend $200 billion, which is equivalent to 20 per cent of total tax revenue.[25]

This situation, characterised by an exploding foreign trade deficit, with a simultaneously rocketing budget deficit, had wide-ranging economic effects. To some it seemed that the policy of the Reagan administration had contributed to American dependence on outsiders, which was regarded as unhealthy. The need to fund a large part of the US budget deficit with foreign capital, and for foreign central banks to buy more than US$150 billion over a two-year period to support the dollar, the US balance-of-trade deficit and growing foreign debt, the accelerating sale of US securities abroad to finance US deficits, together with other factors, had led to a dependence on the policies of other governments and private interests which were now influencing every domestic problem. Indeed because of its financial position as the biggest debtor in the world, no important decision in US domestic politics could be made without international ramifications.

This sounded alarming, but need not have done so. It is true that a large and growing budget deficit considered in isolation has drawbacks, with the burden of debt servicing restricting room for manoeuvre in future financial policy decisions, but in itself it need not constitute any real problem. What really matters is the way in which the borrowed funds are used. If the finance they have provided flows into economically productive sectors, including infrastructures as well as capital investments, the increasing indebtedness of the country may be only a temporary imbalance which will be corrected by the resultant improvement in economic efficiency. To use the borrowed funds, including those borrowed from foreign lenders, within the framework of an integrated strategy for the revitalisation of the US economy would not just have been sensible, it would have involved only slight risks. But this is exactly what was not done. The huge budget deficit was used politically to finance tax cuts, bringing a short-term increase in private consumption and stock-market speculation, and to finance military spending. It was not put to productive use, although huge sums of money accounting for the accumulating budget deficits of the 1980s amounted to well over US$1,000 billion. In other words, these monies were either used unprofitably or, as was often the case, they were simply wasted. There was an acceptance of a substantial future reduction in the US' financial room for manoeuvre, without any attempt being made to tackle the basic economic problems of the country. The Reagan boom of the 1980s was a boom on credit, on tick, financed by eating up existing resources and placing a burden on future economic growth. This type of boom was a sign of weakness, not of strength.

This was, however, only one aspect of the ill-advised policies of the US government. It also undertook to correct its trade deficit with Japan, and to promote the import of capital from Japan into the US by making massive efforts to weaken the dollar in relation to the Japanese yen. The intention was to restore the competitiveness of the US economy, and the balance between dollar and yen did in fact shift dramatically. The 1985–7 period saw the value of the dollar sink from 263 to only 123 yen, while the value of the deutschmark substantially increased during the same period. This attempt to remedy the economic weakness of the US, and to make it more competitive through the political manipulation of a few economic variables, was for the most part a failure.[26]

Within a short time Japanese companies succeeded in adapting to the new rates of exchange which were putting up the price of their exports abroad. They embarked on a massive programme of rationalisation. At the same time they increased their productivity, shifting some of their production abroad, either into countries with low wage costs (such as South Korea) or directly into their export sales markets (the US and EC). The US trade deficit remained around US$120–180 billion per annum. Nor was this the only consequence of manipulating the dollar downwards to try to solve America's foreign trade problems. It also led to a further difficulty which was even harder to deal with. The greatly strengthened yen, in combination with the huge foreign trade surpluses of Japan, meant an enormous increase in Japanese investments abroad both in the productive sector and on the stock exchanges. The financial centre of world business shifted from New York to Tokyo. All this in turn had consequences in terms of power politics. It was the export of capital by Japanese companies into the US that led the American government to allow its budget deficit to reach such dimensions in the first place, and then held it there, so that the US government became increasingly dependent on Japanese funding for its budget as time went on:

> If Japanese investors hadn't bought $90 billion worth of U.S. government debt in 1986, the US budget deficit would have intruded painfully on American life in forms ranging from sharply higher mortgage rates to higher taxes and deeper, more socially divisive cuts in government programs.[27]

Jeffrey Garten – a former member of the White House staff, now an investment banker – has written:

> America today depends on overseas money to finance large portions of its budget deficit. If Tokyo or Bonn took steps to discourage foreign lending, Washington could not finance all its needs from its own savings. The consequent pressure on the domestic supply of funds would drive up interest rates, which could lead to a marked

economic slowdown. Then the dollar would plunge, as investors worldwide lost confidence in the United States.

No one believes that either Japan or Germany would try to orchestrate such a crisis in the foreseeable future. But who can tell whether their political assertiveness will grow, fed by their own view that America is unable to discipline itself? Who can say whether they will react negatively to an aggressive US trade policy or whether some political constellation will develop in either Tokyo or Bonn to put pressure on the United States, as America has pressed them in the past? [28]

In these circumstances the US would have considerable difficulties in waging any serious 'trade war' against the EC or Japan, apart from isolated disputes. Doubtless such a conflict would hit America's trading partners hard, but what is certain is that the US could by no means count on emerging victorious, as it might easily have done at one time. At present it can be assumed that on both, or rather all three, sides the deterrent effect of potential consequences is sufficient to prevent such a trade war.

The deliberate weakening of the dollar, in combination with the continuing Japanese trade surplus, has also had effects on the status of net foreign assets of both countries, effects which have been as crucial as those on US state finances.

Table 8.2 Net External Assets of US and Japan (in billion dollars)

End of Year	US	Japan
1980	106	12
1981	141	11
1982	137	25
1983	89	37
1984	3	74
1985	−111	130
1986	−268	180
1987	−378	241
1988	−531	292
1989	−664	293

Source: Bank of Japan and US Commerce Department, quoted in Konrad Seitz, *Die japanisch-amerikanische Herausforderung*, Stuttgart, 2nd edn. 1991, p. 151.

The figures in Table 8.2 chart the financial rise of Japan and in mirror-image the decline of America. For over half a century, from the end of the First World War till the beginning of the 1980s, America was the largest creditor nation in the world. In 1982 for the first time its net assets abroad dropped slightly, but then the fall accelerated, and in the end they plummeted. During the 1980s the US became the biggest debtor nation in the world, while Japan became the biggest creditor country.

That US government and American financial markets had become increasingly dependent on Japanese capital became known to a wider public only when the causes of the stock exchange crash in October 1987 were investigated. A principal cause was that Japanese investors, acting in cooperation with their Ministry of Trade, were suddenly no longer buying the 30-year US Treasury Bonds which they had previously routinely acquired in large numbers. That a decision of this nature taken in Tokyo should have had such drastic consequences for the American economy spoke for itself. The crash meant that within a short time American stocks taken as a whole lost a third of their value: some US$1,000 billion. But not only did Toyko trigger the stock exchange crash on Wall Street, the recovery of the Japanese Nikkei Index then made the Dow Jones Index rise again. For the first time in history Tokyo's Kabuto Chow Stock Exchange led, and Wall Street followed. That there had been a fundamental shift in power was obvious to all. The financial leadership of the world was slipping from America's grasp into the hands of Japan.

A further index is provided by the dramatic shifts in the positions of the major international banks (see Table 8.3).

By the end of the 1980s all the top ten banks in the world were Japanese. In 1990 no US bank even figured among the top 20. The importance of such shifts in international banking should not be overemphasised, but they clearly illustrate economic trends.

The changing situation since the end of the 1970s, with the once-dominant partner not only losing its former independence in central areas of financial and economic policy but also being forced at least into cooperation, if not into dependency, should not be ascribed to any particularly 'unfair' Japanese practices – an accusation frequently made in the US. It has resulted from a combination of intelligent Japanese economic strategy and a virtually suicidal US economic policy under the Reagan administration. American complaints about Japan are generally misplaced. A country which so energetically contributed to its own economic weakness as the US did during the Reagan period inevitably loses not just the means to confront its rival economically, but also the justification for complaint.

Table 8.3 The 10 largest Banks in the World, 1982 and 1988

Position	1982 Bank	Country	1988 Bank	Country
1	Citicorp	US	Dai-Ichi Kangyo	Japan
2	Bank of America	US	Sumitomo Bank	Japan
3	Banque Nationale de Paris	France	Fuji Bank	Japan
4	Crédit Agricole	France	Sanwa Bank	Japan
5	Crédit Lyonnais	France	Mitsubishi Bank	Japan
6	Barclays Group	Great Britain	Industrial Bank of Japan	Japan
7	National Westminster	Great Britain	Norinchukin Bank	Japan
8	Dai-Ichi Kangyo Bank	Japan	Tokai Bank	Japan
9	Société Générale	France	Mitsui Bank	Japan
10	Fuji Bank	Japan	Mitsubishi Trust	Japan

Source: Daniel Burstein, *Yen! – Japan's New Financial Empire and its Threat to America*, New York, 1988/90, p. 127, and Seitz, *Die japanisch-amerikanische Herausforderung*, p.139.

The American journal *Foreign Affairs* summed up the altered economic relationship as follows:

> Currently the United States is also at a relative disadvantage because Japan and members of the European Community finance the American deficit – out of self-interest, certainly, so as to sustain a still-rich market important to them. But it is a relationship with a colonial aspect, as is the American trade relationship with Japan, wherein Japan buys low-value-added food and raw materials from the United States while selling to it increasingly high-value-added high-technology manufactures. Such a relationship multiplies Japan's advantage greatly; hence the United States risks falling further and further behind.[29]

There is considerable public awareness in the US of the changing relationship with Japan. As early as June 1990, 58 per cent of Americans regarded Japan's economic strength as being 'a greater threat to US security than the military power of the Soviet Union'. Only 22 per cent regarded the Soviet threat as more menacing than that seen to emanate from Japan.[30]

These popular sentiments were reflected in academic and even intelligence circles. One study, *Japan: 2000,* presented the results of a conference the CIA had sponsored on the future role of Japan. It combined economic worries with racist theories:

> Economic domination could precede the imposition of substituted value systems [by Japan]. This is particularly troubling because of the absence of any absolutes or moral imperatives in the Japanese paradigm, unlike [in] the Western paradigm, anchored on the Judeo-Christian ethic.

The report puts forward the thesis that most Japanese would not only support the idea of economic domination over the world, but also 'are creatures of an ageless, amoral, manipulative and controlling culture – not to be emulated – suited only to this race, in this place'. But the authors do not lose sight of economics and strategy. The Japanese – 'our economic competitors' – have acquired America's most important technology, 'and they are using it to defeat us, to lower our own standard of living, and to threaten our national security.'[31]

The shift of economic power between the US and Japan has produced hysteria, but hardly any practical changes of course. Washington still does not appear to give serious thought to evolving a practical new policy which might provide a way out. The Clinton administration at least gives the impression of having understood the economic problem, but anything resembling a solution is still lacking.

However, the impression must not be given that Japan would or even could aim at supplanting the United States in its role as a world power. There can naturally be no question of this. The United States' relative loss of power compared with Japan and the countries of Western Europe took place against the background of an overwhelmingly strong initial position and in no way implied that the US would become a second-rate power, either economically or in any other sphere. The transition outlined, from one-sided US domination to mutual interdependence, must not be overestimated either. Above all 1992 was to make it very clear that even Japan is not immune to ordinary economic pressures. The drastic fall on the Tokyo Stock Exchange, together with clear signs of a slowing down of growth, were evidence that Japan is undergoing a 'normalisation process' in relation to its main capitalist competitors. This has not reversed the shift in economic power which took place over the previous decade, but it does put any fears in the US and Western Europe into perspective. This will be a continuing evolution.

The US Position

The strength of the United States is represented above all by its military apparatus. The size and especially the quality of this military power make it possible for the US to fight a war almost anywhere on the globe within a relatively short period of mobilisation. Its technological expertise, its armed forces' high degree of mobility and its overwhelming superiority in weapons of mass destruction, with missiles and an air force guaranteeing their use, make the US by far the most powerful nation in the world in military terms. This factor is of great importance in international politics, and it must not be overlooked when considering the weakening of the relative economic power of the US in other contexts.

Nonetheless, the cost of this military apparatus (US$288.8 billion in the financial year 1990/1) provides only limited high-technology spin-offs and is one of the main burdens on the US economy. It can only be paid for by increasing debt.[32] By the end of the Cold War the purpose of this armed might was increasingly open to question. Assuming that the United States is not itself militarily threatened, with no threat arising in the foreseeable future either, and that it will not be involved in a war against the European states or Japan (or Russia), then it must be concluded that American military strength can in no way constitute a solution to the country's most important problems, nor can it prevent the weakening of the United States' position in the world as a whole. It is true that its military superiority enables the US to intervene effectively in the Third World. Once again, however, this does not eliminate the most serious threat to the US position, which, as already discussed, is posed not on the level of a military threat but on that of economic efficiency. The most dangerous opponents of the United States are not Russian or Iraqi tanks, or Latin American guerrillas; they are Japanese (and, some way behind these, West European) high-tech companies and banks. American troops are of no use against these opponents. On the contrary, they further handicap American action. The decisive power struggles of the future will take place on the world market and on the stock exchanges of Tokyo, New York and London. As early as 1989 an American investment banker was writing to the effect that: 'the real power in the world is coming to consist of surplus capital combined with national self-discipline, advanced technology and superior education'.[33] Financial power and technology will decide the outcome of these struggles, not intelligent cruise missiles – unless the latter lead to a technological advance in the economy as a whole. There is, however, no empirical evidence to suggest that this can happen.

Naturally, in this situation the United States has endeavoured to compensate militarily for its loss of economic position. Without its military presence in Europe, Japan and many other regions of the world, including the Persian Gulf, and without its superiority in high-technology weapons and nuclear capability, the US today would just be one power among others, perhaps a little bigger but otherwise with no particular advantages. Even the former and so vital advantage of a very large domestic market will vanish as the EC develops. The US owes its privileged role in the world chiefly to its military power. In this situation too it is behaving as it did in the Reagan boom of the 1980s with its budget deficit, in that its present strength and position are purchased by borrowing on the strength of future assets. The huge US military apparatus is today the answer to the wrong question, aimed at certain symptoms of US power loss, not its causes.

The international system in the 1990s and beyond will be multipolar, and not dominated by the US or Japan. Within the fore-seeable future, no one country will be in a position to structure and manage the world on the basis of its own ideas. We shall see attempts made to replace the bipolar system with one which could be described as a trilateral condominium under US leadership, consisting of the United States itself, the EC and Japan, acting as a common manager of the international system, with Russia or other regional powers being brought in according to necessity in individual cases. There is much to suggest that these endeavours will meet with only limited success. Both Japan and the EC constitute ordering factors on a regional rather than an international scale. Neither is likely to have either the will or the means to fulfil a role which would weaken its new-found power by overstretching it. This would obviously not be in their interests.

The cautious conclusion can be drawn that 'world management' will be even more difficult to achieve in the future than it was in the past epoch of superpower rivalry. Instead, what we are likely to see, in parallel with the further evolution of a multipolar world system, is a trend towards increasing regionalisation, with the EC and Germany acting as regional ordering factors in Central and Eastern Europe and surrounding areas, with Japan playing an increasing ordering role in the Pacific, with France continuing to do so in parts of Africa, and with the US operating in the Near and Middle East (with

European participation), the Caribbean basin and parts of Latin America.[34]

Some observers have already interpreted economic trends as heralding the creation of new power blocs. Joseph Brand has stated simply: 'Our world today is dividing into trading blocs.' He continued by saying: 'If by the new political world order we mean increased American hegemony disguised as international cooperation, we may come to know the new economic world order as regional hegemony disguised as free trade.'[35]

This does not necessarily mean that fixed 'zones of influence' will formally become established, but at the very least there will be a form of division of labour, whereby the United States will continue to play an important role in the Pacific and elsewhere. Such regional ordering arrangements (with the 'ordering' function ranging from economic support to military intervention) would be more flexible than the old superpower structure, and it would presumably give local players more freedom for action in certain cases. Such a scenario would also favour the rise of regional powers in the Third World, since these would be better able to exploit the economic and political rivalries within a multipolar world than they were under rigid bipolar conditions.

9

The New Interventionism and the United Nations

The end of the Cold War did not end Third World and regional conflicts. Instead it triggered a new wave. And this in turn contributed to a new debate and new strategies on how to intervene. Several old conflicts changed their specific character, but continued nonetheless. Angola, Afghanistan, and Cambodia are examples of this. Other conflicts disappeared or were reduced in scope; for instance, in Mozambique and Central America. And still others were begun because of or in the context of the end of the Cold War. The wars of former Yugoslavia, Somalia, Moldova, Tadzhikistan, and the Caucasus are cases in point.

The public debate in the West and most of the world focused on very few of these wars. Afghanistan, Mozambique, Central America and Tadzhikistan were mostly ignored – the world had somehow lost interest in these and four dozen other wars. Media attention was sporadic, public interest and the political initiatives of governments minimal. Who was paying attention to the suffering and death of people in southern Sudan?

High on the list of most favoured wars were those in Somalia and Bosnia.

A Tribal War in Europe?

With the conflict in the Middle East barely over, the stage was set for the next major crisis, this time in Europe. The process of the disintegration of Yugoslavia led to civil wars, especially in the new states of Croatia and Bosnia. It soon became clear that the old ethnic and nationalist conflicts in the Balkans which had exercised such a destabilising influence on European politics in earlier decades had not been resolved by Tito's communist government, but simply deep-frozen. With his death, and with communism in Eastern Europe in complete disarray or dissolution everywhere, Yugoslavia broke into pieces. As usual in these kinds of conflicts, severe economic problems and uneven economic development played a major role; here they were politically formulated in ethnic and nationalist terms.

It should be noted that the ethnic differences which former Yugoslav politicians and Western media held responsible for the civil wars did not really exist, or, to be more precise, existed only as psychological phenomena. It is even less plausible seriously to view them as *causes* of these wars. Serbs, Croats and Bosnian Muslims all share the same language, the same traditions and culture. In the late twentieth century historic differences between Serbs and Croats had narrowed so much that it was hardly possible for the people involved to determine who was Serb and who was Croat. In some cases there were small linguistic differences, or variations in names (the names of Bosnian Muslims in particular differed somewhat from Serb/Croat ones), but generally these had more to do with local differences than with ethnic ones. Serbs used 'Croat' words in some places, and vice versa, depending on the region of their origin. Muslims are mostly ethnically Serb, a minority Croat, but this did not save them from being slaughtered by their fellow ethnic groups for being different. Religiously the three groups did vary, however: Christian Orthodox, Roman Catholic and Muslim. It is very interesting that the warring parties decided to wage not a religious war but an ethnic one , when their main differences were religious. To be sure, the religious aspect was present, but it was interpreted as an element of national identity.

So, differences did and do exist between different groups of the population. But they were less than crucial as causes of the war. There is no civil war in Switzerland, not even in the US, despite the fact that ethnic or linguistic variations in both these countries are much more sharply developed than in Bosnia.

To be sure, leaders and ideologues of most of the parties involved prefer to be perceived as ethnic freedom fighters, struggling for a just cause, with all the weight of history behind them. It is much nicer to appear as representing a civilisation in struggle, rather than just power-greedy.   .

The civil wars in former Yugoslavia are fights for power, they are struggles dividing the spoils of a country which has broken into pieces. They are struggles for control and dominance. At the same time there *is* a struggle for identity. But this only became necessary because the historic identities – the ethnic ones – had been subverted by history and weakened so that they were on the verge of disappearing, while the seeds of a new, Yugoslav identity had disappeared with the communist system. And this struggle for identity is a part of the power struggle. The fight for control and power implies the questions: for whom and in whose interest are we fighting? The only two plausible answers are religion or ethnicity. To legitimise war you have to have a cause, or at least pretend to have one. And it is necessary to identify friends and enemies. Without the politics of identity it would be very difficult to wage war, to force war on to society.

So there was an important connection between the war and ethnic identity. But it functioned in such a way that war was waged because of the weakness of this identity, not because of its strength. On the other hand, the war created the basis for opposing national/ethnic identities, which previously had been an artificial invention. After all the massacres and suffering, with all the ethnic cleansing and growing hatred, Croats, Serbs and Bosnian Muslims have developed into separate and antagonistic groups, with opposing viewpoints, opposing traditions. In this way, war brings about the very thing that supposedly caused it: different ethnic and national identities.

One should not take the propaganda of the opponents at face value. Their self-interpretations are self-serving, not analytical. As in the Cold War period, when the selfish power struggles of tribes, clans, ethnic groups, parties and politicians were often camouflaged and presented as struggles for democracy, human rights, Marxism-Leninism or pro-letarian internationalism, today they have to be presented with different legitimations in order to be credible and 'just': as ethnic or national struggles.

The point here is that these identities are of major importance to the conflicts, but they mostly are invented. As soon as they are used as political categories, ethnic or religious identities, in contrast to economic ones, become social inventions to serve specific purposes. Pierre Hassner has rightly remarked that 'all political ethnicity is, in a sense, a "fictional identity" or an "imaged community"'.[1]

Such categorisations generally use existing, real differences between groups of people (for example, colour, language, religion, culture), but these differences do not constitute ethnic identity by themselves, they only provide its raw material. Differences or similarities of language, culture, or colour do not by themselves make people friends or enemies. But they may provide an excuse for differenti-ating between 'us' and 'them', and so allow expectations of good to be projected upon one's own group, while bad is projected upon the other. That these differences in some cases hardly exist or are artifi-cially based on second-rate criteria has been brutally demonstrated by German fascism.

In former Yugoslavia mediators from the UN and the EC are working closely together, but success is nowhere in sight. On the contrary: the necessary humanitarian operations may be in place, but the UN troops are not able to provide the appropriate emergency aid. A political solution, or even the stabilisation of the security situation, is not likely – never mind an armistice or peace. At this point the UN would be content to keep its own blue helmets from becoming war victims. The latter are still in the country principally because a retreat would mean a loss of face and the situation possibly becoming even more unstable. Yet even the control and guarding of heavy arms is beyond the UN forces' capabilities.

The UN's paralysis in this case is a particularly clear reflection of the limited interests and lack of imagination of the powers that dominate it. The few ideas about a political solution that were even discussed (the Vance–Owen Plan) essentially consisted of ratifying of Serbian-Croatian conquests. If any political solution is negotiated, it will be along these lines.

The international and Western response to the wars in former Yugoslavia has been characterised by helplessness. This is not meant as total criticism, because it is highly questionable, whether any Western or UN strategy would have been able to end the war or its disastrous results. The reasonable wish to end widespread suffering and epidemic crime does not necessarily produce the instruments for achieving this goal. It is difficult to see how any policy or military option of the UN or NATO, let alone individual governments, could have ended the war. Most scenarios that have been suggested have even entailed the risk of aggravating the situation still further. Nevertheless, we have seen a long-running debate about international passivity and helplessness.

Helplessness in the UN, EC, NATO and the US there was. But this was not primarily the result of political mistakes by this or that government. Mistakes did happen of course, but they only made things worse; they did not create the problems in the Balkans. The helplessness of outside powers resulted from the internal dynamics of the conflict in Bosnia, which made any successful attempt at conflict resolution or intervention almost impossible. The point may be illustrated by comparing the Bosnian war to the US war against Iraq. As we have seen, militarily the Gulf War was clear-cut: Iraqi divisions waited in the desert to be bombarded by US and allied firepower; the lines of battles were clear, and friendly and enemy forces were clearly separated; topographically, no mountains or forests made air bombardment difficult; the Iraqi soldiers were delivered to the US forces on a platter by the Iraqi high command and its dictator. Armed resistance was limited, casualties one-sided.

In Bosnia, on the other hand, the lines are often blurred. Small areas might be inhabited by three different ethnic groups and even more fighting entities. It is often hard to distinguish between military and civilian personnel, and many of the atrocities are being committed by civilians, neighbours killing neighbours. The physical terrain is difficult, as is the distinction between friend and enemy. And often it is less than clear who is in control of some of the militias or military units. Even worse: there has been no clearcut military mission. In Iraq the goal was to destroy most of Baghdad's military capacity, but only up to the point where it still could deal with Kurdish and Shi'ite insurgencies. That was easy to measure. But in Bosnia, exactly what could the mission be? To stop the rape and the massacres? This is a good goal, but it would imply occupying the whole area and placing soldiers in nearly every hamlet. And this would turn the invaders into the enemy and the target of all parties in the conflict.

In ethnic-religious civil wars, with their 'uncontrolled' and spontaneously committed massacres, with much of the fighting left to bands or clans, with the ethnic minorities not only or not primarily persecuted by a brutal government, but rather killed by their own neighbours, it is very difficult to define precisely the concrete tasks of an intervention force. It is easy to be against injustice, violence and murder, but which group, subgroup or persons should one confront? And in which way? It may appear relatively simple to discipline an insubordinate government (although not even the Gulf War was able to force Saddam Hussein to adhere to a pro-Western line or resign), but to force a society in ruins to make peace is as difficult as it is desirable.

This problem is posed with even greater urgency when the killing is no longer taking place under the orders of political authorities or military commanders, but instead is attended to at the grassroots of a society by the civilians themselves. Truly 'popular warfare', or a 'democratization' of war, is the final stage of social disintegration.

To believe that diplomatic initiatives or military intervention can resolve these kinds of problems is wishful thinking. Both instruments of international politics demand internal conditions that do not necessarily exist in places like Afghanistan, Lebanon in the late 1970s and 1980s, or Bosnia. Helplessness results, often camouflaged by tough talking. Politicians do not like to be perceived as paralysed or helpless by the public, so they tend to present solutions that do not exist. But that has much more to do with domestic politics in North America or Western Europe than with the regional conflicts concerned.

Somalia

The Horn of Africa was an area of the world where (in Ethiopia), ethnicity, tribal/clan relationships and the Cold War were once regarded as being of primary importance. With the Cold War over and the dictatorship in Somalia crumbling (Siad Barre fled the country in January 1991), clan politics and violent competition among warlords in the country remained. The state apparatus disintegrated and disappeared, society became fragmented and war was the rule of the day. Famine resulted. Perhaps half a million out of a population of 7 million people died of starvation in 1991 and 1992, perhaps many more, but for a long time few people outside either noticed or cared. This was Africa, not Europe, so for white Americans and Europeans famine at first seemed to be nothing special, just a part of the African experience. A couple of hundred thousand dead bodies would have been considered a local affair, but when the famine got completely out of control the international media discovered that something was going on. And suddenly TV crews from all over the world covered the disaster, bringing colourful pictures into American and European living rooms. The media forced the hand of governments. 'Something' had to be done.

Somalia is an awkward place for people who want to believe that new conflicts arise principally for ethnic, nationalist or religious reasons. If this notion is dubious in Bosnia, in Somalia there is nothing to support that illusion. For 97 per cent of the population speak Somali, 98 per cent are ethnically Somali and nearly 100 per cent are Sunni Moslems. That is as homogenous as a society can be. And still Somalia is completely factionalised, with civil war destroying large parts of the country. The point of general importance is that one does not need ethnic, national, linguistic or religious differences to invent an identity, to break up a state and to start killing 'outsiders'.

The war in Somalia is neither ethnic nor religious, and its cause is not the clan system either. Its roots are political, psychological and economic. The Siad Barre dictatorship had used the Cold War environment to allow his clan and its allies effectively to control the state and most of the other clans. That had thrown the equilibrium of the Somali clan system off balance. The moment the clans successfully overthrew Siad Barre in early 1991, they began to fight among themselves for control of the state.[2] All the clans wanted to take Siad Barre's place, but none had the strength to achieve this. This power struggle kicked off the war. Increasing economic hardship made the struggle escalate; with resources becoming scarcer and the state infrastructure collapsing, clans fought for food and other goods as well as power. So, Siad Barre's dictatorship had subverted the traditional system of clans, which was interested in autonomy and keeping each other in check. It was the resulting disfunctioning and perverting of this system that caused the war – not the system itself. And without the assistance of outside powers, first the USSR, then the West, Siad Barre could never have achieved his position of preeminent power.

This was to be the reference point of any humanitarian operation, no matter whether sponsored by non-governmental organisations (NGOs), the UN or the US, and no matter whether it involved simply the delivery of food or military intervention. The basic question was whether outside involvement would aim at reconstructing the clan system and help make it function again, or whether outsiders would help destroy it further, willingly or unconsciously, and then substitute something else. The first option required patience and diplomatic skill, but as the Algerian UN special envoy to Somalia, Mohammed Sahnoun, demonstrated between April and October 1992, the approach was promising and could work. Sahnoun begun a process of political stabilisation in some areas of the country by working with the clan elders, and he convinced most of the warlords to allow and even to support humanitarian assistance instead of plundering it. His success was far from complete or overwhelming, but things slowly started to move towards building a new, functioning equilibrium.

The advantages of this approach were that it might very well have functioned, that it went beyond humanitarian goals and aimed to reconstruct a functioning political environment. Its disadvantage was that it was slow and not very spectacular. It offered little that looked impressive on TV.

UN Secretary-General Boutros Boutros-Ghali first supported Sahnoun and his approach, and then suddenly rejected both. Sahnoun's delicate handling of the different clans and warlords was aimed at convincing them to cooperate and at creating incentives for more peaceful behaviour. That was how he achieved General Aideed's consent for 500 Pakistani soldiers to guard the airport and the harbour as UN blue helmet units. But right in the middle of further negotiations for an additional 3,000 troops, UN headquarters in New York announced that the UN would deploy the troops anyway, with or without the consent of Aideed. The negotiations were broken off, and attacks on Pakistani troops began. Sahnoun could do nothing about this; his credibility in Somalia had been destroyed from New York. Shortly afterwards he resigned.

With Sahnoun out, his approach of restructuring a functioning political equilibrium between the clans and warlords was dead. The only alternatives left were either a hands-off policy or military intervention. In other words, it was not that the internal situation in Somalia had required an military intervention, but that the lack of understanding and political mistakes in UN headquarters, shared by the big powers in the Security Council, had made it necessary.

In this way, the US intervention was triggered on the one hand by the UN's blunder, and on the other by domestic pressure resulting from increasing media coverage in the US, which in the summer of 1992 began to draw public attention to Somalia.[3] US troops went in early in December 1992; six months later the operation was handed over to the UN.

Again, it was vital that the intervention force should either deal sensitively with all the clans and warlords, or try to force them all to their knees. The only remaining alternative was to cooperate with some warlords and clans against the others. With the intervention in place, it was virtually impossible to continue Sahnoun's strategy. The US and UN military operations were simply too large and too dominating not to disturb the local balance of power and struggle. With big money and big guns entering the country, most clans and warlords became much more interested in exploiting the newcomers for their own interests, rather than continuing Sahnoun's fragile negotiation process. All parties concerned tried to utilise the intervention forces to strengthen their own positions, some quite successfully. But often this tactic led to frustration, and slowly the UN blue helmets were perceived as just another party to the war. Many people came to consider the UN as an occupation force. This process was supported by the fact that the blue helmets often behaved as if they were. Human rights abuses, indiscriminate killings, theft and racist attitudes by some of the UN troops contributed to this. There were instances reported of blue helmets carrying out acts, such as an attack on a hospital which caused casualties in Mogadishu in June 1993, which appeared to violate international law and had no proper justification. Less than two weeks before this attack, four unarmed Somalis had been killed and more wounded when UN troops had opened fire on a minibus.[4] These acts were bad enough, but they were compounded by the fact that UN spokespeople generally deny cases like these, despite numerous eyewitnesses and other proof, and that no case of soldiers being punished for such attacks has been reported up to now.

The UN and Peacekeeping

The general euphoria about the UN's new, active role as a prominent factor in a New World Order has been replaced by a similar measure of sobriety. A central hope after the end of the Cold War was that the UN could take over the essential task of ending armed conflicts.

In lengthy or trying situations it could at least ease the lot of the population through 'humanitarian interventions'. In this way time could be gained for political solutions.

After the end of the Cold War the continuous stalemate in the Security Council disappeared and the UN thereby became a potentially active instrument of international politics. The paralysis of the world organisation brought about by the mutual obstruction of the two superpowers vanished with the disbandment of the Soviet Union. The UN Security Council was a central political arena in the crisis and war following Iraq's occupation of Kuwait in 1990: the US, Great Britain and France worked for a broad international alliance against Iraq, including Russia and many countries of the Third World, and at least not excluding the People's Republic of China. The fact that this alliance came about and that it was hatched in or around the Security Council of all places was quite original. At the time many observers believed that the UN would gain a new importance through its role in the Gulf War and that this was the beginning of a new era of international conflict resolution mediated by the UN. At times George Bush's 'New World Order' seemed synonymous with increased implementation of international law by the United Nations. The London *Economist* accurately noted that the prestige of the UN as an international peace factor had never been greater in all its history.[5]

The world organisation really did adopt a more active role in local and regional conflict resolution after the end of the Cold War. The scope and quality of its activities expanded considerably. This was already apparent before the Gulf War – with regard to Afghanistan, Angola, Namibia, Cambodia and Central America – but the process gained even more momentum after these initial excursions. At the time of writing the UN is working on more than a dozen peace missions – about as many as the total it dealt with in its previous 40 years. This should be a good sign.

In this context it is useful to examine more closely the euphoria and criticism surrounding the UN. The euphoria is quickly dealt with, since it is a thing of the past. It was a result of two mutually strengthening factors. The first was the relief felt at the end of the Cold War and the discontinuation of the bloc system. This led to wild and fantastic hopes, to the most beautiful of wishes for peace, friendship and other noble goals that could be achieved on our behalf by the UN. A death toll of 200,000 in the Gulf War was a trifle and not enough to spoil the mood, since it was just an expression of wishes and feelings and had nothing to do with real developments anyway. The second factor in this public mood was connected to political calculation. Power elites often consider it advantageous to present their national power politics to the world under the guise of internationalism, and the UN was their best option for achieving this. The Gulf War is again the best example of how this is done.

Afghanistan, Angola, Cambodia, Somalia, the conflicts in the CIS, Nicaragua, Bosnia – the record of the UN as a peacekeeper in most recent years is rather mixed, to put it mildly. And as a 'peace enforcer' it is disastrous. It might have served the interests of a few big powers, but it did not manage the peaceful resolution of regional conflicts in the Third World.

However, this is not the time for *schadenfreude*. In many countries the United Nations comprised the last or only hope for a political solution to long-smouldering conflicts or for humanitarian help. Yet it does not help to close one's eyes to failure either. It is more important to look for the reasons behind it. Leaving aside several difficulties, some of which we have already mentioned and which could be resolved relatively easily with the necessary political will (for example, lack of funds, inefficiency, misbehaviour of personnel) two serious problem areas remain.

Can All Conflicts Be Resolved? And How?

First of all the question arises whether all conflicts that are brought to the UN can ever be resolved and, if so, how. After all it is conceivable that the obvious failure of the UN in many situations might have something to do with the fact that expectations are too high. There is a tendency immediately to call for the UN whenever a war or a civil war breaks out in any region in the world. Is this realistic?

In the past the involvement of the UN was often very limited. For instance, the famous blue helmets were only deployed if all the conflicting parties agreed and if there was a solid and continuing consensus on the matter in the Security Council. During the Cold War these conditions often could not be met. It is no coincidence that there were no new blue-helmet peace missions between 1978 and 1988. The positive side of this limitation consisted in the fact that as a result UN peace missions were only sent in when the environment was relatively favourable – when no objections were made by the superpowers or the regional conflicting parties. This opened the way for political opportunities. Furthermore, the risk of failure was relatively small: expectations were low, the role of the UN limited. Even if not much was achieved, this was scarcely seen to be the fault of the UN.

Today the situation is different. Expectations have rocketed. Today the UN is supposed to force conflicting parties to peace, to supervise elections or even carry them out, to disarm the military and guerrilla forces, to provide humanitarian aid under armed protection or to help destroy weapons of mass extermination. And it is not prepared for any of this. Much more importantly, some of these tasks could not be – or could barely be – managed by any institution at all. Let us look at the disarmament of a guerrilla force. A prerequisite is usually the latter's agreement. If, however, the Khmer Rouge in the Cambodian jungle, for example, evades disarmament or refuses to comply – what then should the UN do? To confine itself to political appeals, calls and talks is to demonstrate its impotence. The alternative would be military action, forcible disarmament. But this is much easier said then done. The US in Indochina, France in Algeria, the Soviet Union in Afghanistan, India in Sri Lanka – any number of examples could be cited to demonstrate the inability of large powers with over-whelming firepower to crush or disarm far inferior guerrilla forces. Just finding them is often impossible. To demand that the UN disarm the Khmer Rouge forcibly and therefore use violence means nothing less than instructing it to wage another war in Indochina – but this time with only 22,000 soldiers, no money and no military strength. The same would hold true for Angola, Afghanistan and many other conflict regions. Moreover keeping one's hands clean while waging a guerrilla war is impossible; every instance has proved a bloody and protracted affair, with little chance of success. In all likelihood such involvement would turn the UN into yet another party of war and place it in a hopeless position.

It is not only a matter of guerrilla wars. To attempt to force conflicting parties to make peace if they have absolutely no interest in peace – a situation not uncommon in regional conflicts – is also a hopeless undertaking. With any luck the only result is the disgrace of failure; at worst one is caught politically and militarily between the warring fronts. Which means of power could the UN then apply in order to force an agreement (instead of mediating)? Economic sanctions which the organisation's own member states usually do not adhere to and which bring the danger of affecting the civilian population more than those politically responsible? Military action against both (or more) conflicting parties? Or is it better to support one side against the other?

The situation has become more complicated since calling for military interventions came into fashion. Of course, these are only demanded for peaceful purposes, for humanitarian reasons or other praiseworthy motives. But the propagandists of such proposals are usually quite vague about what military intervention really should and could effect in concrete terms and how exactly the general goal of a proposed operation could be implemented in practice. Often, these calls are little more than helpless cries, somewhat like calling for a 'strong man' to take over in domestic politics. This is not a pacifist argument. Military action does of course have effects, both positive and negative ones. But the new interventionist fashion is only a sign of bankrupt politics – a substitute for politics after their failure. At the same time it is being used by others as a new, fashionable and 'humanitarian' legitimation for the same old military interventionism.

The point we are making here is that in many conflict situations finding a solution can be difficult, time-consuming and even unlikely. This also holds true for dreadful situations where terrible atrocities are committed. The desire to help does not automatically bring the tools of success with it. And even 'well-meant' interventions can make a situation worse. This topic of 'humanitarian interventionism' will be dealt with in a separate booklet,[6] so it will not be examined further here.

The UN as an Instrument of Power

We have mentioned that the reality of the UN is now determined by growing expectations of its work and by innumerable regional conflicts. On the other hand, its room for manoeuvre depends on a very small number of great powers in the UN Security Council. Here the question of power has been clear since the collapse of the Soviet Union (or even longer): the US dominates with the assistance of Great Britain and France; Russia is economically, and to a certain extent politically, so dependent on the West that it can not deviate fundamentally from its line; and the People's Republic of China uses as a political bargaining counter its agreement or refusal – trading compliancy for an end to the isolation resulting from the 1989 massacre in Beijing, for instance. The UN Security Council makes the decisions concerning the actual activities of the UN and at present it is dominated by the US and its allies. This may be a result of the structure of the organisation and the oligarchical role of the permanent members of the Security Council, but more importantly it is a reflection of the presentday balance of power in the world. The UN is naturally not responsible for this.

The result is obviously and regrettably that the UN has become the tool of a few states. First of all one should remember that the United Nations is not and cannot be an independent, autonomous organisation: it is after all an amalgamation of governments. The UN has never been more than its most important member governments have allowed it to be. And since the collapse of the Soviet Union caused a drastic shift in the balance of power between the key governments, this has also affected the terms of power within the UN.

This is not the place to examine in detail the various cases in which the UN has been or is being instrumentalised by the dominating powers. References to the Security Council's bizarre and dubious enforcement of international law with respect to Libya[7] or certain elements of the policies on Iraq can serve as examples. In these cases the UN resolutions were often little more than the authorisation of policies that had already been agreed on in Washington or London. They were often kept so general that almost anything decided on by the larger powers in the light of these resolutions would be legitimate ('by all measures deemed necessary'). Moreover, the allies in the Gulf War often went far beyond these authorisations, though still referring to the UN – as in the air attacks on Iraq in January and June 1993 which had absolutely no foundation in international law whatsoever. This tendency is not only dubious but also leads in the mid-term to developments that weaken or devalue the UN as a potential organ of arbitration and mediation.

Let us take an example. Of course the Iraqi government is a particularly repressive and brutal dictatorship. Had anyone been interested, they could have had access to sufficient proof of this before August 1990. Iraq's research into and development of weapons of mass extermination was also nothing new.

As a result of the second Gulf War Iraq is de facto under the guardianship of the UN; this having been justified by the protection of its minorities and the elimination of its mass-extermination weapons. The Iraqi government – no doubt a criminal one – has little sovereignty left to speak of in its own state territory. The weakening of such a government is not a disadvantage in itself. But why not treat in the same way the equally brutal and dictatorial regimes in Syria or Saudi Arabia, or Turkey, which is also massacring Kurds (and maintaining a violent occupation of Cyprus), or innumerable other states of a similar category? Syria, Egypt, Libya, Iran and Israel all possess weapons of mass destruction – why aren't they being forced to destroy them? In any case, why is it legitimate for countries who have their own gigantic supplies of such weapons to destroy similar weapons in other countries and not at home? The answers are simple: it is not a question of international law, or dictatorship or repression. It does not even really have that much to do with mass-extermination weapons. The real issue is national power interests. And that is the UN's problem today. In Iraq's case the UN is supposed to enforce principles in a single country that could apply to three dozen others. In practice this means that what is involved is not the principles – which are certainly just – but rather weakening of a country for political reasons, which is why other criminal governments are allowed to participate in this highly moral event. In this way the UN becomes a colonial body constantly referring to international law and other useful regulations while working for the power politics of the predominant large powers.

One result can already be observed today, everywhere, in the Third World. It is that no one takes the UN seriously as an independent and neutral body anymore; it is considered a tool of the West. This opinion does not only hold sway in countries which are not close to the West; even massively pro-American or pro-French diplomats from the Third World readily agree to this verdict. Even most of the governments who participated in the broad Gulf War alliance against Saddam are of this opinion. Yet if the UN is to play a constructive role in mediating in Third World conflicts in the future, it is vital that its independence and neutrality are credible and can be seen in action. The moment the UN appears to be little more than the continuation of Western politics by other means, it will no longer be capable of fulfilling its functions. Today we stand at the very threshold of such a situation.

A Future for the UN?

The question is whether the UN can really become or be turned into an instrument that could represent a counterweight to the imperial politics of nation states. Tendencies threatening to undermine or encumber the international system have arisen from two areas since the end of the Cold War: on the one hand, the outbreak of several new and old ethnic, nationalist or religious inspired conflicts; on the other, the threat of an era of informal recolonisation, a historical period in which a few large powers regulate the rest of the world. The UN then can only be a factor in real peacemaking politics (instead of an agent of conflict management under the orders of the larger powers), if it fulfils a few practical conditions.

First of all, an instrument must be created to ensure protection from arbitrary decision-making by the UN Security Council itself. What should small countries do if the Security Council makes decisions based on tactical or political grounds that are either contrary to international law or simply accommodations to the larger powers? How can such countries protect themselves from attacks or unjustified interventions on the part of the UN? Just as the citizens of a state need the right to legal protection against their government or even their parliament, in the same way we need a safeguard here.

Second, we must ensure that the UN does not only discipline small or weak countries (for instance, to prevent them violating international law), but does the same to all countries in equal measure. It is not just the principle of equality that demands this, but common sense too: transgressions by stronger powers are both more likely as well as more dangerous than those of smaller ones. Therefore the debate should focus on this point: how to control and contain the dominating powers.

Third, UN peacekeeping or combat troops should be kept strictly under UN control. UN military operations should be completely in the hands of the UN, and any influence or control of individual governments, including the permanent members of the Security Council, denied. At the same time UN troops must adhere to the most rigid and highest ethical and legal standards. Human rights abuses, personal or organisational misbehaviour or partisan activities should be strictly monitored and checked, and the personnel responsible should be brought to court – and be convicted, if found guilty of any illegal act. Only if UN troops fulfil the standards of international law, and respect human rights is there any hope that the armed forces of governments can be held accountable to the same standards.

All of these points are easier to formulate than resolve. It is true that 'Realpolitik' or the current balance of power make quick solutions unlikely, but this only demonstrates the importance of the points raised. They are closely connected to a democratisation of the UN – a concept that is the subject of much talk, but very few useful ideas. How should one democratise an organisation of frequently dictatorial governments? This can hardly be achieved along the lines of 'one country, one vote', since then both India and Kiribati would have the same influence, the US as much voice as Vanatu. Furthermore, the many repressive governments in the world could form a majority against democratic reform, which would hardly be an expression of a more democratic UN. Yet the opposite scenario is no better: to calculate the vote according to population would mean that together the People's Republic of China and India could more or less dominate the rest of the world. This is not a pleasantly democratic prospect either.

The UN has failed in fulfilling its new role and fails anew almost every day. But its failure can only be attributed to its own mistakes to a certain extent. It results mainly from the fact that the UN is being entrusted with increasingly complex problems without the necessary conditions of success and without the necessary tools. Furthermore, the UN is failing to fulfil strained and unrealistic expectations. But the bottom line and chief problem is that the UN today is not much more than a tool of a few large powers and that the scope of its abilities is for the most part oriented towards their national interests.

10

The Future of a New World Order

The era of multipolarity began with an unipolar moment. The tendency in the 1970s and 1980s for the bipolar postwar order to be eroded and for the subversion of both superpowers' ability single-handedly to control their respective allies and dominate the rest of the globe had finally been fulfilled by the end of the Cold War. The era of bipolarity was over. The end of the principal disciplinary force which had conserved the superpowers' preeminence and had kept rising powers in check reinforced the existing trend towards a multipolar world system. Ironically, the last remaining superpower, the United States, gave the impression of now being in control, of being able to create a unipolar structure of world politics. US politicians felt able to proclaim the 'next American century'.

The starting point for the discussion of this New World Order was the Gulf War. This war gave rise to assessments which emphasised the special role of US power in international politics. This was under-standable in the context of a military victory.

Paradoxically, however, a very different conclusion can be drawn from the events of the war. In the first place, the war against Iraq would not have been necessary if the US could have imposed its will at less cost. The rise of Iraq to the point of becoming a regional superpower completely dominating the Persian Gulf was in itself a symbol of the fact that Third World countries, under certain conditions and exploiting specific mechanisms within the international system, could get 'out of control'. The war against Iraq was in a sense the last-minute application of an 'emergency brake', a last resort to prevent Baghdad from becoming an independent regional power with enormous weight. Iraqi power would appear to have been largely neu-tralised, but is it realistic to assume that the United States will be willing and able to wage a war on this scale whenever a regional power gets 'out of control'? And would it be realistic to expect the other states on the UN Security Council to back the US whatever the region and other factors involved? To both questions the answer is so obviously 'no' that the scenarios they evoke can be excluded in most conceivable cases.

Second, it is noteworthy how the US government created the international framework for the war. It did this with great diplomatic skill and success, but its very diplomacy laid bare Washington's weak points. The great importance which, up to the end of November 1990 (when Resolution 678 was passed), the US attached to diplomacy within the framework of the UN, and to cooperation with the Soviet Union and China, was due to its absolute need to legitimise its own policy. Without the clear approval of the other powers and the United Nations, it would have been extremely difficult for the US to wage the war against Iraq in the face of domestic and foreign opinion. Thus, for Washington, one political condition for the war was its international legitimacy, – that is, the approval of other powers. At the same time, despite the military success of the US, the war has raised the question of whether the United States would have been able to fund it without the material backing of its allies. The war was financed by Saudi Arabia, the Kuwaiti government-in-exile, other Gulf states, Japan and West Germany. Given the huge budget deficit of the US government, it is at least doubtful whether America would have been able to pay for the conflict itself, or whether the people of the United States would have been ready to pay higher taxes or accept an even higher national debt in order to finance it.

Thus the US achieved a decisive military victory in the Gulf, but this would have been impossible to achieve unilaterally, since the political and material conditions for this were lacking. Nor did the further evolution of the crisis, with the Kurdish uprising and the flight of refugees into Iran and Turkey, exactly give the impression that the US had the situation under control. The London *Economist* succinctly and accurately summarised the nature of the US leadership role in the Gulf crisis when it pointed out that:

> It is leadership only if America is convinced that others will follow – that is the contingency. They can follow in kind, like Britain is doing in the Gulf, or they can follow in cash, like Japan and Germany. But they must follow somehow. Domestic politics dictates that ... This is especially the case in hard economic times. So the domestic political and economic cost of go-it-alone adventurism is one constraint on America's freedom of action overseas.[1]

The Gulf War itself, which apparently provided the strongest argument supporting the thesis of a 'unipolar' world system, upon closer examination shows the weaknesses of such a thesis. More precisely, it illuminates the contradictory and conditional nature of the American leadership role today. The US is capable of spectacular actions, is militarily powerful, noisy and full of ideology, but it has to depend increasingly on the approval and financial support of other nations.

Within the US establishment, the question has already been raised as to whether the Gulf War was not in fact a further step towards the American armed forces and American security policy becoming mercenaries. William Pfaff, writing in the journal *Foreign Affairs*, has expressed this problem in a somewhat understated form:

> The United States, the debtor, furnishes the forces that provide the lender's military security, in exchange for the latter's purchases of U.S. treasury bonds not otherwise so easily marketed. [Pfaff is thinking of Japan here.] An equivalent relationship has now developed with Saudi Arabia, which is purchasing its defence from the United States just as it is accustomed to purchasing other services from other foreigners.[2]

This argument is persuasive. After all, there is every reason to think that the sums contributed towards the costs of the Gulf War by Saudi Arabia, the other Gulf states, Japan and West Germany actually exceeded the total cost. Saudi Arabia and Kuwait promised the United States US$16.4 billion each, the United Arab Emirates pledged $3 billion and West Germany some $10 billion. The war-related financial support from Turkey and other countries must not be forgotten either. The contributions amount to a grand total of around $53 billion.[3] According to the same source, the costs incurred by the US in the war can be estimated at $45.5 billion, although there are grounds for considering that the true total amounted to less than this. In any case, there is every indication that the Gulf War was not only militarily successful but indeed profitable for the United States.

William Pfaff:

> The Gulf deployment was accompanied by an appeal for other nations to pay for it, a demand the United States would never have made in the past, and one that itself amounted to a tacit renunciation of superpower standing. Superpowers pay their own way.[4]

Nonetheless, the US should not be regarded as having simply supplied a 'mercenary army'. It should not be forgotten after all that the US fought the war for reasons which were decided on in Washington, not in Riyadh or Tokyo. Saudi Arabia and the Kuwaiti government-in-exile financed the US for a war which they themselves could not fight, and this naturally does suggest a 'buying' of military security. But if the war had not served US interests then Arab money alone would not have made it happen. Conversely, the fact that the Japanese and Germans supplied funds can hardly be interpreted as being intended to push the United States into the war. On the contrary, both these countries were clearly dubious about whether the war was necessary or logical. For Japan and Germany the funds which they supplied were rather intended as a means of avoiding having to make a direct military contribution of their own and of meeting the criticism of the US and other allies. In other words they 'bought themselves out'. This too is not typical of a mercenary–client relationship.

What Characterises the New World Order?

To take the Gulf War as the main point of reference for the New World Order leads to highly erroneous conclusions, if it is a question of assessing the real evolution of the international system. More logical points of reference are the shift in world economic power towards Japan and Western Europe at the expense of the United States; the dissolution of the Warsaw Pact and the Soviet Union, and the uncertain future of the CIS and Russia, related to the areas of more recent crisis in Eastern Europe; together with the First World's gradual and relative loss of control over the Third World since the Second World War. These three processes are not without inner contradictions, and all are subject to constant stops and starts, but they nonetheless constitute the three most powerful factors influencing the future of the structure of the international system. These are not historical movements which are, like forces of nature, outside the control of governments or political movements. On the contrary, the economic decline of the United States, for example, could be halted if the US political system were able to decide on and implement appropriate decisive countermeasures. So far there is little sign of this happening. After all this would require not only a substantial reduction in the national debt – difficult and uncertain enough, and probably impossible without unpopular tax increases – but also an active state industrial policy to reactivate the national economy and restore competitiveness. The current economic ideology, which is opposed to a strong, active and innovative role of the state in the economic field, and completely orientated towards a free-market economy, aggravates the problem rather than resolving it. It favours the most powerful, and today in many sectors of economic activity the most powerful player is not the United States.

The political structure of the US, as enshrined in the constitution and embedded in the political culture of the nation, makes it more difficult to implement the required measures. Congress is structurally designed as a counterbalance, a check to the administration, and is very strong in blocking or subverting integrated programmes that might be proposed by the White House. In no way is it a body capable of initiating far-reaching measures of national importance. It is much too fragmented and essentially a collection of representatives of competing interest groups. The main structural strength of the US Congress is its ability to block any wide-ranging reform. If the US administration, which is almost as fragmented as Congress is, attempted to introduce far-reaching measures to restructure the economy, it would, as soon as it became apparent that these would damage specific interest groups, immediately come up against the delaying and destructive power of Congress again (as was the painful experience of President Carter with his energy policy). Thus although a thorough revitalisation of the US economy may be possible in principle, and it is conceivable, this is unlikely to come about because of the way in which political power is distributed internally. The relative power loss of the United States is thus likely to continue for the foreseeable future. Whether a Clinton administration has the force to break out of this situation seems doubtful. Not everyone who talks about 'change' really wants change or can make it happen. Any US administration can act forcefully in foreign and military affairs; it can send troops to combat and invade foreign countries without even asking Congress, as long it does not intend formally to declare war. But in domestic matters, in economic or other areas of importance, compared to its Japanese or European counterparts the US government appears virtually paralysed. The military giant does not have the basic structural tools to regulate and revitalise its own economy.

The future of the CIS and especially Russia will constitute important structural elements in a New Order of the international system. Despite their crises, because of their sheer size they are a weighty factor. Russia alone, because of its arsenal of strategic and tactical nuclear weapons, is an important consideration in the power game. In Africa and Latin America, Russia may no longer have any significance, but this is not the case in Europe and Asia. The precise way in which the country will bring its importance to bear depends on its future internal political evolution. If there is a complete internal collapse, the principal manifestation of this will be the exporting of people and instability over its frontiers. If the group gathered around

President Yeltsin does in fact succeed in carrying out the economic reform of the country while maintaining democratic forms of government, which seems increasingly unlikely, this would mean a trend towards the 'Westernisation' of Russia, in economic and political terms. However, the political defeat of Yeltsin has already begun. It now seems fairly probable that there will be a political reaction within the country, either in the form of a new authoritarian regime, perhaps clustered around nationalist and neocommunist forces, or the installation of a hybrid democratic-authoritarian government centred on the conservative opposition and big business. But in any case it seems likely that the further development of a capitalist economy in Russia cannot be stopped and will assume increasingly authoritarian or even dictatorial forms. It is hard to know whether in this context a formal framework of a parliament and occasional elections will coexist with the process of becoming more authoritarian.

A capitalist-development dictatorship in Moscow, not necessarily involving much bloodshed, would also bind the country to the West European economy and the world market, but it would presumably have to keep its distance politically more than is the case at present. A 'Stalinist' or nationalist reaction in Russia would for a time reduce the country's influence abroad compared to the other options (without completely eliminating it), but would fairly certainly be the signal for a period of internal disturbances, greater political instability and possible foreign policy adventures.

Between the shifts in economic power in the West and the internal developments in the CIS, there are a number of links and interactions. If the West European economic and power bloc were to succeed in organising Eastern Europe, including the main CIS states, as its economic hinterland (which is just as possible with successful democratisation as under a capitalist dictatorship), it would have significant competitive advantages over its Japanese and American rivals. Such a scenario cannot be completely excluded, since hitherto the United States and Japan, for different reasons, have not seriously competed with the EC in Eastern Europe and would furthermore be handicapped by geographical and cultural disadvantages if they tried to do so. All this naturally also depends on whether the EC can overcome its current crisis over the problems with Maastricht and the exchange rate mechanism and can once again become capable of action. It depends too on whether the German giant in the centre of Europe can economically digest its new eastern provinces without overstraining itself both economically and politically in the domestic sphere.

The Future Role of the Third World

The process of differentiation of the international system, of developing real multipolarity, also depends on a range of factors which are very susceptible to influence by governments and movements. The means by which the Third World is controlled are numerous and often effective, it is true, but results are not guaranteed. Foreign debt as a means of imposing discipline seems at present to be one of the most effective tools, but it does not work in every case. The up-and-coming countries of East Asia are hardly likely to be controllable in this way over the longer term. Nor are those few countries which are still isolated or not seriously encumbered by debt, such as Syria, Iran and North Korea. In the recent past the Gulf War has clearly shown that non-military methods of imposing discipline are sometimes not enough. What will be decisive in terms of medium-term control over the Third World will not primarily be the level of weaponry in the countries concerned, because this will continue to be inferior to that of the capitalist centres. The revolution in military technology in which intelligent weaponry plays an increasingly important role preserves the lead of America, Europe and Japan over the Third World (and Russia) in this field. There is little prospect of success in attempting to compete with the West on a military level, as Iraq has learned. It is true that the South will continue to work towards acquiring nuclear, biological and chemical weapons of mass destruction, as well as missile technology, and it may well succeed in this. This does not mean, however, that within the foreseeable future Third World countries will be able to stand up to the West in direct military confrontation (save for guerrilla wars), provided that the West has the will and ability to use its full power. To some extent nonetheless a 'deterrent' factor will come into play. It is difficult to assess whether the United States would have forced the conflict in the Gulf to take place as it did, if Iraq had possessed an arsenal of nuclear or biological weaponry capable of being used, and the technology to make its use effective over long distances.

The relative loss of control over the Third World is, however, far from being a matter of military power and technology. The decisive loss will be a decreasing ability to control developments inside Third World societies. Often, indeed, those factors employed to control and dominate Third World governments, such as a country's debt, may result in a loss of stability and amenability of the society concerned. This is why 'low-intensity warfare' will continue to be a key element in US and Western Third World strategy in the 1990s and beyond.

This is the only effective way in which the West can have a really effective influence on the internal evolution of Third World societies. In January 1990 the US secretary for defense wrote in his annual report:

> Low-intensity conflict continues to be the most likely form of violence involving US interests. In addition to violence resulting from insurgencies, regional hostilities, and terrorism, US forces face potential threats from drug trafficking and the proliferation of chemical/biological weapons. We must prepare an active and timely defense against such violence, one that presents a credible deterrent and remains capable of using power when necessary. The Department must also address the underlying causes of instability by assisting in the nation-building process through economic, security, and humanitarian assistance, and civic action in support of US foreign policy objectives.[5]

This policy view has not been made obsolete by the Gulf War and the end of the Cold War. In March 1991 the US general staff, in its annual military net assessment, stated that in the future more attention than before would have to be paid to counterinsurgency and the drugs war as well as to 'smaller regional deployments' – that is, to low-intensity warfare.

It would be wrong to think that forms of deployment modelled on the Gulf War (conflicts/wars of medium intensity) will take over from low-intensity warfare as a means of dominating and controlling the Third World. The growing problems involved in exerting control over the South require a supplementing and further development of the tools available, not simply a replacement of one method by another. There is only a very limited number of scenarios in which the deployment of over half a million soldiers with all their high-technology weaponry will be cost-efficient and also effective. In the crisis in former Yugoslavia, in the Lebanese conflict, in the civil war in El Salvador or in Afghanistan, as well as in many other conflicts, such a massive deployment would have been either pointless or counterproductive. The problems which the United States would face if it had to finance deployments such as that in the Gulf War have already been discussed.

In considering the three basic structural factors of the future world order as a whole, therefore, there is no sense in regarding the outcomes of the processes at work as inevitable. All three factors can be politically influenced, and their mutual interactions and influences increase the uncertainties. This in itself does not mean that no conclusions can be drawn about the future international structure. Such projections must, however, be concentrated on the overall framework of conditions, and not on speculation concerning the future of individual aspects. It is essential not to allow oneself to be distracted from an overall view of longer-term trends by a rush of current events, however spectacular some of these may be.

In the Third World, a number of countries have built up considerable economic or military capacities during the postwar period. South Korea, Brazil, India, Israel, South Africa, Nigeria, and Indonesia are only a few examples, and the number of such powers is clearly going to increase. This is not to say that one or other of these countries can equal the US in military or economic power, or even that the capitalist powers Japan and the united Germany can do so. Conversely, however, it would be unrealistic to expect the US to achieve sole domination within a 'unipolar' world system. The processes of differentiation and development of strength in the First and Third Worlds (and this applies even in the CIS or whatever remains of it) have gone too far and are too irreversible for this to be the case.

It is indisputable that the United States is the only superpower in existence today, now that its rival has vanished. But what does this mean? The interesting aspect of this truism is that the sole remaining superpower is not able to operate a unilateral policy, or even to maintain the unipolar world system which has been conjured into existence. If the sole surviving superpower talks about its 'leadership role', it does not do so to imply that where it leads others will have to follow willy-nilly. Leadership today is by persuasion, acting as first among equals. In fact, although this may still be called 'leadership' it is something fundamentally different from the American leadership role of the 1950s and 1960s.[6]

A New Confrontation?

It is always fascinating to observe how struggles for power are elegantly concealed and dressed up as intellectual enterprises. Brutal Afghan drug dealers posing as freedom fighters and true believers; intellectually immobilised geriatrics in the former Soviet leadership talking about 'world revolution'; a government supporting the cruellest dictatorships and breaking international law by waging a 'democratic crusade'; committing wholesale massacres, torture and ethnic cleansing in Bosnia to fulfil the goal of 'national self-determination' – these are just a few examples of how the real goals of power politics are being hidden by sweet-sounding phrases. For us it does not matter whether the respective politicians believe in their own propaganda. But it is crucial not to confuse the big words with actual strategies.

Today we are witness to another phase of doublespeak creation. The West has won the Cold War. What we are seeing now is the fight over the spoils. These struggles go on inside the Third World, between clans in Somalia, between Iraq and Kuwait (and its backers), in Tadzhikistan, in many places. And these struggles take place inside the former Soviet Union, inside Russia, inside the former Eastern Bloc. Bosnia may be a symbol of this. The same struggle goes on between the industrialised North and the Third World, and between the North and the former East. The takeover of East Germany by the West, the US struggle for the control of the Middle East, and the jockeying for influence in Eastern Europe and China are examples of the same process. Finally there are all the struggles inside the former West, in addition to the usual competition to cash in on the common victory. This is what the New World Order, or in Clinton's less original words the post-Cold War era, is all about. Who will grab which part of the cake, how will the future spheres of influence be demarcated and how will the general rules of the game be rewritten after this process is completed? – these are the proper questions. A new American leadership role, the 'next American century': this is the answer that one of the big powers has to offer to the world.

And these are the questions to be hidden by a new surge of an intellectual enterprise. Politicians and intellectuals are busy inventing pretty theories that justify the struggles, make them look 'moral' and prove that the fight for more power is in reality a struggle for good principles. Our own country's bid for power is really an attempt to strive for all (or most) of humanity. Trying to dominate the world naturally becomes a quest for World Order.

The crucial fight today is over control: control of the Third World, control of developments in Russia and the whole of Eastern Europe, control of resources; and control of each other's markets, currencies, and economic and political potential. It is less a fight for territory than to control the structures of the international system, and to set up and control the rules. To integrate other actors into an environment which we have shaped, that is the main goal. This strategy will be based on military means if necessary, but mostly it will be pursued by 'peaceful' means, by economic penetration, by economic and political instruments in general.

The intellectual justifications for the fight over the spoils does require two principal elements. Besides the positive, appealing side, besides the 'human', humanistic and altruistic arguments, a redefinition is needed about who the enemy is. The final step is to integrate these two aspects of ideology. To fulfil our new altruistic and civilising duty to mankind we have to fight the enemy of civilisation and humanity. In the old days, colonialism was presented as a way to Christianise the barbarians, to civilise them. Cold War imperialism was said to be necessary to bring freedom (or socialism) to the world. And in both historic phases the annihilation of one's enemies was deemed perfectly legitimate: the enemies of God might not even have been human, but they were evil. And to kill a communist could not be that bad, when the communists were enemies to humanity and freedom. The Third World in particular has suffered from these ideologies, but fascism and Stalinism both brought the same logic home to Europe.

After the end of the Cold War we experience the intellectual and emotional constitution of new enemies, and also of new civilising missions. The barbarians are back. They must be controlled, checked and kept in place, and if possible civilised. If they resist, they have to be fought. The question remains: who are the new barbarians and how should they be civilised and fought?

One leading example of an intellectual producing these new ideologies is Samuel Huntington. This is not the place to go into this more deeply,[8] so we will restrict our remarks to just some elements of Huntington's theories and ignore other authors of similar concepts. Huntington's great advantage over others is the clarity of his words. When other authors are vague, he gets right to the point:

> The great divisions among humankind and the dominating source of conflict will be cultural. Nation states will remain the most powerful actors in world affairs, but the principal conflicts of global politics will occur between nations and groups of different civilizations. The clash of civilizations will dominate global politics. The fault lines between civilizations will be the battle lines of the future.[9]

Clear though he is with regard to drawing battle lines, Huntington is woolly when it comes to defining what he means by 'civilisations'. If in his view this category is of such crucial importance, it is strange that it is extremely vaguely defined. 'A civilization is a cultural entity', which is not very illuminating. It is 'the highest cultural grouping of people and the broadest level of cultural identity people have short of that which distinguishes humans from other species'. To call this definition vague is putting it politely. This is reflected in the examples Huntington has to offer. So he mentions the special civilisation of the Anglophone Caribbean, alongside the Chinese civilisation. At the same time he differentiates three Islamic subcivilisations:

Arab, Turkic and Malay. The Persian or Indian Islamic traditions for some unclarified reason don't qualify as civilisations.[10]

But Huntington's approach is not oriented towards conceptional clarity or analytical usefulness, it aims at defining enemies. It wants to fill the gap that has been left by the breakdown of the Soviet Union. Something has to take the place of the old communist threat: 'The fault lines between civilisations are replacing the political and ideological boundaries of the Cold War as the flash points for crisis and bloodshed'. And in regard to Europe: 'The velvet curtain of [Christian Orthodox and Muslim, as opposed to Roman Catholic and Protestant] culture has replaced the Iron curtain of ideology as the most significant dividing line in Europe'.

These intellectual exercises are preparation for a more specific definition of enemies. The vagueness of terms in this context is not a handicap, but an advantage: the enemy can be anybody Huntington chooses to make it. In the past, Western ideology and Western identity were contrasted with communist ideology. Today, the same values are contrasted with foreign cultures. On the one hand, Huntington perceives Western individualism, liberalism, free markets, human rights and all the other values he chooses to regard as 'Western'. On the other, these values 'often have little resonance in Islamic, Confucian, Japanese, Hindu, Buddhist, or Orthodox cultures'. In this way Japan, Russia, Serbia and most of the Third World are portrayed as cultural opponents of 'Western civilisation'.

But Huntington's principal choice as enemy is Islam, a culture he considers as dangerous as he considered communism. 'Islam has bloody borders.' His main argument is the history of Christian-Muslim military confrontations since the Middle Ages. It is quite remarkable that he ignores the simple fact that most wars have been fought inside either the Western or the Islamic cultures, not between them.

After discovering Islam to be an enemy, Huntington elaborates on this theme. He actually invents a 'Confucian-Islamic connection', because Islam alone probably would not be threatening enough. It has to be linked with China (and indirectly Japan) to gain credibility as a threat to the West. His 'Confucian-Islamic connection has emerged to challenge Western interests, values, and power'.[11] This new threat, in his view, entails a growing military challenge, including missiles and means of mass destruction.

Huntington also has advice on how to deal with the dangers ahead. Among other things he considers it clearly in the interest of the West ... to limit the expansion of the military strength of Confucian and Islamic States; to moderate the reduction of Western military capabilities and maintain military superiority in East and Southwest Asia; to exploit differences and conflicts among Confucian and Islamic states; to support in other civilizations groups sympathetic to Western values and interests.

His argument boils down to the conclusion that the West should 'maintain the economic and military power necessary to protect its interests in relation to these civilizations'. This position is hardly surprising for a person who works as a consultant to the US Defense Department.

The whole exercise makes little sense academically or analytically, because it is full of contradictions and vagueness, and does not provide evidence for its main points. But, on the other hand, it is very strong politically. It uses age-old perceptions and stereotypes of the enemy, brings them up to date and fills the gap in threats and fears that has opened up with the end of Cold War communism and the Soviet Union. In this context, the woolly character of Huntington's notions are not a weakness but a necessary ingredient. An overwhelming threat, if it is not real, has to pretend to define the enemy precisely, but give lots of room for fantasy at the same time.

Hardly anybody would seriously consider the Islamic states a credible military threat to the West, at least for the next generation or two. The same does apply to the 'Confucian' states. And, by the way, there are hardly any 'Islamic states' anyway. The Iraqi state is no more Islamic in character than the US or French states are Christian. Even if it were, just a few years ago it was amply demonstrated that the West could singlehandedly destroy Iraq's armed forces without much resistance. And remember that in terms of manpower and technology the Iraqi military was quite impressive, compared to all other 'Islamic' armies.

The whole point is not that Middle Eastern or Asian governments could or will seriously challenge and threaten the West. Most are close allies of the West anyway, fighting side by side with it against other 'Islamic' states and begging for Western support against their regional 'Islamic' enemies. The 'Confucian-Islamic military connection' of Huntington is a pure invention, without the potential to threaten the West.

The reality behind this is quite different. It is plain fact that the international system is in the process of differentiation, of becoming increasingly multipolar. Countries in the Middle East and Asia are gradually becoming more independent of Western domination.

They might even begin systematically to behave like independent nations, deciding their policies according to their own interests and not according to Western wishes and desires. This is the development which Huntington and many policymakers in North America and Europe are afraid of, and which they want to stop or slow down. In order to produce a legitimation for this which sounds less imperial and more acceptable to the public, a 'clash of civilisations' is being proclaimed by Huntington and others. The real fight, once again, is for control, and not for 'values' and 'civilisation'. It is for the control of natural resources in the Middle East, for oil, and for control of Asian markets. In these struggles the countries of the Middle East ('Islamic civilization'), together with China, Japan and the 'four little dragons' of Southeast Asia ('Confucian Civilizations'), are the main potential adversaries. They are to be substituted for the disappeared 'Soviet threat' ('Communism') of the past. In this context Huntington has properly defined the enemies, and that he does not tell us or even know what 'civilisations' really are does not matter at all.

Control is the catchword, and the struggle to control the game. A 'clash of civilisations' is one of the many artificial justifications for it, trying to unify the West behind its leading power. The remaining superpower desperately needs a rationale to hold on to its leadership role, to preserve its military might after the Soviet demise and to keep its allies in line. It needs a common enemy. If there isn't one, it has to be invented and the threat blown up out of all proportion.

But if this struggle for control is going on and will escalate, how is it being done? Some of the principal traditional tools of the 1980s and early 1990s have been discussed in this book. Foreign debt, low-intensity warfare and direct military intervention will remain crucial instruments. Trade policy has already become more important since the end of the 1970s, especially against Asian countries. Two additional strategies and concepts will gain importance as an expression of this struggle. The 'Democratisation' of the Third World is one of them, and a redefinition of international law and the United Nations the other.

Democracy has traditionally been denied to most people in the Third World by their own ruling elites and by the imperial powers in the North. Their joint interest has been to keep Third World peoples in check for strategic, economic and political reasons. Democracy was a thing to talk about loudly during the Cold War for ideological or propaganda reasons, but to ignore or subvert as soon as it became inconvenient. The coups in Guatemala (1954) and Chile (1973), the military invasion of the Czechoslovakia (1968) and similar cases were just the tip of the iceberg. There was a consistent policy always to place national and strategic self-interest way ahead of wonderful principles like democracy and human rights.

Essentially, this has not changed. But the way it is done after the Cold War is quite different. 'Democracy' in the Third World today is being taken more seriously than in the past, and can be, because today the countries of the South can no longer turn to an alternative superpower for protection against pressure by the other. The West has won the Cold War, so it is less restricted in its actions. But the term 'democracy' does not always mean what it seems. It is not always about self-rule, self-determination. Often it is about quite different things. In the West there is a tendency to consider democracy, human rights and similar concepts as 'Western' values. And the converse is also true: if a country is perceived as pro-Western, it will often automatically be certified 'democratic'.

So, more often than not, for the North, democratisation does not imply that the people of the Third World are empowered to rule themselves and determine their own fate, but that the South will be Westernised. Democratisation in this context means 'to make the Third World like we are'. The problem obviously is that it lacks the economic basis for becoming like us. Democratisation often means introducing free-market economies, because Western ideologues conveniently like to equate democracy with freedom, and freedom with free markets. And free markets obviously imply that big Western companies have free market access to fragile Third World economies. In many cases too, Western intellectuals and politicians have discovered that freedom is being subverted by state bureaucracies. So, democratisation also implies the weakening of the state apparatus in the Third World and the shift of responsibilities to private actors: companies or NGOs. As a result, democratic election processes and other wonderful things are only to be applied to an ever-shrinking sector of society, to a state and government that are becoming less and less able to deal with economic and social problems, and so are more and more irrelevant. The final result is that most of the formal trappings of Western democracy can be introduced, yet the execution of power is not being democratised but privatised and often shifted to external actors, like foreign companies, international financial institutions (such as the World Bank and the IMF) and foreign governments. In this way 'democratisation' of the Third World can easily become an instrument of controlling the Third World more efficiently, instead of empowering its citizens. Democratically elected governments now have to push through all the damaging structural adjustment programmes that the North deems useful in keeping control of and remodelling the South.

In addition, there is a tendency to strengthen the UN and to reinterpret international law in a way that makes both tools of the
dominant powers. In principle, again, there is nothing wrong with
strengthening the UN and developing international law. Quite the
opposite. But the problem arises when this is done in a way that makes
both the UN and international law more subservient to the West,
instead of making them serve and protect all countries in the same
way. The UN is badly needed as a counterbalance to keep the transgressions of individual powers in check. The usefulness of the UN is
based on not being partisan, on its ability to apply the same standards
to all member states evenhandedly, whether they are big or small,
powerful or weak, North or South. When the UN is being hijacked
by a few big powers, as it currently is, it becomes worthless and even
harmful. And, as we have discussed earlier, today the US, Great
Britain and France (which means NATO) are dominating and utilising
the UN to serve their national and joint interests. The recent practices
of the UN have provided legitimacy to national power policies
instead of checking them. They have made the organisation another
instrument for controlling the Third World. The strengthening of
the UN should be made conditional on the strengthening of its non-
partisan and unbiased status and practices.

As a result of this, international law has suffered and it too has
become an instrument of the same process. Instead of applying
equal criteria to all states and governments and their behaviour, international law has increasingly become a weapon of the strong against
the weak, the rich against the poor. This has worked in different ways.
The main technique is to apply international law to the weak countries
and make the big powers enforce it, while these powers themselves
are above the same laws. Invasion or intervention in other countries
is often legitimised and goes without punishment, as long as it is
undertaken by the great powers or their allies and friends. But the
same brutal and illegal practice might lead to a major war if committed
by an unruly Third World country. This kind of double standard has
recently been adopted by the UN Security Council too, which has
not held back from breaking or manipulating international law.
What makes things worse after the Cold War is a new tendency to
reinterpret and develop international law to make it more 'flexible';
that is, easier to manipulate. Old and basic principles today are up
for 'adjustment to new realities', and some of these new realities are
the changes in international power relationships. 'National
sovereignty' is being reinterpreted, officially for humanitarian and
human rights reasons. In the future the UN and other actors might
be allowed legally to intervene in the internal affairs of countries.

We have already seen the first instances of this, with the classic case being UN Security Council Resolution 688, concerning the Kurds in Iraq. Its official goals are wonderful and would be shared by anybody. But a few tricky problems arise, and it might very well be that again good principles are being applied for harmful strategies and bad results. How and by whom will it be decided whether an intervention in some other country's internal affairs is justified for 'humanitarian' reasons? Who will decide in which cases the principle of non-intervention in the internal affairs of sovereign states will be ignored and when they will be applied? Again, the answer is the UN Security Council, which in practice means a few powerful governments. And how can it be ensured that these few governments with all their individual foreign policy interests will not manipulate 'humanitarian' arguments for their own national advantage? How can it be ensured that the same (humanitarian) standards will be applied evenly with regard to friends and enemies? And, even more difficult, what can be done if a 'humanitarian' intervention in a big power's internal affairs becomes necessary? Who should, would and could carry it out? Or are these forms of intervention only applicable to 'small' countries, to be implemented by 'big' ones?

The bottom line is that the continuing creative way of reinterpreting international law and, among other things, making interventions in other countries easier, will provide the big powers with the additional weapon of law, because they are the only ones who will be able to exercise it. Interventions will be more easily permissible. The capability to undertake them and the power to define what 'humanitarian' means in specific cases, and whether or not military means are necessary, will be exclusively in the hands of the dominating powers. The result is that the 'humanitarian' arguments in terms of power will only strengthen the strong and hand them another instrument for domination.

The New World Order of George Bush was about creating another Pax Americana, another American century. This is not going to happen, and the new international system will not be structured along such simple lines. It is true that following the Soviet collapse the US is and will for a while remain a leading world power. But it cannot dominate the world unilaterally.

Notes and References

Chapter 1: The Birth of the Postwar Order

1. For a general analysis of the bipolar structure of the postwar international system, see R. Harrison Wagner, 'What Was bipolarity?', in *International Organisation*, Vol. 47, No. 1, Winter 1993, pp. 77–106.
2. Raymond Vernon, 'Same Planet, Different World', in William Brock and Robert Hormats (eds), *The Global Economy – America's Role in the Decade Ahead*, New York 1990, p. 17.
3. William P. Bundy, 'The 1950's Versus the 1990's' in Edward K. Hamilton (ed.), *America's Global Interests – A New Agenda*, New York 1989, pp. 52 et seq.
4. David P. Calleo, *Beyond American Hegemony – The Future of the Western Alliance*, New York 1987, pp. 27 et seq.
5. See George G. Kennan, *Memoiren eines Diplomaten (Memoirs of a Diplomat)*, Munich 1971.

Chapter 2: The Shifting Centres of Power

1. Robert Gilpin, *The Political Economy of International Relations*, Princeton, NJ, 1987, p. 331.
2. Ibid.
3. North Atlantic Assembly, Economic Committee, Information Document – Sub-Committee on Transatlantic Trade Relations, EC/TTR (87) 1, May 1987, p. 1.
4. Mike Mansfield, 'The US and Japan: Sharing our Destinies', in *Foreign Affairs*, Spring 1989, p. 3.
5. Michael B. Smith, 'US-Japan Economic Relations in the 1990s: a Crossroads?' in William Brock and Robert Hormats (eds), *The Global Economy – America's Role in the Decade Ahead*, New York 1990, p. 82.
6. Data from *Encyclopedia Britannica World Data Annual 1990*, and World Bank, *World Development Report 1990*, as published by PC Globe, Inc (copyright).
7. Konrad Seitz (former chief of planning at the German Foreign Office), *Die Japanisch-amerikanische Herausforderung*, 2nd edn., Munich 1991, pp. 32 et seq.
8. 'The World Economy: Perspectives for a Divided Responsibility', Richard R. Burt: USIS, *US Policy Information and Texts*, 4 November 1987.
9. Alec Nove, *An Economic History of the USSR*, London 1969, p. 287.
10. Michael C. Pugh, 'Prospects for International Order', in Michael Pugh and Phil Williams (eds), *Superpower Politics – Change in the United States and the Soviet Union*, Manchester 1990, pp. 176 et seq.

Chapter 3: The Postwar Order in the Third World.
1. Callum A. MacDonald, *Korea – the War before Vietnam*, London 1986, p. 3.
2. Ibid., p. 10.
3. Ibid.
4. Peter Wyden, *Bay of Pigs*, New York 1979.
5. Jerome Levinson and Juan De Onis, *The Alliance that Lost its Way*, Chicago 1970, p. 138.
6. Fred Halliday, *Cold War, Third World – An Essay on Soviet-American Relations*, London 1989, p. 29.
7. Concerning this phase of American policy towards Angola and the CIA operation there until it was stopped by Congress, see John Stockwell, *In Search of Enemies*, New York, 1978.
8. One example of this was the well-known War Powers Resolution of as early as November 1973. Another was the Clark Amendment of 1976, which forbade any undercover operations in Angola on the part of the administration.
9. James Earl Carter, 'A Foreign Policy Based on America's Essential Character', speech of 22 May 1977, in *Department of State Bulletin*, Vol. 76, 13 June 1977, p. 622.
10. Quoted from Michael T. Klare, *Beyond the Vietnam Syndrome*, Washington 1981, p. 32.
11. *New York Times*, 29 January 1981.
12. Stephen V. Cole, 'The New Soviet Bases on Our Continent – a Soviet Invasion', in *American Opinion*, June 1984, p. 7.
13. 'The Russian Knife at America's Throat', in *Reader's Digest*, August 1982, p. 89.
14. A private, conservative, group that ideologically and politically prepared the Latin American policy of the incoming Reagan administration.
15. Committee of Santa Fe, 'A New Inter-American Policy for the Eighties', published for the Council for Inter-American Security, Washington, May 1980, 2nd edn. 1981, pp. 3, 32.
16. US Department of State, *Current Policy*, No. 275, April 1981.
17. Committee of Santa Fe, op cit., pp. 1, 2.
18. Joseph E. Hopkins, 'Cuba: Moscow's Marionette', in *Parameters – US Naval Institute Proceedings*, July 1982, pp. 60, 62.
19. Committee of Santa Fe, op cit., p. 17.
20. *Wall Street Journal*, 28 February 1985.
21. George Shultz, 'Low-Intensity Warfare: the Challenge of Ambiguity', in US Department of State, *Current Policy*, No. 783, January 1986, p. 4.
22. Military Operations – US Army Operational Concept for Low-Intensity Conflict, United States Army Training and Doctrine Command (TRADOC) Pam 525–44, 10 February 1986, p. 3.
23. Caspar Weinberger, in US Department of Defense, *Proceedings of the Low-Intensity Warfare Conference*, 14–15 January 1986, Washington, pp. 2, 1.
24. 'Low-Intensity Conflict', Vol. 1 of *Main Report*, prepared for the US TRADOC, 30 July 1983, by Robert Kupperman Associates, p. VIII.
25. Thomas A. Cardwell III, 'Strategy for Low-Intensity Conflict', in Ninth Air University Airpower Symposium, *On the Role of Airpower in Low-*

Intensity Conflict, Maxwell Air Force Base, Alabama, 11–13 March 1985, Appendix 2, p. 13.

26. Felix F. Moran, 'Security Foresight: a Rational Defense against Terrorism', in Ninth Air University Airpower Symposium, Appendix 1, pp. 30, 31.
27. Clarence O. Herrington, 'B-52s in an Anti-Terrorist Role', in Ninth Air University Airpower Symposium, Appendix 2, pp. 387 et seq.
28. Deryck J. Eller, 'Doctrine for Low-Intensity Conflict', in Ninth Air University Airpower Symposium, Appendix 2, p. 48.
29. 'Low Intensity Conflict', Vol. 1, *Main Report*, pp. 23, 26, 62.

Chapter 4: The Conditions

1. Jürgen Nötzold, 'Economic Problems of the Soviet Union under Gorbachev as Starting Point for Changes in East–West Relations', SWP-LN 2455, December 1985, p. 3.
2. Hans-Hermann Höhmann, *Structures, Problems and Perspectives for a Soviet Economic Policy after the XXVII Party Conference of the CPSU*, Berichte des Bundesinstitutes für Ostwissenschaftliche und Internationale Studien, Cologne 1986, p. 11.
3. A. Izmujov and A. Kortunov, quoted in Jörg Kastl, 'New Thinking in Soviet Foreign Policy?', in *Europa-Archiv*, no. 20, 25 October 1988, p. 576.
4. Claudia Urbanovsky, 'The Soviet Officer Corps – Time for Reform?' in *Jane's Soviet Intelligence Review*, April 1991, p.157.
5. Interview with the former Soviet Secretary of State Edward Shevardnadze, in *Der Spiegel*, 27 May 1991, p. 179.
6. North Atlantic Assembly, Political Committee, 'Draft General Report on the Challenges for the Alliance: Northern Security – The Gorbachev Era', by Loic Bouvard, *Rapporteur*, September 1987, p. 12.
7. Shevardnadze interview, *Der Spiegel*, pp. 179 et seq.
8. Ibid.
9. Western European Union Assembly, General Affairs Committee, 'Development of East–West Relations and Western European Security', Working Paper by Mr Pontillon, *Rapporteur*, (undated), p. 25.
10. Elizabeth Kridl Valkernier, 'Die Wirtschaftsbeziehungen der Sowjetunion zur Dritten Welt: Vom Optimismus zur Ernüchterung', SWP-AZ 2424 April 1985, and her book *The Soviet Union and the Third World – An Economic Bind*, New York 1983.
11. Paul Kennedy, *The Rise and Fall of the Great Powers*, New York 1987.
12. Shevardnadze interview, *Der Spiegel*, pp. 183 et seq.
13. Kastl, 'New Thinking in Soviet Foreign Policy?', p. 575.
14. 'Soviet Economy Disintegrating, CIA Official Says', in USIS, *US Policy Information and Texts*, 21 May 1991, p. 30.
15. Mortimer B. Zuckerman, 'Rethinking Aid to Russia', in *US News and World Report*, 21 September 1992, p. 90.
16. 'A Friend in Need – Single-minded US Support for Gorbachev at Home could Backfire', in *US News and World Report*, 3 December 1990, p. 48.
17. *Economist*, 11 January 1992, p. 42.
18. Address to the UNO, manuscript pp. 24, 25, 27.
19. Press Release No. 1022/87 of the West German Foreign Office, 1 February 1987, text of speech of Foreign Minister Genscher at World Economic

Forum in Davos: 'Gorbatschow ernst nehmen – Gorbatschow beim Wort nehmen'.

20. One example of this position is in Rodney Leach, 'Should We Save Gorbachev?', in *National Review*, 19 February 1990, pp. 27–9.
21. 'Kimmitt Says Too Early to Call Soviet Threat Reduced.' Under Secretary of State for Political Affairs' testimony to Senate Appropriations Subcommittee. USIS wireless file 10 May 1989.
22. 'Scowcroft Says "Cold War" Not Yet Over', in USIS, *US Policy Information and Texts*, 23 January 1989, pp. 11, 12, 14.
23. Ibid.
24. Paul D. Wolfowitz, 'US National Security Strategy for the 1990s'. Adapted by the author from a speech by the Under Secretary of Defense for Policy to the National Defense University. USIS wireless file, 13 December 1989, pp. 1–20.
25. Retranslated from Baker, 'American-Soviet Cooperation Regarding Regional Conflicts Necessary', USIS wireless file, 24 October 1990, pp. 6, 4.
26. Ibid., p. 5.
27. 'NATO Meeting "An Important Milestone"; Cheney Says', in USIS, *US Policy Information and Texts*, 3 June 1991, p. 22.
28. Ibid.
29. 'Hopes for New Order Depend on Ending Iraqi Occupation, Excerpts: Baker to North Atlantic Council on Dec. 17, 1990', in USIS, *US Policy Information and Texts*, 19 December 1990, p. 23 et seq.
30. 'Two Summits, One Question: Aid for Gorbachev', in *Business Week*, 9 July 1990, p. 28.
31. 'US Will Shoulder Responsibility for World Leadership, Text: Christopher Remarks in Minnesota', in USIS, *US Policy Information and Texts*, 1 June 1993, p. 4.
32. 'Talbott Addresses Senate Committee on Aid for Russia, NIS', in USIS, *US Policy Information and Texts*, 10 September 1993, p. 18.
33. Steven Rosefielde, 'Russian Aid and Western Security', in *Global Affairs*, Fall 1992, pp. 113, 114.

Chapter 5: Initial Trends in the Third World

1. 'Von Gorbatschow bitter enttäuscht', in *Frankfurter Allgemeine Zeitung*, 27 June 1991, p. 14.
2. Stephen R. Galster, 'The Great Game – Afghanistan, the Superpowers, and the Prospects of Peace', Working Paper No. 3, German Institute for International Relations (Wuppertal), 1988.
3. A high-ranking official of the US Defense Department, talking to the author in 1986.
4. USIS, *US Policy Information and Texts*, 15 April 1988, p. 18.
5. Marlin Fitzwater, USIS, *US Policy Information and Texts*, 28 March 1989.
6. Michael Kramer, 'Anger, Bluff – and Cooperation', in *Time*, 4 June 1990, p. 23.

Chapter 6: The Ideology of the New World Order

1. George Bush, 'State of the Union Address', USIS, *US Policy Information and Texts*, 31 January 1991, pp. 17 et seq.

2. Lawrence Eagleburger, 'New World Order: Democracy, Freedom from Aggression', in USIS, *US Policy Information and Texts*, 1 March 1991, p. 45.

3. See Chapter 7 on Gulf War.

4. 'Taft Talks about European Security in New World Order', in USIS, *US Policy Information and Texts*, 10 February 1991, p. 41.

5. 'President Bush on New World Order', in USIS, *US Policy Information and Texts*, 15 April 1991, p. 11.

6. Bush, 'State of the Union Address', 29 January 1991, USIS, *US Policy Information and Texts*, 31 January 1991, p. 18.

7. 'Bush Says US Welcomes Emergence of United Europe (Boston University Commencement Address)', USIS wireless file, 21 May 1989.

8. Walter Russell Mead, 'An American Grand Strategy – the Quest for Order in a Disordered World', in *World Policy Journal*, Spring 1993, p. 10.

9. 'Bush Outlines New World Order, Economic Plans – Text of State of the Union Message', in USIS, *US Policy Information and Texts*, 29 January 1992, p. 3.

10. 'Bush: Unique Chance for Worldwide Cooperation, US President Addressing the UN General Assembly', USIS wireless file, 25 September 1991, p. 4.

11. 'Bush Outlines Challenges in Post-Cold-War Era – Text, Address to Naval Academy Commencement', in USIS, *US Policy Information and Texts*, 29 May 1992, p. 11.

12. 'Bush Says US Must Continue World Leadership Role', in USIS, *US Policy Information and Texts*, 13 March 1992, p. 5.

13. Brent Scowcroft, 'US Goals: Democracy, Liberal Trade, Leadership', in USIS, *US Policy Information and Texts*, 24 June 1992, p. 5.

14. 'US Will Shoulder Responsibility for World Leadership: Christopher Remarks in Minnesota', in USIS, *US Policy Information and Texts*, 1 June 1993, p. 4.

15. 'Christopher Outlines Clinton Foreign Policy Elements', in USIS, *US Policy Information and Texts*, 3 June 1993, p. 18.

16. Ibid., p. 20.

17. 'New World Order: What's New? Which World? Whose Orders?', in *The Economist*, 28 February 1991, p. 47.

18. '"US to Stay Engaged in Creating New World Order." Deputy National Security Advisor Robert Gates' Comments before the American Newspaper Publishers Association', in *USIS*, 9 May 1991, p. 3.

19. 'All Chips Are Not Alike', in *Newsweek*, 17 June 1991, p. 41.

20. Steven R. David, 'Why the Third World Still Matters', in *International Security*, Vol. 17, No. 3, Winter 1992/3, pp. 127–59.

21. On Islam as the new enemy image to the West, see Jochen Hippler and Andrea Lueg, *Feindbild Islam*, Hamburg 1993; translation into English in progress.

22. '"Kimmit Says too Early to Call Soviet Threat Reduced." Under Secretary of State for Political Affairs' Testimony to Senate Appropriations Subcommittee', USIS wireless file, 5 October 1989, p. 4.

23. '"US National Security Strategy for the 1990s". Under Secretary of Defense for Policy, to the National Defense University', USIS wireless file, 8 December 1989, p. 2.

24. Ibid., p. 4.

25. The US position on nuclear proliferation is summarised in Spurgeon M. Keeny and Wolfgang K.H. Panofsky, 'Controlling Nuclear Warheads and Materials: Steps toward a Comprehensive Regime', in *Arms Control Today*, January/February 1992, pp. 2–9.

26. '"Bush Cautions US Must Maintain Strong Defense", Speech by President Bush to Commonwealth Club of San Francisco', USIS wireless file, 7 February 1990, p. 4.

27. For a realistic assessment of the danger of Third World missiles, see Lora Lumpe, Lisbeth Gronlund and David C. Wright, 'Third World Missiles Fall Short', in *Bulletin of the Atomic Scientists*, March 1992, pp. 30–7.

28. Quoted from 'President Bush's Middle East Arms Control Initiative: One Year Later', in *Arms Control Today*, June 1992, p. 11.

29. 'Administration Advances Strategy for a Solo Superpower's Global Military Role', in *Washington Post*, 19 May 1991, p. A14.

30. 'Threats to US Security Have Grown, Not Shrunk; Excerpts: Woolsey Confirmation Hearing', in USIS, *US Policy Information and Texts*, 4 February 1993, pp. 9, 10.

31. 'US Faces Four Post-Cold War Security Threats: Aspin May 16 Commencement Address', in USIS, *US Policy Information and Texts*, 19 May 1993, p. 16.

32. 'Pentagon Charts Plans for Future Force Structure, Excerpts: Defense Department's "Bottom-Up Review"', in USIS, *US Policy Information and Texts*, 3 September 1993, p. 4.

33. Ibid.

34. This process has been analysed earlier in regard to the German Greens, see Jochen Hippler and Jürgen Maier (eds), *Sind die GRÜNEN noch zu retten? – Krise und Perspektiven einer ehemaligen Protestpartei*, Cologne 1987.

35. The title of a shallow but still broadly discussed article: Francis Fukuyama, 'The End of History?', in *National Interest*, Summer 1989, pp. 3 et seq.

36. Joel Rocamora, 'Third World Revolutionary Projects and the End of the Cold War', in *Debate – Philippine Left Review* (Amsterdam), March 1991, p. 44.

37. Ibid., p. 45.

Chapter 7: The Ordering of the New World

1. In Washington's eyes, Saddam was not always an enemy; in fact, three presidents counted on him to keep Iran's brand of Islamic radicalism in check. See 'A Man You Could Do Business With' in *Time*, 11 March 1991, pp. 53 et seq.

2. USIS, *US Policy Information and Texts*, 25 July 1990, p. 12.

3. International Institute for Strategic Studies (London), *The Military Balance 1990/91*, London 1990; and 'Iraq's Armed Forces – Equipment', in *Jane's Soviet Intelligence Review*, October 1990.

4. Jochen Hippler, 'Iraq's Military Power: the German Connection', in *Middle East Report*, Vol. 21, No. 168, January/February 1991, pp. 27–31.

5. 'Bush Doubts Sanctions Alone Will Force Iraqi Pullout (Statement and Conference)', USIS wireless file, 30 November 1990, p. 3.
6. 'Read My Ships', in *Time*, 20 August 1990, p. 11.
7. Walter Russell Mead, 'An American Grand Strategy – the Quest for Order in a Disordered World', in *World Policy Journal*, Spring 1993, p. 30.
8. On US-Soviet communication during the Gulf crises see 'The Moscow Connection', in *Newsweek*, 17 September 1990, pp. 6 et seq; important insight in Yevgeni Primakov, 'The Inside Story of Moscow's Quest for a Deal', in *Time*, 4 March 1991, p. 32; and Primakov, 'My Final Visit with Saddam Hussein', in *Time*, 11 March 1991, pp. 48 et seq.
9. '"Baker Says Present, Future Gulf Aggression Doomed", Secretary of State Baker's News Conference in Brussels Following a Special Meeting of the North Atlantic Council', in USIS, *US Policy Information and Texts*, 10 September 1990, p. 2.
10. USIS, *US Policy Information and Texts*, 5 September 1990, p. 34.
11. USIS, *US Policy Information and Texts*, 10 September 1990, p. 13.
12. Ibid., p. 14.
13. *Der Spiegel*, 21 January 1991, p. 18.
14. 'A Quagmire After All', in *Newsweek*, 29 April 1991, p. 12.
15. '"Superpowers are odious to me" – UN General Secretary Javier Perez de Cuellar on the Crisis in Yugoslavia and the UNO after the Persian Gulf War', in *Der Spiegel*, 1 July 1991, p. 126.
16. Mead, 'An American Grand Strategy', pp. 31, 32.
17. The fact that Iran supported Hamas with millions of dollars did not help the PLO's position.
18. For the implications of the 1992 elections in Israel, see Leon T. Hadar, 'The 1992 Electoral Earthquake and the Fall of the "Second Israeli Republic"', in *Middle East Journal*, Vol. 46, No. 4, Autumn 1992, pp. 594–616.

Chapter 8: The New Order of World Power

1. Stanley Hoffmann, 'The Case for Leadership', in *Foreign Policy*, Winter 1990/1, p. 23.
2. Peter W. Ludlow, 'Managing Change: the United States and Europe East and West', in William Brock and Robert Hormats (eds), *The Global Economy – America's Role in the Decade Ahead*, New York 1990, p. 67.
3. 'The Community Blueprint for the Future', in *Time*, 24 December 1990, p. 30.
4. On 31 May 1989 at Rheingoldhalle, Mainz; text in several issues of USIS, *US Policy Information and Texts*.
5. '1992 International Affairs Budget Overview', in *US Department of State Dispatch*, February 1991, p. 90.
6. 'Deutsch-polnischer Vertrag unterzeichnet', in *Frankfurter Allgemeine Zeitung*, 18 June 1991, p. 2.
7. 'NATO: Out of Area or Out of Mission, Text: Lugar 6/24 Overseas Writers Club Speech', in USIS, *US Policy Information and Texts*, 8 July 1993, p. 38.

8. 'The Future of NATO, Text: Slocombe Remarks to Senate Panel', in USIS, *US Policy Information and Texts*, 2 July 1993, p. 21.

9. Sir James Eberle, 'Die Sicherheitsinteressen Westeuropas', in *Europa Archiv*, 25 February 1991, p. 123.

10. Heinz Schulte, 'After the Warsaw Pact – What Next?', in *Jane's Soviet Intelligence Review*, April 1991, p. 186.

11. An example is Konrad Seitz, who was director of political planning at the German Foreign Ministry in Genscher's time; see his book: *Die japanisch-amerikanische Herausforderung* (The Japanese-American Challenge), Bonn 1991.

12. 'Hopes for New Order Depend on Ending Iraqi Occupation – Excerpts: Baker to North Atlantic Council', in USIS, *US Policy Information and Texts*, 20 December 1990, pp. 23 et seq.

13. '"Gulf War Proved NATO's Security Approach is Valid" – William H. Taft Address', USIS wireless file, 23 May 1991.

14. 'NATO Meeting "An Important Milestone", Cheney Says', in USIS, *US Policy Information and Texts*, 3 June 1991, pp. 21 et seq.

15. 'NATO Trims Down', in *Newsweek*, 10 June 1991, p. 9.

16. Ibid.

17. 'The Future of NATO, Text: Slocombe Remarks to Senate Panel', in USIS, *US Policy Information and Texts*, 2 July 1993, p. 18.

18. Germany, France, Italy, Great Britain, Belgium, the Netherlands, Luxembourg, Spain and Portugal.

19. Karl Feldmeyer, 'Die NATO und Europa', in *Frankfurter Allgemeine Zeitung*, 24 May 1991, p. 1.

20. 'Baker: Nuclear Deterrence Keeps Peace in Europe', in USIS, *US Policy Information and Texts*, 24 May 1989, pp. 21 et seq.

21. 'Taft Talks about European Security in New World Order', in USIS, *US Policy Information and Texts*, 10 February 1991, p. 41.

22. See 'Amerika befürchtet seine Ausgrenzung – Eine Demarche', in *Frankfurter Allgemeine Zeitung*, 9 April 1991.

23. Christopher Layne, 'The Unipolar Illusion – Why New Great Powers Will Rise', in *International Security*, Vol. 17, No. 4, Spring 1993, pp. 33, 34.

24. Statistical Office of the European Community, *Statistical of the Community*, 27th edn., 1990, p. 40.

25. 'Rekorddefizit im amerikanischen Haushalt', in *Frankfurter Allgemeine Zeitung*, 30 October 1992, p. 15.

26. Daniel Burstein, *Yen! – Japan's New Financial Empire and Its Threat to America*, New York 1990, pp. 139 et seq.

27. Ibid., p. 79.

28. Jeffrey E. Garten, 'Japan and Germany – American Concerns', in *Foreign Affairs*, No. 5, 1989, p. 93.

29. William Pfaff, 'Redefining World Power', in *Foreign Affairs*, No. 1, 1991, pp. 37 et seq.

30. Figures quoted from I.M. Destler and Michael Nacht, 'Beyond Mutual Recrimination – Building a Solid US-Japan Relationship in the 1990s', in *International Security*, Winter 1990/1, p. 92.

31. 'Quoted from 'Paradigm Paranoia', in *Far Eastern Economic Review*, 27 June 1991, p. 15.

32. Michael B. Smith, 'US-Japan Economic Relations in the 1990s: A Crossroads?', in William Brock and Robert Hormats (eds), *The Global Economy*, New York 1990, p. 81.
33. Felix Rohatyn, 'America's Economic Dependence', in *Foreign Affairs*, No. 1, 1989, p. 59.
34. Earl C. Ravenal, 'The Case for Adjustment', in *Foreign Policy*, No. 81, Winter 1990/1, pp. 11 et seq.
35. Joseph L. Brand, 'The New World Order of Regional Trading Blocs', in *American University Journal of International Law and Policy*, Vol. 8, Fall 1992, pp. 163 and 164.

Chapter 9: The New Interventionism and the United Nations

1. Pierre Hassner, 'Beyond Nationalism and Internationalism: Ethnicity and World Order', in *Survival*, Vol. 35, No. 2, Summer 1993, p. 49.
2. Jonathan Stevenson, 'Hope Restored in Somalia?', in *Foreign Policy*, No. 91, Summer 1993, p. 142.
3. Peter Schraeder, '"Cynical Disengagement" or a New Doctrine of Humanitarian Intervention? The Case of US Intervention in Somalia in the Post Cold War Era', unpublished manuscript.
4. African Rights, *Somalia – Human Rights Abuses by the United Nations Forces*, London, July 1993.
5. *The Economist*, 30 November 1991, p. 17.
6. Quoted by Bernhard Graefrath, 'Leave to the Court What Belongs to the Court – On the Libyan Case', unpublished manuscript.

Chapter 10: The Future of a New World Order

1. 'New World Order: What's New? Which World? Whose Orders?', in *The Economist*, 28 February 1991, p. 45.
2. William Pfaff, 'Redefining World Power', in *Foreign Affairs*, No. 1, 1991, p. 38.
3. Figures quoted from *Time*, 11 March 1991, p. 40. In the case of Japan the financial commitments had been in yen, so the precise figures might be somewhat different because of currency fluctuations.
4. Pfaff, 'Redefining World Power', p. 37.
5. Quoted in *Europa-Archiv*, 10 December 1990, p. D587.
6. 'Strategy for Solo Superpower', in *Washington Post*, 19 May 1991.
7. William G. Hyland, 'America's New Course', in *Foreign Affairs*, Spring 1990, p. 3.
8. Andrea Lueg and Jochen Hippler are preparing a book on Islam as a new enemy of the West, which will follow up this point.
9. Samuel P. Huntington, 'The Clash of Civilizations?', in *Foreign Affairs*, Vol. 72, No. 3, Summer 1993, p. 22.
10. Ibid., p. 24.
11. Ibid., p. 45.

Index